The Inner Life of Children with Special Needs

Edited by Ved P. Varma

W

Whurr Publishers Ltd
London

© 1996 Whurr Publishers
Copyright of Chapter 7, Paul Cooper
Copyright of Chapter 9, Wendy Rinaldi
First published 1996 by
Whurr Publishers Ltd
19b Compton Terrace, London N1 2UN, England

British Library Cataloguing-in-Publication Data
A catalogue record for this book is available from the
British Library.

ISBN: 1-897635-43-5

Printed and bound in the UK by Athenaeum Press Ltd,
Gateshead, Tyne & Wear.

Contents

Foreword

The title clearly indicates the strength of this book. All the chapters demonstrate the importance of paying attention to, and listening to, the individual. The case studies can be sad in themselves but there is also something inspiring in the sensitivity of the studies, something from which many more people than specialists can learn.

The term 'Inner Life' is a significant one but not unproblematic. More than one chapter slips into the term 'secret lives'. Inner life is a defined psychoanalytical term that suggests not only those forces, experiences and attitudes that form a view of the world, but that they are beyond normal articulacy. But, as this book implies, inner life can also mean real life as experienced by the individual; not the measurable amount of facts learned or the time spent 'on task' but understanding, not the 'delivery' of a curriculum, but what is actually learned. The difficulty is that what is learned often remains a secret.

Secrets imply that there is something there that could be conveyed. Winnicott reminds us that there is a part of everyone that is unknowable both by others and by themselves, but there is much more to be learned about everyone if we only listened. The inner life is not a separate one. As these chapters demonstrate, inner lives are at the same time social and cultural ones. One cannot isolate the individual from the circumstances that have formed and informed him or her. The inner world is the interplay between the one and the other, the formation of attitudes and opinions and the development of the individual gaze. This close attention to the world is shared by all, whatever the barriers to their expression.

This is why language, at whatever level, is so important. Nothing is more frustrating than the inability to communicate, to oneself as well as to others. The greatest difficulty of special needs is the disjunction between the need for expression and the difficulty of giving it free rein. We sometimes forget that, from the point of view of the individual with special needs, this frustration is not just a matter of finding the right words but of finding an ear that will listen to his or her voice. What the case studies do amply demonstrate is the sadness of a pervasive fear.

The authors here all reveal their sensitivity to the individuals, but as one of them remarks, such a provision is, for many children, a matter of chance, a lottery. There are many reasons for this but one of them is the way in which 'special needs' are associated with a deficit, a certain percentage of the population that do not cope. Whether the percentage is that of the embrace of the Warnock report, or the grudging one driven by the resources that surround Statementing, it is still driven by the tendency to isolate. As with social workers whose time is spent entirely with problems and difficulties, failures and inadequacies, there is a tendency to forget that they are part of a greater whole, that viewing the world beyond their professional compartments could be enlightening.

It is a curious symptom of our society that the greatest attention given to the individual voice and inner feelings is given not by the education system but by psychiatrists and psychologists, as if people are only listened to when things go wrong or there are difficulties. There is a lot to be learned in this book that goes far beyond the difficulties that are described. Recognition of the importance of inner lives is not only a matter of respecting the dignity of the individual but an attitude that could have practical and dramatic effects on the education system as a whole. The term inner lives also reminds us how widespread special needs are.

Cedric Cullingford
University of Huddersfield

Contributors

Helen Barrett,
PhD,Honorary Research Fellow at Birkbeck College, University of London and Lecturer in Psychology at Thames Valley University.

David Bond,
Headteacher (formerly Specialist Educational Psychologist and Audiologist), The Royal School for Deaf Children, Margate, Kent.

Jill Boucher,
PhD, Director, Speech Science, Psychology Department, University of Sheffield.

Paul Cooper,
PhD, Institute of Education, University of Cambridge.

Gianetta Corley,
PhD, Educational Psychologist, London.

Ali El-Hadi,
MB., Bch., MRCPsych. Consultant Psychiatrist/Psychotherapist, London.

David Jones,
PhD, Senior Lecturer in Psychology, Birkbeck College, University of London.

Patricia Kiff,
Instructor in Communication, The Royal School for Deaf Children, Margate, Kent.

Penny Lacey,
Lecturer, School of Education, University of Birmingham.

Ludwig F. Lowenstein,
PhD, Director, Allington Manor School, Hampshire.

Tim Miles,
PhD, Emeritus Professor of Psychology, University of Wales, Bangor.

Alice Morris,
MA, Psychodynamic Psychotherapist, Devon.

Linda Pring,
PhD, Senior Lecturer in Psychology, Goldsmiths' College, University of London.

Wendy Rinaldi,
Doctoral Candidate, Speech and Language Therapist, I CAN Training Centre, Surrey.

Michael Smith,
PhD, Principal, National Star Centre College, Cheltenham, a national specialist college for the physically disabled.

Ved Varma,
PhD, (London) was formerly an educational psychologist with the Institute of Education, University of London, Tavistock Clinic and the London Boroughs of Richmond and Brent. He has edited or co-edited more than 30 books in education, psychology, psychiatry, psychotherapy and social work, and he is an international figure in the area of special needs.

Acknowledgements

We would like to acknowledge the written work or narrative reports of the people with autism on whose accounts Dr Jill Boucher's chapter in this book is based. We thank the authors and publishers who gave permission for extracts of their work to be quoted.

Likewise acknowledgement is made to quote two tables by Juliet Goldbart in Penny Lacey's chapter.

Dedication

This book is dedicated, with affection and esteem, to the inner life of children with special needs.

Ved P. Varma

Introduction

This volume is an anthology of essays on the inner life of children with special needs. As the reader will see elsewhere in the book, the inner life of children contains dreams, fantasies, hopes, fears, beliefs and their unconscious life. These can be inferred from their preoccupations, stories, plays, games, conversations and behaviour. Thus this is rather a complex subject. It is a somewhat sad subject too because most inner life of children with special needs contains elements that are both permanent and damaging. The reason for this is that these children are often confused, frightened, anxious and angry. Nevertheless, many of them put out clear signs of wanting to be understood and helped.

This interesting book will enable professionals working with these children to find out what they are thinking and feeling and why they behave as they do. The contributors include a psychiatrist, a psychotherapist, nine psychologists and four educationalists, all of whom are leading authorities in their fields. This is why their views command every respect and attention. Therefore, this warm and authoritative book will appeal to students and professionals in psychiatry, psychology, psychotherapy, counselling, medicine, education and social work. May all who read it realise that the world belongs to those who work for the suffering.

The editor would like to thank the reader for taking the trouble to read this book. He would also like to thank Colin Whurr and all the contributors who have worked with him in this context.

Ved Varma London, September 1995

Further reading

Segal, J. (1985). *Phantasy in Everyday Life*. Harmondsworth: Penguin.
Varma, V.P. (Ed.) (1992). *The Secret Life of Vulnerable Children*. London: Routledge.

Chapter 1
The Inner Life of Visually Impaired Children

GIANETTA CORLEY AND LINDA PRING

Children who are visually impaired seem to suffer the greatest trauma in the early years of life and it is at this time that it is hardest of all to get a window on their feelings, thoughts and inner world. Children who are born blind often show autistic tendencies, failing to react to the natural emotions of love, warmth and affection, and instead preferring some strange 'aloneness'. Many have suggested that such infants and young children can find no consistency or pattern in the world around them and, without such a framework, the world becomes an unpredictable and perhaps a scary place. As the child develops there can often be seen strange ritualistic movements or ritualistic behaviour which may provide the consistency the child is looking for. However, as the mental abilities of the child develop and more is begun to be understood, then slowly the world becomes more comprehensible, the role of family and friends more natural and the child begins to come back towards the environment that was rejected early on. Congenital impairment of this kind does provide severe difficulties but we know from the work of Fraiberg, for example, that blindness does not produce consistent developmental patterns and such a heterogeneous group, therefore, makes it hard to generalise about the effects of visual impairment. It seems every case may demand an alternative appraisal but we will start to set the scene by providing a small range of vignettes.

The first image which comes to mind in thinking of the inner life of visually impaired children is the picture of a circle of five-year-olds, five boys and a girl, sitting around their teacher and helpers, one morning at register time. They do not look up when the visitor comes in but they listen to find out where she will sit. They hear her say her name. As they answer the register and sing their nursery songs, a small hand reaches out to make contact with her. He knows she is next to him and he feels his tactile greeting returned. This provides him with the information he needs for the moment. Later that morning he returns to feel her hair and face. He asks his helper where she is. He also asks where other people are, as though checking his internal inventory for the day. This little boy

1

is active and trusting in his search for information. He cannot see what clothes she wears, nor the expression on her face, but he reaches out and makes contact through the delicate sensitivity of his fingers, and by so doing he learns something about her. This active search for knowledge enables this child to build up an inner picture of his home, his class and school, his parents, his friends and teachers, the garden and the world beyond. He is aware of newness and change and tries to accommodate these into his present internal world. He also has the language to ask questions: two ways of making contact – one proximal, the other distal. He can assert his existence, know and be known in his world of light and dark.

In the early years of the twentieth century, in the post-Nietzsche era, when literature was shaped by the philosophy that God was dead and man inhabited earth, alone with the creatures, Rainer Maria Rilke, a German poet, described in the first of the Duino Elegies his immense sense of aloneness. He was acutely aware that even if he were to cry out, no one would hear him, not even the 'angels', those beautiful and powerful beings, whose very presence could terrify and destroy. He sensed that nothing in the universe was alive unless someone was aware of it: beings came alive only if they were experienced and sensed by some other living creature. Without that knowledge of being in someone else's awareness and thoughts, the person was desolate indeed.

Edvard Munch, the Norwegian artist of the same era, painted 'Der Schrei', 'The Scream', in which a gaunt and haunted figure, foreshadowing the appearance of those who survived the holocaust, uttered a silent, wordless scream. His figure was bent and twisted, as though in torment, and his skeletal eyes and mouth formed a long howl, taken up by the bending and twisted landscape.

These images, too, became associated with the cries of visually impaired children, for distressing though it is to include in this exploration a mention of screaming, it is nonetheless the case that some young visually impaired children scream a lot: they are sometimes even referred to as 'screamers'. When young children without sight scream, parents and carers know it signals pain, protest, hunger, frustration, misery or delight. Those who know the child well can tell which message is intended by the tone of the cry. There seems to be no universal cure for screamers – and perhaps that is as it should be, for in the case of the child with no words, it describes an inner experience. Children grow out of screaming, often when speech develops, but what does it signal of their inner world? The child usually has no words and in this respect is like a baby expressing primitive and powerful survival needs. When there are no words available the child cannot ask for food, nor speak of pain nor fright. Much screaming occurs at night when the child awakes and finds him- or herself totally alone. For the visually impaired child without speech, there is a double communication loss; he cannot see anything outside himself, nor can he hurl words into the void to make contact with the 'outside' world, to see if there is an echo, a human response. Maybe the lack of sight denies him any realisation that there is a world beyond himself. All that is there for him at the time is what he can feel, smell, hear and touch. At night he may hear nothing, and so is in a state of relative sensory isolation, like the man in Rilke's poem or in Munch's picture. Interestingly the most recent research suggests that language development in the visually impaired is not very different, nor indeed necessarily delayed, compared with their sighted counterparts (e.g. Landau and Gleitman, 1985) so there are many visually impaired children who learn to verbalise their needs very readily.

An eight-year-old partially sighted girl, with good ability to speak, described her terror of going swimming, even in the paddling pool, because once in the middle of the pool she lost contact with other people. Unless the adults kept shouting her name, she could not see if they were there or not and she felt she had been abandoned. Another younger partially sighted child wept inconsolably when a favourite toy was removed; it was as though she had been robbed of her most trea-sured possession and could not see who had taken it, nor where it had been placed.

But then, there are the screams of pleasure and delight when a child discovers a new sensation, often a visual one, and repeats it over and over again – perhaps a bright, shiny surface which stimulates the eye. It is like drawing in the rich smell of coffee or newly baked bread and expe-riencing again the use of an underused sense. The silence which follows screaming comes as suddenly as the screaming itself, as the hungry chil-dren eat their lunch or as the tired and frightened child falls asleep, stilled.

These children have had experiences of pleasure, pain, hunger, joy, frustration or fright. They have responded to the experience by emitting a sound: this is a powerful signalling device to convey the child's reac-tion to the experience. There is an internal stimulus and a personal response. At this level, the child may lack awareness. Associations are made, however, between the scream and what happens next so that eventually the child will be able to predict the outcome and scream deliberately, with intention and planning. The crying sounds are made without tears. Even though a child may be unable to speak, this aware-ness of cause and effect is still able to grow, and a form of survival communication develops. Nowadays this awareness of cause and effect can be transformed in a variety of ways to harness speech synthesised systems or switch mechanisms.

A child's play reflects his inner world. He acts out with toys, in games and in make believe his understanding of what adults do and how he fits in. Some play, of course, is really making use of mastered skills: riding a bicycle, for example, or putting sand through a hole in the funnel. The child has a sense of security and purpose in pedalling backwards and forwards, round and round, or can enjoy scooping up the soft sand and feel it running over his hand. Make believe play amongst the small group of five-year-olds was not greatly evident: one child insisted that everyone wore their glasses, as he had heard his teacher tell the pupils many times to do. Another child built things with giant lego and found he could push them on the table, like a train. He could also pass a lego bridge over his head to signal his attempt to crawl through and under the bridge. A little girl insisted that both she and her visitor wore hats from the dressing up chest. Another lay on the floor and pretended to 'sit' on his toy car. These descriptions are to some extent contrasted by a very different pattern that can emerge for many a congenitally blind child. In terms of play it has been noted that this child has difficulty using toys or indeed allowing any object to 'stand for' another thing. Thus dolls may have less appeal to a blind child who might try and get into a baby bath rather than put a doll into it. Similarly playschool reports suggest that big cardboard boxes which for sighted children might easily represent a car or a train are not used for this symbolic purpose. Instead visual impairment may hinder imaginative play of this sort and more down to earth games may be preferred. This concrete approach to many things is remarkable. One young blind child emerged from a classroom to say that another was making a 'funny' noise, though this was, in fact, quiet weeping. A visually impaired child was reported to remark on the strange taste of a plastic biscuit used in a game, not realising it should not have been eaten!

Watching children at play can be revealing, but young visually impaired children are often restricted by a difficulty in negotiating the physical environment. Nonetheless, they skip, run, play ball, scoot and cycle, throw bean bags and generally practise and display their developing motor skills. But it is not only through play that an insight can be gained into the inner life and world of the visually impaired child. This can also be achieved through looking at what the child has drawn or by listening to what the child says. Sadly much of the drawing of young visually impaired children has been heavily influenced by help from the teacher. The drawings are no longer truly 'naive' or 'primitive'. Moreover, many visually impaired children do not enjoy paper and pencil tasks when they are young, perhaps because the feedback from the page is not visually rewarding. Much more is gained by listening to a visually impaired child's questions and by trying to paint a visual picture of what those words suggest.

The word reflects the child's inner world and how he construes the external world. Visually impaired children love to talk and to ask questions. The questions compensate for the loss of visual detail and visual information available to the child. 'How old are you?' reveals that the visually impaired child does not readily pick up the visual cues of wrinkled skin or white hair and so the answer may be to try to link oneself to what the child knows: 'as old as your Granny.' 'What are you going to do when you get home?' requires a description of shopping and housework, dusting and tidying up. 'What does your home look like?' demands at least a description of the colour of the front door, the carpet and curtains.

The adult has to paint a picture in words for the child, filling in factual information normally picked up incidentally from pictures, from television or from direct experience. Gaining information on her own from inspecting pictures can be a long and tedious process for a partially sighted child. With this in mind, one child's parents only allowed her access to books with realistic pictures of whatever was the topic in question, let us say, animals, so that whenever she made that effort to decipher the picture, she would gain a real life inner idea of the pictured object, not a cartoon, nor a stylised image. Blind children also gain and show a remarkable knowledge of what things look like (Pring and Walker, 1993).

Asking visually impaired children what certain words mean can be very illuminating in disclosing what they have entered under that word in their internal lexicon. For example a cow 'lives on a farm, gives you milk and goes 'moo'' but a donkey only goes 'heehaw'. Less is known of the donkey at present. The visual detail of long ears has not yet been assimilated to the inner picture. Each child draws on her own experience in developing this lexicon and the child who knows a lot about being in hospital describes 'brave' as 'If you have an injection, it pricks a little bit and you have to be very, very brave'. Constantly the child reveals that he knows the context in which words have been used, and he draws upon these recollections of contexts in order to provide the meaning. The precise meaning of the word on its own may not have been fully identified at this stage – the interconnections may not have been established in the internal lexicon.

Strange misconceptions arise if visual information is lacking. A seven-year-old partially sighted child was heard to ask her teacher 'Is a butterfly as big as a bird?' By asking the question, she was ordering her internal lexicon and her inner world. Most children would learn the relative sizes of flies, butterflies, bees and birds by seeing them, or by seeing pictures. Without this knowledge, the partially sighted child has to ask. This information is then added to what is stored about the item in question, but this may be information without any experience attached to it. Questions and how they are interpreted and answered are essential windows into the inner world of the visually impaired child. They reveal activity on the part of the child in trying to expand and order his knowledge: they indicate that cognitive discrepancy has arisen which the child is trying to resolve.

Thought reflects experience: the child is aware enough to reflect on what he has done: he can remember, recreate and repeat experiences.

Words reflect that thought and that experience. Words are not the same as the experience but they arise from it. Occasionally, it is evident that words do not, in fact, reflect experience but they are learned, echoed phrases without substance.

Visually impaired children can learn a considerable amount from watching TV and video but it may not always be well understood. For example a young visually impaired child was asked what she would do if she saw thick smoke coming from the house next door. Drawing in her breath in horror, she replied that 'they could phone an emergency'. When asked what an emergency was she explained that 'if smoke goes up your nose, you have to go to hospital'. It is not clear if she realised exactly what the danger was, but she did realise that thick smoke was something to take very seriously. In this case it had probably been learned from a TV programme.

The import of this is that visually impaired children must be provided with real experiences and must be allowed to interact in ways which extend their world and their store of knowledge of how people and things work. One way in which sighted children do this is by means of the mechanism for being aware of familiar people and distinguishing them from strangers. They then try out on the familiar items or people those reactions which they feel from their knowledge will work. Somehow they have to incorporate the unfamiliar into their framework. One question which arises is how young visually impaired children identify the familiar and unfamiliar.

In one experimental study, six-, seven- and eight-year-old partially sighted children were asked to examine photographs of each other taken the previous week. It was clear that they identified people not by their features but more often by their hair, by significant clothing or spectacles: 'That's Peter. I can tell by his jumper.' 'It looks like a girl. I can't tell any more. Is it Jenny? I knew it was because she had bunches.' 'It looks a bit like Mary. I thought so because she's got those sort of glasses with metal frames.' Additionally, there was also some recognition of people by their colour. This was the commentary when an eight- year-old was asked to identify the picture of a young Ghanaian girl in his school: 'Can't tell. Is it Mark, dark Mark? It's someone dark. I can tell that. It must be a girl because not many boys are dark. I can't tell.' Further commentaries of this kind reveal the kind of detail visually impaired children perceive when they look at pictures. If vision is severely impaired then the process of identifying a pictured object is not the instantaneous process carried out by sighted people. It is a step by step process of building separate details into a whole. A young visually impaired child looking at a picture of an 'ostrich said that it looked 'round at the back', 'along at the top' and 'a head like a horse', then eventually pieced this together and said 'it's an ostrich'. This painstaking picture recognition is described in more detail by us elsewhere (Corley and Pring 1993a, 1995). There we pointed out that visually impaired and partially sighted children often fail to use picture material when the opportunity arises. The difficulties described already may contribute to their feeling that it is not a medium which will provide the information and experience which they need most. Parents and teachers can often mistake just how much a child is using visually derived information and this can lead to important misunderstandings.

Listening to visually impaired children talking as they describe what they see enables the listener to understand the categories they are using, and then how they go about categorising the item before naming the individual member. Shape and line are the first features to be identified but these can give rise to error if not fully investigated. Congenitally blind children, in a study by one of us (Pathak and Pring, 1989), were asked to identify and then later recognise by touch raised line drawings of common objects. When it came to finding the match by touch the children had to make a selection from amongst the originals and distractors, some of which resembled the originals in shape; for example, a flower with a stem for a toothbrush. When the blind children failed to find the original item, they selected most frequently the distractors which were similar in shape, not those which were totally dissimilar. This signifies that even if they had not got so far as to identify all aspects of the target and name it, they had recognised and remembered the first level features of shape and line.

From this we learn that visually impaired children grow to experience the world and pictures of the world by building up a series of pieces of significant information about the object. If they have too little time for this investigation, their knowledge remains partial and there is a danger of premature identification on the basis of insufficient information. Too great emphasis may be placed on one aspect whilst ignoring another which has a bearing. It is often said that visually impaired children take more time to process information. The importance of this is seen clearly here, for it is not just the identification of objects which has to be undertaken, but their grouping into ideas, associations and categories available for later recall and use. Without this constant sorting, sifting and grouping of incoming information, much of it is lost, unassimilated or wrongly filed.

As language reflects a person's experience and knowledge, so for a visually impaired person language is likely to reflect their unique experience of a world which is only partially or very obliquely perceived visually. There are many observations in the literature on visually impaired children and young people that the quality of their language differs from that of the sighted person. There are what are known as 'sighted' words, which have a high visual component. It is difficult to catch this difference in quality without long and careful listening, but when it occurs, it reveals that the child has partial knowledge of the item derived perhaps from touch or from hearing about it. For example, Kelli used 'see' to mean very much the same thing a sighted child would mean i.e. perceive with the dominant sense (Landau and Gleitman, 1985). The word 'beard' is an instance of a 'sighted' word. Most young sighted children of seven have an idea of what it is. For visually impaired children of the same age, a beard is often only associated with Father Christmas and is often made of 'fur'. They have not seen a beard, and unless their father or other relatives have a beard, they have mostly not touched one. They have just heard about it at Christmas time. Other attributes may be missing, such as where it is located on a person or what it is like texturally.

Sally, a twelve-year-old blind child, described a raised tactile picture of a tree she had just drawn on German film as 'a shortish round cylinder, with triangles getting shorter as it goes up, like a pyramid.' In other words she focused on shape and described a rather stylised, geometric tree. A slightly younger sighted child who had also drawn a tree on German film described her drawing as: 'bushy, green leaves with lots of sticks and twigs and branches inside'. She used colour as well as her knowledge of the structure of a tree, its component parts as well as its form (Pring, 1992).

Sally, the young blind artist, drew a picture of the sun and from her circle came lines. She said she had been told that this was how a sun was usually drawn. When pressed to say what the lines represented she was able to say: 'I think they are the light or heat from the sun'. She was able to relate information from various sources when urged to do so. This example serves to reinforce the notion again that talking, listening and making links between encapsulated pieces of knowledge is vital for visually impaired children in making their internal representation of the world coherent and richly furnished. We tend to think that the loss of vision influences the development and use of knowledge. Its greatest impact is on the loss of a channel of information, rather than on the use of the channel itself. Raised pictures can provide both a supplement to ideas of form but also to the relationship between form and function. Indeed pictures can be considered to play an even more important part for the visually impaired child than for the sighted child, but perhaps only in an interactive context with a caregiver. Indeed the element of sharing a book is something that may not be as available to a visually impaired as to a sighted child and this seems a tremendous loss for both social and intellectual well being. The use of tactile pictures is particularly advantageous for congenitally blind children whose spatial picture of the world has to be entirely constructed without internal light.

How do congenitally blind children know where things are or how to react to the environment? So much is learnt by use of vision and by copying others, how does learning occur if this means is prevented? Many conventions are taught and this is how Sally knew to draw lines coming out of her drawing of the sun. But why should those lines be there? Sally had to learn the explanation probably at another time and then link it to her existing knowledge, modifying the existing schema to include the new insight.

Many visually impaired children have difficulty in interpreting facial features and expressions. They do not readily alter their own facial expressions, but do other things to reflect feeling and emotion. For example, they might laugh or bang the table top with enjoyment. They might touch each other's hands to make contact instead of looking at each other as they talk. In the playground they will walk about in twos and threes hand in hand or arm in arm, rarely is a child on his or her own and 'out of touch'.

Navigating across open space is a test of how the child has organised his or her picture of that space. Mobility training is designed to enable the child or adult to build up a picture of a room, a route or a locality so that it can be rehearsed and 'seen' in the mind's eye. Happily there is an overlap between spatial information derived by sight and that derived by movement or touch as all three senses use sequential coding. Building up such an internal picture is a detailed and structured process. Changes in layout or routine can be frustrating and anxiety provoking.

Recently one of us watched a seven-year-old partially sighted child who had been away from school for a week making her way around the playground on her first day back after this short absence. Out of the door into the open air, she walked against the wall of the block, touching it all the time for safety, until she reached the corner. She then walked slowly and tentatively on her own away from the building to the climbing frame and slide. There she met a friend and she was again more confident as she could once more feel something familiar and swing on the low over-head bars or slide down the slide. It was the open space of the play-ground which had become unfamiliar and a little daunting. This is so for many visually impaired children when they first go into an unfamiliar room. They may first anchor themselves by a feature, such as a window or a door. Then they learn to walk round the walls and explore the shape of the room in detail. Location in space can be established by use of echo and resonance and with practice a child can learn to hum or clap and pick up the solid surfaces from the resounding sounds from the environ-ment. Sophisticated sonar devices are now available for adults to enable them to detect obstacles in advance.

Walking with a visually impaired person along a new route requires a detailed plan of training. The journey is divided into 'chunks' at first. Then each separate section is identified with a distinctive marker, a gate, a kerb, a crossing or a traffic light, for example. The visually impaired person, whilst learning this route, has to visualise these features and markers in sequence so as to be able to travel the same way alone in future. This person has to be an active learner taking in and recording verbally and experientially the important features. The new and unknown can be frightening and overwhelming, for what the blind person may only be able to perceive is faint light or even just darkness. A good description of how safe travel is taught and internal spatial maps developed is provided by Steve Lockett (1989).

We know the world through our senses – sight, touch, smell, hearing, muscle movement. These senses each have their own recording system, and memories are lodged in our internal lexicon of what we have experienced directly through our own senses, or what we have learned about through someone else's portrayal. We have direct sensations or images, each stored in the modality in which we received them. Connections and associations have to be forged between the separate pieces of knowledge in order to access the full richness and scope of our knowledge. In some cases the links and associations have been well made, in others not. Reliance on one modality to the exclusion or diminution of others can lead to seemingly simplistic unelaborated, inner pictures. Young children, for example, may be taught to draw pictures of a house and garden where the sky is blue and the grass is green. This does not allow for the fact that the sky may often be grey, cloud covered or dull and the grass parched and dry. This process of elaboration must continue throughout life for everyone. For the child with impaired vision, loss of the major sense which co-ordinates and links other sensory impressions, can inadvertently lead to the persistence of 'primitive' or 'naive' inner landscapes.

We have tried to investigate by means of structured experimental tasks how a visually impaired child's inner landscape is constructed. We have explored how a child without sight interprets a two dimensional drawing or how he learns the intricacies of Braille reading. We have explored how a partially sighted child inspects pictures and reconstructs what is seen into a meaningful whole. Here then is integration in its essence.

Underpinning these scientific investigations have been the current models and theories derived from the world of psychology about how the sighted populace goes about the same tasks. It is exciting to find that in the most unattainable and unknowable part of man's mind, all of us, sighted and blind alike, often use the same strategies, but in different measure.

In the case of processing words, we have based our respective work with young blind and partially sighted children on the information processing model presented by Ellis (1984). This in turn summarised the findings of the previous decade and is still being amplified and reshaped in the light of new knowledge. The questions being asked were whether readers did use two forms of processing. The first would be based on stored knowledge about the printed or Brailled word, an equivalent to a 'look and say' strategy where the association is learnt between the 'look-touch' of a word and its meaning or name, sometimes called lexical reading. The second is a different sort of mechanism which does not rely on memory to any great extent but instead allows the child to use rules to move from letters to their associated sounds, blend them together and produce an appropriate pronunciation which in turn is recognised. Work on the effect of analogy established that there were interactions between the two processes when it came to the written word, but for the skilled reading of print it was possible that the second process of decoding was redundant. We established that if the skills of young blind readers were put under pressure by so reducing the Braille dots that normal tactile means were insufficient to read the text, then these readers did turn to decoding or phonological processing to support their weakened ('touch-say') tactile reading. The second strategy was there, it seemed, as a backup (Pring, 1982).

Another group of partially sighted children with whom we worked represented a different method (Corley and Pring, 1993b). They were one class in a school where they had been taught to read by a strongly 'phonic' method. They had been taught to sound out the words letter by letter, letter group by letter group. This was partly inevitable as their use of the closed circuit television monitor so enlarged the print that it was often difficult to take in a whole word at one glance or fixation. The question we asked was whether these readers would ever become lexical readers, using visual processing only, or would they always employ the processing strategy they had been taught so rigorously in their early reading life. This issue relates to the one brought up by O'Connor and Hermelin (1978) where they argued that the familiarity of the blind with certain kinds of information, but not others, might affect the way they naturally dealt with new information. For example, the visually impaired would be far more familiar with sequential, temporally based information arriving at the senses a bit at a time. This is the natural form for language processing, many types of movement processing and indeed exploration strategies. However, it contrasts with 'gestalt based', holistic strategies often predominant in our perception of the visual world, where information seems to be processed in one bite, in a parallel way.

We looked at how the partially sighted children dealt with different types of letter strings, for example 'pseudohomophones' such as BLOO, which makes sense when spoken aloud but are nevertheless misspelt. We also compared their reading of words which are considered 'regular' since their letter to sound associations can be decoded correctly by a beginner e.g. cat or thespian, to 'irregular' words where the letter to sound association is anomalous, for example, yacht or have (the '-ave' combination is usually pronounced to rhyme with wave). Finally we also investigated whether or not disrupting the 'look' of a word by changing the case of the spelling units systematically would affect reading (e.g. chURch keeps the units intact but still looks strange relative to cHUrcH which disrupts the units but also is unfamiliar).

To summarise our results, we found that partially sighted children could use a non-sequential strategy in reading words. That is they appeared to recognise the words as 'wholes' and did not have to decode them always in a letter by letter fashion. Nonetheless, they still relied on this sequential phonic approach rather more than did their sighted counterparts. This result surprised their teachers because greater similarity was found between the reading of partially and fully sighted children than had previously been imagined. This was strengthened by finding that 'pseudo-homophones' did not necessarily present a more difficult problem to partially sighted than to a matched group of fully sighted children of the same age. The result was unexpected, since we thought that the partially sighted children would be less likely to spot the spelling error and simply use the 'sound' of the word to provide its meaning (e.g. the bloo sky became overcast, correct/incorrect). Finally, we looked at spelling units such as ea or ee and the way that the visually impaired would deal with them. Again no difference between the partially and fully sighted was revealed. It seems that any problems that might at first disadvantage a partially sighted child are overcome relatively quickly. We could see that the partially sighted children were working towards reading fluency using both lexical and non-lexical, decoding skills, albeit in slightly different balance from that of sighted children of the same age.

When it came to comparing how partially sighted and fully sighted children viewed and processed pictures the findings were very different (Corley, 1992). Here, the model provided by Paivio (1986) was a useful framework within which to investigate the processes. In this model there is a representational level at which sensory input can be matched and recognised. There is also a referential level at which links can be made with material in the same modality (words with words) or between modalities (words with pictures). Two sets of experiments were planned to see whether partially sighted and fully sighted children differed in their abilities in both these spheres. Sets of black and white line drawings were assembled which had been rated for their familiarity and complexity (Snodgrass and Vanderwart,1980). When it came to matching or recognising pictures they had seen before, the partially sighted children were as good as the fully sighted ones, both immediately and after a delay of some 20 – 30 minutes. However, differences between the two groups showed when it came to recalling studied pictures. To be able to do this effectively required the child to name the picture within the limited viewing time of five seconds. This was of course difficult for the partially sighted children, particularly as hard-to-name pictures had been selected. It was studying the nature of their responses to this task which was the most illuminating part of the study in terms of learning how they categorised information in their inner lexicon. Unlike their equal ability to recognise pictures, partially sighted children were significantly worse than fully sighted ones when it came to recalling them. This was so whether the children were simply left to view the pictures for the five seconds allowed them, whether their viewing was preceded by orienting questions, or whether the viewing was followed by an elaborative sentence. Partially sighted children recalled most when just left to view at study time, but fully sighted children were assisted by the relevant elaborative sentences, designed to aid visual rehearsal. The fully sighted seemed to have taken in the picture so quickly and easily that the elaborative sentence could be processed easily, the words enabling the picture to be reviewed. The partially sighted were probably still struggling to make out what the lines and shapes were. The words spoken after the children had viewed the picture could not be processed so quickly. Indeed one partially sighted child specifically complained that they followed too soon. The lines and shapes of the pictures had been so poorly discerned that the words did not make much sense and so did not aid recall.

It was in their verbal recall and in the names the children ascribed to the pictures that important information about processing lay. There was, for example, a picture of a peach. In the short time available the partially sighted children could see it was a round shape, but they did not identify the small indentation which to the sighted viewer indicated fruit of some kind: the circle was not a perfect one. If the shape was identified as a circle or as round then it might be entered into memory as a ball. If the small dent in the circle was seen, the picture might have been identified as an apple, or even as a peach, and entered into memory as such. All depended on seeing the minute but significant detail in the first place. It was this attention to small detail in the time available that was so difficult for partially sighted viewers. It was this which shed light on the nature of some possible confusions in their inner categorisation system.

This same kind of difficulty in seeing small distinctive detail affected the children's ability to make quick, accurate category choices in every sphere. Does a short haired girl in jeans look more like a boy or a girl? Does a four legged animal look more like a dog or a donkey or a pony? For the sighted person such visual discriminations can be achieved in milliseconds but for the visually impaired person it takes several seconds, at least.

Curiously, we fall into assuming that the only way of perceiving the richness of our world is by sight, for the sighted are in the majority and it is they who have constructed environments and a culture designed in the main to be seen. We think too readily of those without sight as being deprived of this heritage. But here, in this chapter, we have begun to learn of alternative ways of perceiving things, providing the time is there, and opportunities for exploring and experiencing exist in abundance.

References

Corley, B.M.G. (1992). Partially Sighted Children: The Visual Processing of Words and Pictures. (London University: unpublished PhD thesis.)

Corley, G. and Pring, L (1993a). Partially Sighted Children: The Visual Processing of Words And Pictures. Paper presented at the British Educational Research Association Conference, Liverpool. UK.

Corley, G. and Pring, L. (1993b). Reading strategies in partially sighted children. *International Journal of Rehabilitation and Research* 16, 209-20.

Corley, G and Pring, L. (1995). Visual Memory and Partially Sighted Children. *Journal of Visual Impairment and Blindness.* In press.

Ellis, A. W. (1984). *Reading, Writing and Dyslexia: A Cognitive Analysis.* New York: Lawrence Erlbaum Associates.

Fraiberg, S. (1977). *Insights From The Blind.* Souvenir Press (E&A)

Landau, B. and Gleitman, L.R. (1985). *Language and Experience: Evidence from the Blind Child.* Cambridge, USA: Harvard University Press.

Lockett, S. (1989). Mobility Education. In: Gianetta Corley, Donald Robinson and Steve Lockett, *Partially Sighted Children.* NFER-Nelson.

O'Connor, N. and Hermelin, B. (1978). *Seeing and Hearing and Space and Time.* London: Academic Press.

Paivio, A. (1986). *Mental Representation – A Dual Coding Approach.* Oxford University Press.

Pathak, K. and Pring, L. (1989). Tactual Picture Recognition in Congenitally Blind and Sighted Children. *Applied Cognitive Psychology.* 3, 337-50.

Pring, L. (1982). Phonological and tactual coding of Braille in blind children. *British Journal of Psychology,* 73, 351-9.

Pring, L. (1992). More Than Meets The Eye. In: R.Campbell (Ed.), *Mental Lives.* Oxford: Blackwell.

Pring, L. and Walker, J. (1993). Degree of accuracy in perceiving graphic and pictorial information by touch. *International Journal of Rehabilitation Research* 16, 221-33.

Rilke, R.M. (1957). *Duino Elegies.* German Text with English translation, introduction and commentary by J.B. Leishman and Stephen Spender. Revised Edition. Third Impression. London: Hogarth Press.

Snodgrass, J.G. and Vanderwart, M. (1980). A Standardised Set of 260 Pictures. Norms for Name Agreement, Image Agreement, Familiarity and Visual Complexity. *Journal of Experimental Psychology: Human Learning and Memory* 6(2), 174-215.

Chapter 2
The Inner Life of Deaf Children

PATRICIA KIFF AND DAVID BOND

Introduction

'With young children words are valueless unless they are backed by the true coin of things and doings. They have their own place as aids to experience, and to clear thought about experience' (Isaacs, 1930). 'For most children "spoken language" helps to shape thought, creating inner speech, internal dialogues, and codes for thinking' (Wood, 1980).

But what of those children who form a minority group of the population where approximately 1 to 1.2 per thousand have a severe to profound hearing loss? How do differences in perception and acquisition of language affect the shaping of thought, the creation of inner speech, internal dialogues and the codes for thinking?

What sort of 'stuff' do deaf think in? Do they have dreams? What do they imagine? How do they perceive the world? Are there differences in the way that they perceive the world from the way in which hearing people perceive it? If a deaf child has not had the opportunity to develop a natural language for communicating as in the case of a natural sign language, and if the use of spoken auditory/aural communication is limited, are they able to organise their inner feelings and emotions? And do they dream in vivid visual dreams about events they have observed or experienced? Whilst the majority of hearing impaired children and adults integrate and function successfully and independently in open society, there are many studies which indicate a higher incidence of emotional and behavioural problems amongst children and people who are deaf (Bond, 1993).

Is it lack of access to an appropriate system of communication and a system of language to develop thought that has resulted in various writers describing the behaviour of the deaf as being egocentric, possessive, rigid, and selfish, lacking in flexibility, superficial, physical, lacking in imagination, regarding issues as being one or the other with no shades of grey, showing an absence of negotiation skills, and failing to recognise the 'rights and needs of others' (Bond 1993)? Or is it a difference in language and difference in perception of the world and experiences which may lead to some of these observations?

As approximately 90% of deaf youngsters grow up in hearing families, most families have little experience of deafness prior to the arrival of their deaf child, and consequently the relationship between a deaf child and his family may be one of alienation and rejection in view of the problems and inconsistencies of communication and interaction as perceived by the adults and the child. Mutually reinforcing relationships between parent and child through responsive social interaction may fail to develop in the case of the deaf child who does not respond to verbal communication and the exchange of feeling between mother and child. Parents and families who don't develop communication appropriate to the child's needs will sometimes use extremes of management to control the deaf child, either allowing them too much freedom without firm consistent boundaries, or 'over disciplining' the child and then exerting substantially more control than they would for their hearing children.

Delving into the mind or the inner world of a deaf person, may to lead to a discovery that the images and memories of the deaf child must be very different from those of the hearing child. For many deaf children, language and communication may be substantially distanced from experiences, particularly in the early years. Thus when attempting to recall those experiences, how much had perceptions changed, and was recall and memory affected by this delay?

The factors which may affect the deaf person's perception of the world around them

The cultural environment

Differences in experiences and perception of the world around them and the effect of hearing loss on social, emotional responses and experiences, and interaction with the cultural environment in which the individual develops, are different from those of the hearing person. For deaf people who grow up in a cultural environment where parents and friends are deaf, and are able to create a responsive, communicational and interactional environment, there is evidence of distinctly better mental health and higher levels of attainment than for deaf children growing up in a hearing cultural environment. As noted in Bond (1993) there may be other factors which also contribute to this difference.

Observations of hearing parents working with deaf children indicate that hearing parents are less likely to respond to children's initiatives in communication unless they are specially trained. Their interactions with the deaf child are more likely to be 'controlling' than responsive and reciprocal. Wood (Wood *et al.*, 1986) indicates that a three-year-old hearing child controls approximately 75% of his interactions with adults. The deaf child on the other hand has most interactions 'controlled' by supervising adults. In communication and interaction with deaf children there is more likely to be a higher level of physical contact in order to establish attention, control and communication. Differences in behaviours such as these may lead to differences in interpretation of socially inappropriate or other behaviours, and may in some respects be responsible for placing deaf children in a position of vulnerability and risk, e.g. where deaf children may accept touching or inappropriate contacts and inappropriate controls because of the high level of control which is applied to them from an early age, and the lack of opportunity to control interactions and communication through socially appropriate behaviours. Thus deaf children may view themselves in a negative role, accept the directions and controls of others, blame others for their behaviours – and have difficulty in accepting or understanding their own actions.

Many deaf children grow up in an environment where they do not have access to deaf adults. Parental wishes and aspirations for their child to have 'normal' hearing and speech may affect the child who is deaf, and these influences may combine with a lack of models of successful deaf people. In these situations deaf children may view themselves as a failure, they may absorb parents' feelings of guilt, denial, anxiety, etc. and feel individual guilt about being deaf. They may also think that, because of the absence of models of deaf adults, they are going to grow out of their deafness when they get older, sometimes in order to fulfil the wishes of their hearing parents.

Other difficulties in the perception of the world around them will sometimes occur through displacement of blame which appears (from a clinical and observational viewpoint) to occur with much higher frequency amongst deaf children than it does in hearing children, where blame is ascribed to others without taking responsibility for one's own behaviours and actions, e.g. 'he told me to' or 'I was only copying him'. How much of this behaviour arises through control of the child by others from a very early age? Is this high level of control also a major contributory factor to the behaviour of those deaf children who have difficulty in accepting responsibility for their own behaviour, and difficulty in developing a moral, ethical code of behaviour with consequent responsibilities to the society in which they live, showing a degree of guilt only when they are 'caught' doing something they shouldn't? Often these individuals will repeat behaviour for which they have been previously 'corrected' when they think they may not be caught!. Whilst these patterns of behaviour are also evident in hearing society, they appear more prevalent amongst children who are deaf and who have long histories of rejection or alienation.

Perceptions and inner feelings of a deaf person growing up in a hearing world

When language comes after the experience it is sometimes very difficult to recall and to structure the experience. Consequently, when there is a gap between the experience and linguistic development the recall of feelings, using a language which wasn't previously available, may evoke a different image from that which was originally experienced. How does the difference in time between experience, perception and linguistic development result in accentuating or distorting experience and emotion?

The memories of a young deaf adult remain vivid, particularly those memories which reflect the harsh and sometimes punative 'rejecting' behaviours of the society in which they lived.

> I was living in a silent world with no noises around. I didn't feel anything different when my parents tried to teach me to speak, and I struggled to learn the spoken language.

> Before I wore my hearings aids my world was silent. I noticed my parents were not wearing hearing aids so I asked why they didn't wear hearing aids. They tried to explain to me that they could hear and I couldn't. At first I was bewildered, wondering why I was different from them, and why I couldn't hear like them. I wanted to be like them. It had been on my mind for a long time when a teacher used to say to us deaf children that it was important to wear hearing aids as one day we would be hearing like the teacher. When my mother told me that I would always be deaf, I thought it was pointless to wear hearing aids.

> I remembered when I was just 5, and attended an oral school for deaf children where we were not allowed to use sign language. At play time my friends and I were playing gleefully, chatting away and using our imagination. I was using natural gesture and mime, showing how my father drove a car. My teacher called me to her room and gave me five strokes on my hands with a cane. Afterwards my hands were painted red all over to show other teachers and children that I was signing like a monkey (at that time if we used to express something through our hands we were called like monkeys in a zoo). Inside of me I was heartbroken, humiliated, and hated myself for being deaf, and had always thought why me, I am the only one to blame when problems arise.

> My hands were throbbing with pain and I cried my eyes out in private. It was a painful experience for me – some 26 years ago. I compare that to the present time when deaf children are allowed to sign and express themselves in sign language and they are encouraged to feel good and positive about themselves and to communicate freely no matter what mode of communication they are using. This helps to build up their self-esteem and identity which enables them to accept their deafness. They are now able to have deaf role models to work alongside in order to provide them with positive adult role models.

When I was young and realised that I was deaf and different from other children I felt that there was a communication barrier between us. I was bullied and taunted by hearing children. I couldn't understand why I couldn't talk like them and be part of their world. My mother reassured me and encouraged me to gain confidence by mixing with other children. I was isolated and lonely with no hearing friends, but had plenty of deaf friends at school. Sadly most of my deaf friends lived a long way from my home and I wasn't able to share or meet with them at holiday time. I kept trying to explain to my mother how I felt, but felt that she couldn't understand my frustrations due to communication difficulties. I didn't really know how to express myself, and I felt rather oppressed by hearing people when I was little. I don't blame my parents, as I realise now they didn't have much support from professionals. I was asked to join groups like Guides, but when the girls and the leader couldn't communicate what I was supposed to be doing, I became more and more frustrated. Eventually I built up frustrations over a long period and exploded and walked out. It took some time, but I realised that I was not part of the group, and felt very angry and isolated with those girls for making my life hell. Now that I understand more about the hearing world I don't blame them because they were not aware of the effects of my deafness or my frustrations.

When I have talked with other deaf people who went to partially hearing units or mainstream schools, I have found that we have had similar problems and similar experiences. In many cases we were in those days of over 20 years ago encouraged to deny our deafness. We all felt that we had difficulties in integrating fully with hearing children due to different attitudes and backgrounds. I was aware of differences, and these were sometimes highlighted, as in a class when I was studying human biology integrated with hearing girls. One girl asked me if I had a boyfriend, she then said sarcastically, 'well you don't have a boyfriend because you are deaf and different from the others'. The negative things that girls like this said to me made me feel that my life would always have to be different from other adolescents. I wanted to have the same experiences and the same enjoyment as other children in the hearing world; I wanted to enjoy relationships in joining teenage activities, but I felt much of this was being denied me because I was different from the others.

One of the features which stands out in the many personal accounts of school and growing up, which are produced by people who are profoundly deaf, are the years of confusion and unhappiness experienced in the hearing world and at home, before the world started to make some sense to the deaf child.

As they formed relationships with their deaf peers, and as they expanded their skills in signed communication (despite being forbidden to do so in some school environments) they started to develop a base of language and communication, interaction on equal terms, and feelings of achievement and being valued wherever they were given opportunities to succeed.

For other deaf children, now adults, confusions about the world around them were added to by adults who took them from one place to another without adequate preparation or explanation. The experience of being taken to a hospital, and examined by a man in a white coat, sometimes even held down during the examination, with no explanation of what was happening, and sometimes with pain, left indelible memories and confused perceptions. Being left in a hospital for treatment without access to parents or to people who could communicate with them in some cases has left lasting scars, which have only been resolved through very careful counselling at a later stage of development.

Of particular concern are those deaf children who were placed in educational environments where they were not able to succeed, where they didn't have peers with whom they could communicate, identify and compete with on equal terms. Their attempts at communication were not responded to or understood by supervising adults, and they could not understand peers or adults. For many of these children, school and hearing society represented a threatening, sometimes bullying and rejecting environment.

Because the negative behaviours expressed towards them, in the anger of adults and the bullying of other children, were very often physical and visual, they learned and developed inappropriate ways of behaviour. Those who developed these ways of behaving were identified as being problem deaf children, who were subsequently transferred to schools for the deaf or other educational environments on the grounds of their inappropriate behaviour, rather than failure of professional assessment and identification of need and the failure of educational placements to provide appropriately for their needs.

Sadly, inappropriate assessment, treatment and inappropriate management and placement continues to damage deaf children in society today. Lack of appropriate professional knowledge, training, understanding and experience still leads to inappropriate advice to parents, and consequent placement in unsuitable environments.

A few years ago a deaf boy who had some problems in relationships was brought to David Bond's attention by the headteacher of a school for autistic children. The boy had been placed in the school because it was said that he couldn't communicate. He was unable to communicate orally/aurally and required signed communication. In the discussion with him, and in subsequent discussions after he was transferred to a school for the deaf, he commented:

> When they put me in this school I couldn't understand anybody. I couldn't understand why the other children wouldn't communicate with me. I couldn't understand the adults and they couldn't understand me. I thought I was supposed to behave like everyone else. I thought that was why they put me there. I became more switched off. I became more lonely. Later my teacher and the headteacher showed a particular interest in me. I think they understood that I wasn't like the other children. They started to realise that I could learn.

Later, when he had been transferred to a school for the deaf he commented:

> Now I'm in a school where the teachers, the care staff and the other children understand me and I can understand them. I want to be with people who can understand me, and I want to be able to understand them.

This young man, and other deaf people who are placed in environments in which they are unable to communicate because their peer group have different needs from them, and the staff who are working with them are unable to communicate effectively, may develop other patterns of atypical behaviour, including marked difficulties in interrelating and interacting with other people. They may start to develop very negative views of themselves. They see themselves as failures, inadequate, and unwanted. They may view the world as a threatening, confusing and aversive environment. They need to be placed in an environment in which they have appropriate communication in order to develop interaction skills and understanding so they can participate on equal terms with peers, and develop an understanding and appreciation of the world around them. If this does not happen, their mental health may be permanently damaged.

Even when the child who is deaf or hearing impaired has a lot of useful residual hearing, they may still be faced with having to guess what is going on in their home and school environment because they miss out on most of the essential small pivotal words in spoken communication. They may be able to 'get by' in the ordinary class with little tricks, through becoming astute observers of other people's behaviour. This was shown in the case of a boy David Bond was asked to assess. He was in an ordinary class and had a hearing loss in the severe range i.e. in excess of 70 decibels. Aided responses to sound in a clinical setting indicated function within the 30 to 40 decibel range (i.e. with his hearing aids set appropriately). Despite compression of sound, his hearing aid caused difficulties in one ear. He also complained of difficulties in comprehension in a classroom setting. Teaching staff and peers felt that he understood them perfectly, although they couldn't understand him at times. During a period of observation, when the attendance register was being called, he responded at the 5th name instead of the 6th. He didn't know that another child had been admitted to the class that week and the new child's name appeared higher in the register than his. Through careful observation of his behaviour in interactions throughout the day, the young man was seen to flit from group to group in a playground situation and to watch his peers for visual cues. Whenever the whole class was asked to do something, he was always the one who responded a little later, or when instructions were complex he had to check with his peers for each stage of the instructions. In discussion with him (oral/aural discussion), he said that he had learnt that if he watched other children carefully, it saved him from getting into trouble. He felt he wasn't as clever as the other children even though he was much better at mathematics than most of them were. He felt sometimes that they were talking about him (the staff and other children) and when they looked at him sometimes they laughed. He liked the attention that he got from the visiting teacher of the deaf and from the remedial teacher, because they helped him with his hearing aids and his English. Their visits made him feel rather special, but although he tried really hard he couldn't do as well as other children. Sometimes the other children teased him when the adults weren't looking or weren't there. They called him names and tried to make him angry, so that he would get into trouble. Yes, they were his friends, but they didn't seem to like him sometimes. They didn't come to his home.

This young man subsequently moved to a aural/oral school, and then to a grammar school (oral/aural) for deaf students. We understand that he progressed very satisfactorily in that environment, established a more positive self image and continued successfully to higher education. His friends made at the Grammar School (for deaf students) are still friends. Not all deaf people grow up with negative images and negative recall about their past. There are many who have had successful experiences, being founded upon effective communication and interaction from a very early stage of their development. For some of these people early interaction may have been through aural/oral communication, which they were enabled to understand because they were able to make use of their residual hearing, and to understand spoken language. Their parents were very often supported by very experienced teachers of the deaf and educational audiologists who were able to provide them with sound practical and realistic advice, guidance and support in preparing their hearing impaired or deaf child for the world outside (Tucker and Nolan| 1984; Webster and Ellwood, 1985).

Deaf people who have grown up in an environment in which siblings and sometimes parents are deaf, are often placed at a significant advantage, as indicated earlier in this chapter. The combination of a family where other siblings were deaf, with good support for the parents (in helping them understand the importance of communication, interaction, and the difficulties in facing the world from the children's perspective), may have led to the views of Jill, who is severely to profoundly deaf and a bilingual communicator using British Sign Language and spoken English.

> Sure I'm deaf – so what. My parents treated me like any other child, but they gave me a lot of time to talk things through, and to explain things to me. They were helped by the advisory teacher, who has remained a family friend ever since. They also met a lot of other professionals who were very helpful, and although some people gave prejudiced advice, my parents always sifted through it and took what they thought was best for me. They tried to include

me in every activity in the local neighbourhood and with other groups. When people didn't understand, my parents took time out to explain what deafness was all about. It must have been exhausting for them, because I was a very demanding child – I must have caused them to become very exasperated at times.

Yes, we had our ups and downs, I often couldn't understand things that were being said, sometimes I made silly mistakes, and so did my family. They didn't get too worried when I made mistakes, and they laughed at themselves! Ours was a happy home. I liked those long discussions with my mother and father. I am sure there were times where we had misunderstandings. There were times when things went wrong. There were times when I was bullied by children outside, or treated in a cruel and insensitive way by hearing adults. It still happens, it's a fact of life. I think probably that happens to everyone, not just to deaf people.

One of the problems for people who are deaf is that they are in a minority group in society, but probably include the widest range of additional disabilities of other groups of people who are disabled, and have the most heterogeneous needs and range of abilities. Many writers, parents, professionals and even the deaf themselves, fail to appreciate this extremely wide range of needs and abilities. This is sometimes reflected in the different 'camps' of people who claim to represent the interests of the deaf. There are those who suggest that all deaf or hearing impaired people should be educated aurally/orally, or those who think that only sign language is appropriate for deaf people. Fortunately a growing number of parents, professionals and groups of deaf people recognise and emphasise the importance of appropriate communication from a very early age, combined with placement in appropriate environments according to needs, are likely to be the most beneficial.

However, the same problems which have applied in oral/aural communicational and interactional environments in affecting the deaf person's perceptions of the world around them, and consequently affecting their inner, emotional world, have also applied to deaf people who have been placed in signing 'deaf culture' communities where there may also be no recognition or appreciation of their individual differences or individual rights as a human being. Just as the institutionalised abuses by 'hearing society and culture' can adversely affect the development and perceptions of the person who is deaf, institutionalisation and beliefs of 'deaf culture' can have negative effects. This occurs particularly where 'deaf culture' may be equally as restrictive and controlling as hearing society, and where the individual may not be provided with opportunity to develop as an individual and to make decisions which do not fit into the requirements of the 'deaf culture'.

Tom Bertling (1994) lost his hearing after having acquired spoken language and was first admitted to a school for the deaf at the age of 10, a school in which sign language was often used without any spoken language, sign language which he was then unable to understand. He was placed in a class of children about his age and was given work which was substantially below the level at which he had been previously been able to succeed. He describes the experience as 'realisation that I felt that my life was slowly becoming someone else's and my whole world was being shrunk into a closely controlled and monitored situation where decisions I once used to make were being made for me'. Bertling describes innumerable incidents in which he was expected to conform to the requirements of the deaf community and deaf culture rather than being accepted and valued as an individual and given opportunity to make decisions and to take or accept responsibility for his own behaviour.

As indicated earlier in this chapter, there appears to be a significant difficulty for some who work and live with people who are deaf, and amongst the population of people who are deaf, to appreciate the need for a wide range of resources and facilities and provision to meet the very heterogeneous needs of deaf people. The inner feelings of people who are deaf are sometimes very strongly aroused against this lack of awareness and institutionalised abuse, which has been metered out to them in their childhood. Consequently, there is sometimes a tendency to dismiss or uncritically accept provision which bears any relation to that which they had experience of in their childhood. There is also a tendency to generalise feelings about negative early childhood experiences, to make uninformed judgements about the suitability of current educational provision for the deaf children of today, even though it may have (or should have) substantially changed and improved. This is clearly shown in Tom Bertling's book *A child sacrificed to the deaf culture*. It is also apparent in some deaf people who have had negative experiences in the hearing world, who advocate non-use of residual hearing, non-use of hearing aids, non-access to innovations such as cochlear implantation, and only school for deaf education. Both views fail to appreciate the needs of deaf people, and fail to recognise a need to provide people who are deaf and their families with the same range of choices which are available to the hearing, thereby giving them similar opportunities for being valued and for taking responsibility for their own decision making. Is it that high levels of inappropriate control in infancy and childhood result in inappropriate controlling behaviour in adulthood?

How do people who are deaf organise their inner world? How do they dream? What is the stuff they think in?

One of the greatest difficulties in understanding or attempting to interpret the inner world of deaf children is our own limitation in effective communication. Often we have to interpret by observing children's behavioural responses and the grave danger remains that we are projecting our own thoughts, feelings and emotions into the interpretation of the child's reactions and responses to the world around him. The observations provided early in the chapter report a mixture of emotions, feelings and interpretations of experience from a variety of deaf people. They reflect a variety of personalities, just as we would find in a hearing society, although we tend to find a higher level of concentration on negative experiences and feelings of confusion, frustration, rejection and failure. When we have asked other deaf people what they think and dream in, the answers have been varied. Some have said that they dream in colour and through sign language, a few have indicated that they dream that they can hear and understand ordinary speech. Some have reported that they dreamed they were hearing, and have indicated they would like to be hearing even though they enjoy their deaf friends and contact with 'deaf culture'. The picture of what deaf, and particularly profoundly deaf, people think in seems to be a world of visual image, pictorial information, movement – almost like a moving picture, as described by one person. Childhood memories often seem vivid cinemascopes of experience.

Summary

To delve into the inner world of the person who is deaf is an almost impossible task for someone who is hearing, and is still difficult for a deaf person. We have tried to give an insight into some of the feelings of deaf people and some of the factors which may influence some of these feelings. For many deaf people there is a major difficulty in the distance between their feelings and perceptions, and development of language to organise, express, and to assist in the recall of those earlier experiences. Influences of high levels of adult control over the child and experiences of rejection, denial of communication, and failure of placement in inappropriate environments may all serve to create feelings of inadequacy and inferiority, combined with a tendency to be more accepting of inappropriate social behaviours because of the visual and physical images in the world around them. Heightened awareness of adult anger and desensitisation to the inappropriateness of bullying or physical contact and control may lead to these behaviours being accepted into the repertoire of behaviours available to people who are deaf, and may well be a significant social explanation of higher levels of difficult and deviant behaviour which are shown in the population of people who are deaf, as well as the higher levels of abuse which deaf children suffer – a vicious circle of experience.

Very early identification of deafness, appropriate support and communication, whether it be through signed communication or oral communication, but which provides the child with opportunities to have initiatives and communication recognised and responded to, appear to provide a key to a more positive self image and more positive mental health. Well-informed and experienced professional assesment and assistance appear crucial factors in supporting the family and their deaf child and creating a positive enabling environment to ensure that the individual's rights and needs are recognised, and that the deaf person has positive feelings about being valued as a member of society.

Note of thanks

The writers are indebted to the many deaf children they have worked with over the years, and to innumerable deaf and hearing friends, families, and professional colleagues who have contributed to the ideas contained in this chapter. Please forgive us for the many issues which we have omitted. Our learning experience in this area continues.

References

Bertling, Tom (1994). *A Child Sacrificed to the Deaf Culture* Oregon, USA: Kodiak Media Group.

Bond, D.E. (1993). Mental Health and Children who are Hearing Impaired. In: Varma V. (Ed.) *Coping with Unhappy Children.* London: Cassell.

Isaacs, S. (1930). *Intellectual Growth in Young Children.* London: Routledge. (Cited in Woods D.J. (1980.)

Tucker, I.G. and Nolan, M. (1984). *Educational Audiology* London: Croom Helm.

Webster, A. and Ellwood, J. (1985). *The Hearing Impaired Child in the Ordinary School.* London: Croom Helm.

Wood, D., Wood, H., Griffiths, A. and Howarth, I. (1986). *Teaching and Talking with Deaf Children.* Chichester: Wiley.

Wood, D.J. (1980). Models of Childhood. In: Chapman A.J. and Dillon M. (Eds.) (1980). *Models of Man.* Published by the British Psychological Society UK.

Chapter 3
The Secret Life of the Physically Disabled Child

MICHAEL SMITH

From the outset it needs to be stated that the thoughts of a physically disabled child need not be very different from their able-bodied peers. However there exists a large number of areas that can create differences so affecting the psychological development and therefore thoughts of those physically disabled. These differences fall into two main areas; medical and interactive:

Medical differences

Those medical conditions specific to the disability include:

(i)   neurological damage and its effects
(ii) secondary disabilities, particularly epilepsy, learning difficulties and sensory problems
(iii) conditions developing from the particular disability, e.g. bowel and bladder incontinence, kidney infections, skin lesions, hydrocephalus, etc.

Interactive differences

These areas will have the greatest effect on the psychology and secret life of the disabled child. These areas include:

(i)   familial effects and child rearing practices
(ii) societal feedback, expectations and values
(iii) learning environment
(iv) social relationships with peers and carers
(v)   mobility and accessibility.

Assuming that the 'secret life' is only secret because of the differences between this particular minority group and those of the general population then it will be of early value to posit differences that can arise. The requirements to enable healthy psychological development and subsequent living are well documented. If these conditions are met then any child, physically disabled or not, are less likely to need to dwell in an existence that is 'secret' and different to the conventional.

The following differences (see Table 3.1) are expressed as a continuum and very few physically disabled children will be at the negative extremes across the majority of areas.

Table 3.1

Psychologically healthy	Psychologically unhealthy
growing independence	overreliance on others
social confidence	social withdrawal
growing abilities	learned helplessness
optimism	pessimism or even depression grieving, etc.
objective, realistic	overly fantasising
loosening of parental ties	reliance on parents
healthy ego	excessive use of ego defences
optimally positive body image	poor body image
striving	stagnation, regression

Reasons for the presence of these negative states will follow, with examples of the child's apposite thoughts and also some suggestions for amelioration.

Maturation

Retarded or maldevelopment of disabled children is well chronicled in academic literature and with particular relevance by Lewis (1987), Hersen and Van Hasselt (1990).

A child with motoric problems is less able to interact with the environment. To the child a developing accomplishment in making, doing, running or cycling at speed, climbing, testing agility, using strength and construction are all pleasurable experiences. These cannot be fully experienced by the physically disabled but they may have some understanding acquired through other routes, usually as a comprehending spectator.

Parents, other carers and teachers often underestimate the ability to perform or partially perform tasks or even how psychologically and physically robust these children are in meeting failure. It is not unusual for the child to be markedly more responsive in the different settings of home or school. To deny a child the positive experience enjoyed in one setting but denied in the other is developmentally harmful.

For example, the facility to stand vertically is something most of us take for granted. To be looked down upon (sic) when in a wheelchair is psychologically different. Adrian has an acquired brain injury and is paralysed from the waist downwards. He has no residual speech. The parents have massive concern for Adrian's condition, perhaps not least because father was driving at the time of the motor accident. This means however that Adrian has the extreme and intelligent concern of two responsive people. At home Adrian had use of an expensive full standing frame. In his educational setting there was not an appropriate full standing frame for his use. The parents strongly advocated the use of a frame in both settings. Institutional concern was expressed at the cost and limited use of such a frame. Reservations on its usefulness were tempered by the well-known zealous nature of the parents. Eventually the parents hired a van and brought their frame. To see the psychological difference the frame made to Adrian was inspiring, he positively glowed with satisfaction at being 'bigger'. By various means a second and similar frame was purchased and a psychological link made through Adrian standing every evening to write a letter home. A number of lessons were learnt from this episode.

Maturation will be inhibited if an individual has to receive help or care in a large variety of situations. This may be psychologically accommodated but if overcare is regularly experienced then this will be unnecessarily damaging to development and maturation. Psychologically it is the lack of maturation within older physically disabled children that presents the greatest difference with their more able bodied peers. Because of this the summative view at the end of this chapter will comment on the dynamic effect a number of factors has on maturation.

Child rearing

The effect of various child rearing practices and patterns upon the emerging personality of the child is also well documented in the literature. Workers within the field of disability are well used to the extremes of parenting that are witnessed, with of course many examples of more regular parenting also in evidence. Overprotection is much more prevalent than amongst parents of the non-disabled.

A major component of this overprotection by parents is the high standard expected of themselves but also of others too. It is a form of positive intervention driven by emotional concern. This concern may result from early but continuing guilt or simply that the binding ties necessary in the child's infancy have never been loosened. Indeed if the need to care, as with a helpless infant, is required day after day, year after year, the ties cannot be loosened. This very process may reinforce the bond if only in a non-perceived, habitual manner. From such parents trust for the capabilities of other carers and teachers cannot be assumed. For the child, the separation from parents into the hands of others can be particularly traumatic even if this takes place at a time when the young person is leaving childhood for adulthood. So critical is this problem that resolution is not always possible. The relationship is, or has become symbiotic, and parents often cannot handle the void in their own lives that separation presents. Whilst parents may be able to effect the most personalised levels of care, most are not at the same time able to facilitate independence within their offspring.

Invariably this one child will be the only experience the parents will have of physical disability. If the child attends a mainstream educational setting the child's disability will also be of low prevalence to the school or college. Thus, the experience of knowing what is usual, what is possible and what to expect is lacking. To remedy this the parents must actively seek some association with parents of similar children in order to even out some of the misconceptions. The child should also have some substantial benefit from a multi-professional team and this is usually only to be found in a specialist school or college. Not to gain a wider overview on behalf of the child is to labour in ignorance, to a greater or lesser degree. If as a consequence of this ignorance the child does not receive various experiences, learning or therapeutic support or access to opportunities then psychological delay or misconception will take root in the child. The home and some non-specialist settings do not give the developing child sufficient opportunity to participate or fully explore.

It is the writer's experience that by mid or late adolescence most parents painfully recognise the lack of maturity in their offspring. This they translate into a need for training in independence, preferably in a structured, specialist residential setting. By adolescence the extent of their caring is clearly illuminated and parents wish to see some resolution of the perpetual care problems. If this residential experience does take place then massive readjustment is needed by both parents and offspring. This readjustment is a 'new birth' and can lead to new personalities that are not subjected to compromise in either party. A growing apart is seen as emerging maturation and independence but the 'new' personalities also require attention. To some in late adolescence such a separation can be felt to be as bad as death itself, whilst to others as a liberation and a new life.

Educational experience

The educational experience of the physically disabled is nothing short of a lottery. It depends on where the child lives, resources available at the time, societal values, current trends and the assertiveness of his or her parents. Integration, more latterly termed 'inclusion' is becoming the norm for most young physically disabled children, though secondary and/or further education may still be in specialist settings. Clearly the quality of this 'inclusion' will be central to the psychological wellbeing of the individual and to later life chances. The process of integration and inclusion is well documented, if not well researched and further description is considered unnecessary.

Success in education, or at least equal opportunities for success, will have obvious implications for the disabled individuals' self-regard, at least in respect to their academic and educational prowess. Fair opportunity for educational success will not be realised without the following:

(i)   physical access to all necessary educational, comfort and social requirements
(ii)   teachers and support staff having a thorough knowledge of the effects of the disability and consequential needs
(iii) ready availability of physiotherapy, repair and development of electronic and mobility equipment, speech therapy, occupational therapy and aids, specific counselling and nursing support. If not on the educational premises these need to be readily available to reduce educational time lost through 'out patient' appointments
(iv)   appropriate curriculum access to all areas including PE, sport,drama, science and craft
(v)   rest rooms and recovery facilities as required
(vi)   an ability to successfully respond to 'secondary' disabilities such as partial loss of sight or hearing, obscure learning difficulties, epilepsy or emotional difficulties.

Usually the disabled do not expect anything other than equality of access and treatment and education should reflect this basic tenet. Recently, the writer listened to two quite separate accounts from graduates of Oxford universities of how academic success had provided them with a clear mark of acceptability 'as a proper person'. If childhood is seen as an apprenticeship to adult life then as education takes up most of the childhood, any failure will affect the craft of adulthood. Educational achievement usually affects later status, earning power and independence of action. However, there are many non-disabled adults who, rightly or wrongly, perceive education to have failed them. In the later 'secret life' of the physically disabled it would not be psychologically healthy to have a bone of contention about education to add to the many other feelings of deprivation, reliance on others and negative differences.

Carers

Teachers and support staff will be thrust into the role of carers along with parents, other professionals and incidental carers.

The power relationship between the carer and the disabled is a most unequal one. The latter is usually reliant on the carer for even his or her basic needs. This imbalance receives a good deal of covert acceptance from the dependent recipients. Because of the very need it is a disempowerment. The relative comfort of either party in working within this relationship will determine the psychological wellbeing of both. Without this wellbeing the 'secret life' of both will be severely exercised.

Some of the power imbalance that will lead to separate perceptions and the need to sublimate self are as follows:

Table 3.2

Young disabled	Carer
physical dependence	independent
not readily mobile	mobile
relative immaturity	relative maturity
recipient	giver
often the payer	often paid
wheelchair height	erect
continuous needs	continuous labour

The psychological reasons, personal demands and constraints the carer brings to the task of caring will condition the relationship. A professional will be there by choice but not the parent. A professional carer who is there by choice will seek to satisfy the underlying desires that lead to that choice.

The psychological needs of the carer could include the requirement to sublimate self in the service of others, to exert power, as a veneer to a less than satisfactory inner self (correctly perceived or otherwise) or for complex psychosexual reasons. Adults with an inferiority complex may feel safer with the disabled. Such an inferiority complex may be justified! In any of these cases the young disabled person will to some extent be supporting and complying with the carers' often complex and subtle needs. This is in addition to working with their own unformed psyche. Even the most balanced and robust of carers will experience at various times extreme fatigue, boredom, reflected depression and maybe the guilt arising from a perceived inability. McGown (1995) fully describes why 'always being nice to people is not good for you' and of the cumulative harm to carers.

The psychological needs and state of carers are chronicled here because it is the carer or range of carers with whom the young disabled person spends their waking hours. It is the quality of that relationship that can condition the need for a 'secret life' or its very reality.

The carer will invariably bring a distinct persona to the task. Essentially it will be a caring persona as this is the primary role. It is comfortable for the carer to conclude that the more caring the presenting persona the 'better' the carer's role fulfilment. Overcaring is common but stifling to the young person's growth. Some disabled will not even perceive overcaring as they are conditioned to it. A variance to over caring will itself be perceived and often engender a strong reaction. Perceived levels of care needs vary enormously from one disabled child to another and also across tasks. New carers do not always hit the right level and 'overcaring' might appear to be the safer choice. Because the attitude of carers is so important to those dependent upon such care the secret life stemming from extremes of overcaring and undercaring are portrayed.

Duncan was a Junior Leader in the Army and had risen very quickly through the ranks. He then suffered a severe brain injury. After primary rehabilitation he was placed in a vocational specialist college. Duncan had limited wheelchair mobility, speech difficulties and the usual memory impairment. Initially he was treated in a 'generalised' fashion, not least because each person with acquired brain injury has, of course, quite distinct and specific needs. The result of this initial generalised approach was that he was overcared for and this inhibited his rehabilitation. Despite this inhibited progress, Duncan reached the point where he could recognise enough of his former striving self. From this point he eschewed much caring and grew rapidly to a point of gratifying independence. He had not previously received years of 'caring' and was of an independent, resourceful nature as a Junior Leader.

Sharon voiced her unhappiness at perceived parental rejection and was a constant complainer that her needs were not being satisfied by the 'aid carers and professionals'. She was also promiscuous, at only eleven years of age. This way she gained a certain caring and loving and also, to some extent, proved to herself that her disabled body was of some use and attraction. In reality her parents had given her a lot of early love and attention but later, in some contrast, gave her more freedom and less personal care. Such was the degree of contrast that she perceived her parents did not love her. She projected all of her familial love onto her elder brother who was a soldier serving in a peace keeping capacity in Bosnia. Again, the permanence of sustainable love was put into question.

Whatever the disabled young person's perception of their carers, there is always some contrast with the attitude of 'lay persons' within society who do not have to have contact with the disabled. Indeed they may reject such contact.

Sometimes carers will overcompensate for such public attitudes and provide a safe cocoon into which the young disabled may retreat. Ego protection may suggest the disabled take on the value systems of the carers as they are more 'realistic' in fitting in with the perceived needs and wishes of the disabled. Thus a distinct secret life is constructed.

To ensure a caring bond the disabled should preferably be happy at all times, thoughtful, not overdemanding and expressive of gratitude! To higher order carers the learned and repetitive gratitude is nauseating but not easily unlearned by the disabled young person. In showing daily fortitude and resilience in the face of disability a cheery nature is a suitable mask! This can eventually be a mask to the wearer's true opinions, state and means of proper expression. To some the disabled are expected to be fairly cheerful, not to have bad tempers, or worst of all, to express sexual desires. To comply with the societal expectations of some, the persona of the disabled may have to adjust downwards. This can then become a habit (disorder). A tension will then exist with what is 'right'! Whatever the degree of role playing the mask is not real and a secret life is played out behind the mask.

Chasing services

Over the last two decades the financial provisions for the education, health and social services have been severely cut back. These are the services crucial to the wellbeing of the disabled child. Professionals working within these services invariably know the full and often complex needs of the disabled child. And yet how do they prescribe?

The 1981 Education Act was intended to work from an individual need basis. For financial reasons most local education authorities in the UK cannot fulfil these legal obligations. Neither can the social services fulfil obligations, particularly in terms of 'Care in the Community'. In the health services the emphasis is on 'relative cost benefits'. Where is the young client in this?

For the disabled child the educational psychologist is a pivotal professional and the co-ordinator and gatekeeper to many required services. Every day the educational psychologist will face the dichotomy of how to reconcile their professional recommendations with the economic realities faced by their departmental heads. In practical terms this means the school child will not always receive full or sufficient enabling support. This is particularly true in the greyer and seemingly softer areas of dyslexia and moderate learning difficulties though not necessarily so for overt physical disabilities. However, worse than the above, it seems the mediating and facilitating role of the educational psychologist is only rarely available for the young person in further or higher education (Futcher and Carroll, 1994).

Even younger physically disabled children seem fully and painfully aware of unmet service needs, not least because the parents have to frequently ferociously campaign for services and equipment. If the child is left stranded or struggling in certain areas further handicapping from the disability will be felt. If the struggle means inequality in relation to their non-disabled peers it could heighten their anxiety and feelings of little worth. For a child to be left short is to feel somewhat abandoned. The secret life may be tempered by a growing resentment, envy or plain submission to what appears to be their fate.

Societal values

The pervasive negative social attitudes of non-disabled individuals towards those with disabilities and the problems encountered by the disabled in social adaptation have been well chronicled over the years. A quater of a century ago, in a study of societal reactions by Siller, Chipman, Ferguson and Vann (1967) they found the following paramount feelings:

generalised rejection (unpleasant personal reactions)
interaction strain
distressed identification (i.e. anxiety by the non-handicapped regarding their own potential vulnerability)
imputed functional limitations
rejection of intimacy
authoritarian virtuousness (i.e. appearing to be supportive of the disabled but actually negative in attitude)
inferred emotional consequences (i.e. negative character affects, social valence, emotional status)

In a seminal article Asch (1984) stated that:

. . . the presence of someone who actually is or is thought to be disabled arouses in the non-handicapped person a variety of emotions that, at the very least, hinder ordinary social contact with the disabled or behave more formally and in distorted ways if they are forced to interact with handicapped persons . . . (p532).

The writer could reflect from disabled young people several recent instances of each of the circumstances noted by Siller et al and Asch. It shows that over time societal values and attitudes change very slowly or not at all. That today's young people experience the very same responses is disturbing! It does not auger well for the general quality of their life in later years, particularly as the responses to disabled children are of a higher quality than those to disabled adults (as it often is to black babies!).

Much of societal disdain is covert but there can be little more overt than killing of the disabled because of their perceived non-value. Whilst in the western world developing infants are rarely killed it is fairly common for a disabled foetus to be aborted, sometimes fairly routinely. This topic is current and the debate is absorbed by disabled youngsters. This invokes extreme responses and certainly makes them question their own value within society or by their parents. One boy, Martin, asked his parents if they would have aborted him had they known of his disability. He took it as rejection when their reply was one he didn't really wish to hear or know.

This absorption of debate concerning the disabled must inevitably negatively affect the self-esteem of the disabled. Indeed, the recent debacle and duplicity of central government concerning legislative changes must serve as a massive reminder of the dual valuation of some of this country's disabled, of all ages.

Although there is ample reportage of society's negative or distorted attitude toward the disabled, what of leaders in the disability field? To cite some senior educationalists' comments (from within the last twelve months) suggests the professional persona is not always too distant from that of lay people:

Example 1

'I didn't think they (young p.d. students) could produce such good art work', said an independent inspector.

Example 2

'What, physically disabled students studying drama?', exclaimed a senior funding agency administrator.

Example 3

'Can some of your (physically disabled students) really benefit from education', observed a senior inspector.

To be so devalued and stifled on a regular basis is similar to the experience of many blacks and women in the past (and still too much today). Just as the blacks and women can now prove wide competencies it must begin to be the evolutionary turn of the (physically) disabled. Socialisation is proffered through a range of teaching and training packages for the disabled but socialisation cannot be properly learned and practised without much greater equality and respect from within society.

The secret life of the physically disabled has had to accommodate a commonly subservient position within society. General psychological reactions are ones of 'fight' and 'flight'. The wide spectrum of the handicapping effects of disability leave many disabled choosing 'flight', usually in the form of passivity and acquiescence.

Socialisation

Many physically disabled children have weaker social skills. There are a number of profound reasons for this:

    lack of socialisation
    others too ready to think and answer for them
    lower societal expectations and a retreat from rigour
    low self-esteem, particularly of body image
    poor speech and/or articulation skills
    general psychological immaturity

Many of these areas are amenable to remediation but the attitudes and expectations of society in general and parents and teachers in particular must take most of the responsibility for any initial deficits in the child's socialisation. If the child moves in restricted social circles because of mobility difficulties, low peer group interaction or overprotection then social skills cannot be readily acquired or practised. In a specialist school or college the peer group will be more accepting and mobility should be optimally complete. Staff working with a full concentration of disabilities can more readily set realistic expectations - these being usually higher. Likewise the less used to working with the physically disabled the more ready the helper is to 'think and do' for the child, not least as an exercise or proof of caring.

Self-esteem will be discussed more fully later in this chapter, as will 'general psychological immaturity'.

Where, say, a young person with cerebral palsy has speech articulation problems, it does help to communicate with them! Not only for their practice in articulation or use of augmented speech but for psychological reasons. An inability to have a reasonable conversation on a regular basis is more than frustrating. Conversation is the lubricant of life, the main vehicle in social intercourse.

Helplessness

Physically disabled children are handicapped by two main types of helplessness. All helplessness is, of course, comparative.

The first area of helplessness is due to a sheer lack of motoric ability to perform physical tasks due to no or little muscle control, a lack of strength or stamina or motor-perceptual difficulties. Such loss is not likely to be amenable to significant improvement though continuing improvements in enabling equipment and 'smart wheelchairs' reduce physical helplessness and boost psychological wellbeing (Paulsson and Christoffersen, 1987; Nisbet et al, 1995). 'Learned helplessness' (Diener and Dweck, 1980) has been variously described but essentially it comes about because the person is not motivated to attempt or accomplish tasks others believe they are capable of satisfactorily performing. The lack of motivation can be distilled to the following reasons with physically disabled children:

overreliance on others
poor self-esteem and resultant anxiety
depression with attendant apathy
fatigue. Physical disabilities can make daily tasks quite exhausting

It is well accepted by practitioners and in the literature that 'learned helplessness' adds to the handicapping effects of any disability. Indeed, its effects can be more handicapping than the original condition.

Improvements in self-esteem based on real achievements are often able to move the disabled person away from learned helplessness. Clearly if overcaring persists then opportunities for personal achievement are fewer. Enhanced self esteem can also reduce depression and related apathy.

Self-esteem

Gurney (1988)

... sees the self-concept as a symbolic construction built up within a person over a period of years from birth, which is a product of the psychological processes of attention, perception, learning and memory, as they are currently conceived. The self-concept, it is argued, begins as a growing collection of attributes but, in course of time, both overall, and in relation to specific groups of attributes ....

For the older child and adolescent physical attributes are particularly important and for the physically disabled this period poses atypical problems and will affect their emotional state. Self-esteem is the relative degree of worthiness or acceptability which people perceive their self-concept to possess (Gurney, ibid).

It is now generally accepted that the self-concept encompasses different aspects of the self, across situations and concepts and in a wholly dynamic way. The self-concept can change with the 'mood' or current affective state. Because of its affective dynamic and diffused nature, measurement can never be sufficiently objective. This has not prevented a mass of studies using comparative measures. Within this loose theoretical framework two recent studies that attempt to examine the relationship of physically disabled children to their self-concept and self-esteem across settings are recorded by Lalken and Norwich (1990) and Paull (1992). The first study compared the effects of integrated settings, a topic beset by efficacy problems, to self-esteem. Overall general self-esteem was judged to be higher in the fully integrated setting where body image was at its lowest. This usefully suggests that a negative body image need not reduce overall self-esteem.

Paull (ibid) examined the interconstruct correlations across groups in day and residential settings. Children in the residential settings showed lower interconstruct correlations which Paull appears to ascribe to the limitations of the institutional setting. Reality would suggest that generally speaking it is children with more complex difficulties that are found in residential specialist settings. Paull did suggest the latter had blunted cognitive structures and category systems for judging self and others. A lack of differentiation is associated with restricted psychological development.

.... Just as normal children who have not shown any particular interest about their appearance may become preoccupied with it soon after puberty, so children with physical handicaps may, at this stage of life, become acutely concerned about their disability for the first time in their lives. Despite this possibility, low self-esteem is not a frequent occurring characteristic in adolescents with chronic illness .... (Graham (1986))

Perceptions of body image can be subjective and grossly misconceived. Perception is usually by comparison so how do the physically disabled compare themselves? Foundations for comparison and inaccuracies suggestive of some free floating anxiety in this are sufficient to fuel a different 'secret life'.

Fantasy and adjustment to handicap

The opposite to reality is fantasy. The more physically disabled a person is the more they are removed from the reality of everyday tasks, socialisation, exploratory activities and physical access. Their world is not conducted as a first-hand experience but largely gleaned through others. Any image they have of themselves is likely to be distorted; compared and developed from weak and undifferentiated constructs. A severely disabled person is likely to be constantly reminded of what they can't do and what they are not. Nowadays the media presents flashing images of glamour and adventure. How often is the hero grossly physically disabled!?

It is also noticeable that within the young disabled's shaky constructs a change in carer or staff role will elicit a 'different self'. That so many such adolescents construct or allow themselves an active fantasy life is hardly surprising - such a 'secret life' must be a more attractive way of spending time than merely 'vegetating'. The fantasy can be an escape from the unacceptable realities of their everyday life with its hard won achievements. At other times the fantasy can serve as a denial of the disability.

Paul was told by his father he was not different but 'normal' and eventually could walk. Complete paralysis below his waist meant that Paul could only harbour fantasies of walking. He constructed his future around walking. Two other young adolescents, both with severe spina bifida, fantasised about owning Harley Davidson motorcycles. That these youngsters were 'adopted' by the local Hells Angels Chapter gave them roles and socialisation they otherwise would not have experienced. The riders, in a very matter of fact way, simply strapped the youngsters to their backs as they rode the motorcycles. Did this substantiate or enlarge the fantasy?

Adjustment to a disability is relative. Is it healthy to totally accept or totally reject one's physical disability? The level of acceptance is usually on the continuum between these two extremes. How and where it is anchored mainly depends on the mental health and environment of the young person.

The stages of adjustment have been viewed as parallel to those described in trauma literature (Kubler-Ross, 1969; Hersen and Hasselt, 1990). Whilst this is easier to visualise in the case of sudden traumatic injury or death the writer concludes that these stages are also utilised, to a greater or lesser extent, in those disabled from birth or an early age. To some physical disability is a living death. Lewis and Doorlag (1983) suggest that the child suffering or anticipating loss moves through the following stages, not always in strict order or for an equal period of time. Indeed the writer suggests that such is the sense of perceived loss by some disabled young people that they move through or sometimes fixate at one of the levels, or across a small cluster of levels.

Positive improvements in mental health can encourage a general move from pre-morbid conditions for those who do not have a 'valid' reason for grieving. Degenerative conditions such as muscular dystrophy, Duchenne Type, often lead to 'self-mourning'.

Shock and disbelief - this serves as a temporary anaesthesia holding the child's sense of self-esteem together for a brief time.

Crying (sometimes hysterical) - this usually provides the needed emotional release.

Feelings of isolation and loneliness - this may help the child feel the need for others and to experience the discomfort which alienation brings. A degree of personal untidiness may be observed at this stage.

Psychosomatic symptoms - this may momentarily deviate the child's attention from the fatal prognosis to lesser conditions.

Panic - this pushes the child to explore all possibilities and to eventually accept the dying process is occurring.

Guilt feeling - this eventually enables the child to accept the fact that nobody is to blame and that the process of dying is unlikely to be reversed.

Hostility - resentment - the child attempts to defend and protect his ego by projecting these negative feelings onto teachers, parents and friends.

Resists usual routine - the child questions the worth and complains of the difficulty of doing everyday activities in an effort to come to terms with the requirement of continued living.

Reconciliation - this very positive stage enables avoidance of feelings of hopelessness and the inevitability of death.

Acceptance - of living and work yet to be accomplished. The child becomes a deeper more profound person - young in years but old in experience.

Even during transient physical disability, the above reactions are evidenced. Stewart (1991) describes a group of twenty-one athletes who underwent knee surgery. Strong time effects correlated with the mood states as recovery took place. For the permanently physically disabled it is easy to see a fixation with mood states where recovery is not possible.

Berry and Zimmerman (1983) revise a five stage model of grieving which accounts for parental adjustment to the issues of the idealised child and to rearing the disabled child. Professional support practices are also outlined.

Denial is used to protect the disabled from the reality in which they find themselves. This state is dysfunctional where it interferes with rehabilitation, everyday commerce or mental health. With sound mental health this stage will be largely transitional. Some long-term physically disabled youngsters are locked into this stage and the outlook for future adjustment is not always positive.

Anger may be observed as a reaction to a physical or psychological condition or accident and against perceived diminished life-changes, inequalities and reliance on others. Denial may be linked with anger and either or both offer impedance to growth or rehabilitation. Depression reflects the disabled young person's feelings of inability, hopelessness and negative views of what the future can hold. Depression and masked depression is prevalent in the adolescent who is physically disabled. Suicide is sometimes considered though rarely attempted. Indeed, self-harm is not prevalent. Within a sense of futility and hopelessness the secret life will often be a painful one.

Diagnostic criteria associated with depressive conditions are frequently observed in the physically disabled:

appetite disturbances e.g. over and under eating
sleep disturbances e.g. a loss of sleep or excessive sleep patterns
pyschomotor inactivity and overactivity
loss of pleasure in activities
loss of energy
feelings of worthlessness
impairments in thinking and concentration
recurrent suicidal ideas

taken from Graham (1986).

The jolly stampede towards 'inclusion' and 'integration' neglects these unrecognised needs of the disabled child. With such a depressive 'secret life' can such a child be 'included'? Further the physical needs of students have invariably been met by a range of medical and paramedical specialists but the psychological needs are too rarely addressed. It is as important to employ a counselling psychologist as a speech therapist or physiotherapist.

Tiredness and illness

Physical disabilities make everyday commerce and learning hard work. Often rest periods need to be built into the study timetable. Fatigue is not uncommon and not to be confused with depression and apathy that are also common. However, when the disabled young person becomes tired, depression is usually nearer to hand than rank bad temper. Sleep disturbance due to a need for regular toileting or the need to be turned in bed to reduce the prevalence of pressure sores leave a residue of tiredness. Illness is more likely to strike at those who are very tired or inactive. Also the range of secondary disabilities can lead to further treatment needs.

Degenerative disabilities lead to increasing fatigue and the ultimate illness of lung infection, heart failure or kidney malfunction. Birtwistle and Day (1992) suggest ways of developing a network of professional support services for those grieving. Research is urgently needed on the extent of pre-morbidity, grieving and depression amongst the young disabled so that the reality can be openly explored and solutions sought.

Summary

Similarities between the physically disabled young person and their non-disabled peers are much greater than the differences. However, it has been seen that the operational scope and outlook of the disabled establishes distinct components to their 'secret life'. The extent that the 'secret life' is unhealthily different depends on the handicapping effects of the disability. To take an extreme view, if there were no handicapping effects then the psyche and 'secret life' would be no different to that of anyone transiting childhood or adolescence. To reduce the handicapping effects demands:

(i)   truly positive societal attitude and facilitation to interact in all reasonable situations
(ii) through (i) above, integration and inclusion in society including education, this being central in childhood.

At the present time, due mainly to attitudinal and financial limitations neither of the above fully occurs. The physically disabled cannot interact without full physical access, full social acceptance and a range of supporting services attached to a mainstream educational placement. Without time efficient supportive therapies and medical aid the educational curriculum will be only patchily accessed. A diagrammatic explanation by Adelman (1992) well illustrates the dichotomy between in-child factors and those problems created by factors in the environment that serve to be a barrier to learning and development.

Table 3.3 Primary Locus of Cause

Problems caused by factors in the environment (E)				Problems caused by factors in the person (P)
E	(E-p)	E-P	(e-p)	P
Type I learning problems		Type II learning problems		Type III learning problems (e.g. learning difficulties)

This illustrates a continuum of learning problems reflecting a transactional view of the locus of primary investigating factors. Type III learning problems may be experienced by physically disabled young people due to a variety of factors specific to the learner, but to varying degrees:

> interrupted education for medical and therapy reasons
> neurological and perceptual problems
> physical inability to perform tasks
> slow cognition through those of acceptable quality

plus other factors of a more general nature.
Type I learning problems are caused by factors in the environment and could be:

> lack of curriculum access
> unmodified learning materials
> lack of classroom support
> absence of appropriate technology
> lack of training for the teachers
> negative attitude from peers or staff
> transport and mobility problems
> lack of therapeutic support

In barrier-free education Type II is the range of incidental learning problems least problematic.

Any learning difficulties due to factors I or III will lead to inward struggles and a secret life of coping, or otherwise. Because of the range of psychological problems it is clearly necessary to continue to focus on the overt physical needs but also to pay more attention to psychological counselling. Pelletier (1985), Smith (1985), Thurer and Rogers (1985) and Rogers (1986) are among a growing number of professionals who recognise the urgent need to focus on the mental health of the physically disabled.

Certainly the incidence of psychiatric disorders is higher. Graham (1986) reports that adolescents with spina bifida have high rates of depressive disorder and 40% of children with cerebral palsy show significant emotional or behavioural problems. Certainly where the central nervous system is damaged a vulnerability to psychiatric disorder is more likely. Until adequate mental health support for the physically disabled becomes the norm then their lives will be harder and more 'secret'.

References

Asch, A.(1984). The experience of disability: A challenge for psychology. *American Psychologist.* 39,529-36.

Berry, J. O. and Zimmerman, W. W. (1983). The stage model revisited. *Rehabilitation literature* 44,275-7.

Birtwistle, J. and Day, S. (1992). Some children die. *School Psychol. Int.* **13**, 61-71.

Diener, C. L. and Dweck, C. S. (1980). An analysis of learned helplessness: II. The processing of success. *Journal of Personality and Social Psychology* **39**, 940-52.

Futcher, A. E. and Carroll, D. (1994). Delivering a service in further education: EP's into FE. May go at a cost. *Educ. Psych. in Practice* **10**(1), 19-26.

Graham, P. (1986). *Child Psychiatry: A Developmental Approach.* Oxford: Oxford University Press.

Gurney, P. W. (1988). *Self-esteem in Children with Special Educational Needs.* London: Routledge.

Hersen, M. and Van Hasselt, V. B. (1990). *Psychological Aspects of Developmental and Physical Disabilities.* London: Sage.

Kubler-Ross, E. (1969). *On Death and Dying.* New York, USA: Macmillan.

Lalken, Y. and Norwich, B. (1990). The self-concept and self-esteem of adolescents with physical impairments in integrated and special school settings. *European Journal of Special Needs Education* **7**(2),131-45.

Lewis, R. B. and Doorlag, D. H. (1983). *Teaching Special Students in Mainstream.* Columbus, USA: Charles E Merrill.

Lewis, V. (1987). *Development and Handicap.* Oxford: Blackwell.

McGown, A. (1995). Always being nice is not good for you. *Carers World.* February/March. 35-6.

Nisbet, P., Craig, I. and Odor, P. (1995). Taking Control. *Special Children* March, 29-31.

Paull, M. E. (1992). Personality, attitudes and self-concept in physically disabled children: a study using repertory grids. *European Journal of Special Needs Education.* **7**(2), 131-45.

Paulsson, K. and Christoffersen, M. (1987). Psychological aspects of technical aids: how does independent mobility affect the psychological and intellectual development of children with disabilities? In *Proceedings 2nd International Conference of RESNA,.* 282-5.

Pelletier, J. R. (1985). Barriers to the provision of mental health services to individuals with severe physical disability. *Journal of Counselling Psychology.* **32**(3), 422-30.

Rogers, E. S. (1986). Mental health needs of individuals with severe physical disabilities. *Rehabilitation Counselling Bulletin.* **29**(4) 240-50.

Siller, J. A., Chipman, A., Ferguson, L. and Vann, D. H. (1967). *Studies in reaction to disability: Vol 2, Attitudes of the non-disabled toward the physically disabled.* New York, USA: New York University School of Education.

Smith, C. D. (1985). Adolescent spinal cord injury and paralysis: Understanding the psycho-social aspects. *DPH - Journal* **8**, 16-23.

Stewart, R. M. L. (1991). Emotional reactions of athletes during recovery from knee surgery. University of Western Australia. Unpublished M.Ed. thesis.

Thurer, S. and Rogers, E. S. (1985). The mental health needs of the physically disabled persons: Their perspective. Paper presented at the Annual Convention of the American Association for Counselling and Development. New York, USA. April 2-3.

Chapter 4
The Inner Life of Children with Moderate Learning Difficulties

HELEN BARRETT AND DAVID JONES

Broadly speaking, the term 'moderate learning difficulties' (MLD) refers to global, rather than specific, cognitive and intellectual difficulties. Children with MLD typically have verbal and performance IQ scores in the 50-70 range, that is, two to three standard deviations below the population mean. Approximately 2% of people are estimated to have moderate learning difficulties.

In recent years there has been a move away from labelling based on psychometric assessment alone and attempts have been made to avoid the negative or stigmatising aspects of previous terminology. These developments have tended to make definitions less clear-cut so that, since the 1981 Education Act, a child has been considered to have a learning difficulty if '(a) he has a significantly greater difficulty in learning than the majority of children of his age; or (b) he has a disability which either prevents or hinders him from making use of educational facilities of a kind generally provided in schools, within the area of the local authority concerned, for children of his age' (DES 1981, Section 1). Sharp distinctions are no longer made between the profiles of children with MLD and those with mild, specific or even severe learning difficulties. Learning difficulties are now seen as arising from an asymmetric relationship between the child and his or her educational environment rather than from within the child relative to the more abstract norms associated with IQ measurements.

These definitional problems are further compounded by the fact that the UK classification system differs considerably from that employed in other parts of the world. In the US, for example, the DSM-IV classification of 'mild mental retardation' refers to children with IQs of 50/55-70 (American Psychiatric Association, 1994). In this system, three criteria are essential for diagnosis of mental retardation: (a) significantly subaverage intellectual functioning; (b) concurrent deficits or impairments in present adaptive functioning in at least two areas (communication, self-care, home living, use of community resources, social/interpersonal skills, self-direction, work, leisure, health or safety); (c) onset before 18 years.

In the research literature, though, this category features less frequently than the term 'learning disabilities', which often includes children with specific disabilities in one or more learning process (therefore eliding the specific and global difficulties categories). Level of achievement has also provided a less formal classification with 'low achievers' usually being identified primarily by teachers' ratings, so that it is not always clear whether low achievement is due to unidentified learning disabilities, low ability or motivational factors.

One outcome of these definitional problems is that interpretation of the research findings from different cultures is difficult. But there are more important implications with regard to the welfare of these children within the education system. Given the emphasis upon integration, most children with MLD, particularly in the early years of their education, will be provided for within mainstream schools. While learning difficulties can be falsely identified, there is also some evidence to suggest that the number of children with mild or moderate learning difficulties may be underestimated (Zigler and Hodapp, 1986). Unfortunately, unrecognised needs cause individual children at least as much, if not more, stress than recognised needs, particularly if recognition leads to appropriate or effective intervention.

To these definitional issues is added the important debate over whether mental retardation can be conceptualised as due to delayed or defective development (Baumeister, 1987). For those who take the developmental delay position, children with moderate learning difficulties are seen as developing along the same lines as children without learning difficulties: they are simply regarded as functioning at an earlier developmental stage than children of the same chronological age. For those who take the defect or difference position, it is more than mental age which distinguishes between children with and without learning difficulties: the type of processing engaged in by children with learning difficulties is thought to be qualitatively different from that of normatively developing children due, for example, to functions such as impaired short-term memory or attentional deficits. These two positions clearly have different implications in terms of children's experiences or inner life. Delay theorists would expect only timing to differentiate between children with and without learning differences in cognitive functioning but there may be problems associated with the lack of synchronisation between physical and cognitive development and secondary differences due to social comparison processes. Defect theorists, on the other hand, seeing children with learning difficulties as having unique ways of making sense of their world, would envisage quite considerable differences. At this point, it is not possible to determine which of these positions is more tenable. But in practice the difference between the two positions may be minimal since delay may be caused by differential maturation of areas of the brain or other organs, in which case uneven development conceivably also arises from the delay model.

At this point, having dwelt on the difficulties which beset us in our approach to a discussion of the inner life of children with moderate learning difficulties, it seems apposite to consider what can be said with confidence about this group. Three points can be made with certainty: first, there is a strong association between the presence of MLD and social disadvantage (at least for a large number of children with MLD); second, a substantial proportion of children with MLD have social skills deficits; third, children with MLD constitute a distinctly heterogeneous group.

Relationship between MLD and social disadvantage

It is well recognised that moderate learning difficulties are often associated with negative sociocultural variables (Rutter *et al.*, 1975; Scarr and Yee, 1980) such as poverty (Mercer, 1973), cultural deprivation (Itskowitz *et al.*, 1986), father's occupational status (Pihl and McLarnon, 1984), mother's IQ (Heber, 1970), economic difficulties, family difficulties and lack of educational stimulation (Toro *et al*, 1990), impoverished language environment (Montgomery, 1990) and abuse of all kinds (McCormack, 1991; Sinason, 1994).

Another link between learning difficulties and environment has also been traced to the teaching environment, for ineffective teaching strategies can seriously affect children's achievement levels (Brennan, 1979). Setting children tasks which are beyond their capabilities may well lead to attributions of low self-efficacy which become self-perpetuating, a point which will be taken up again later in this chapter.

From this description of the close relationship between environmental factors and learning difficulties, it becomes evident that there is an essential confounding of within-environment and within-child influences. This presents obvious problems of interpretation when it comes to considering effects on the child's sense of self-efficacy and responsibility. For those working with children with MLD from deprived backgrounds, it is often difficult to know whether to attribute the origins of their learning difficulties to socio-emotional or cognitive sources. Misattribution may be capable of causing a disjunction in the relationship between the child and his or her learning processes. This ties in closely with the notion of 'secondary handicap' (Sinason 1986, 1992) in which one's own response to other people's treatment of a primary difficulty has the effect of exacerbating or qualitatively altering the nature of the primary difficulty in a disempowering way.

Relationship between MLD and social skills deficits

There has been much debate about the degree to which social skills deficits can be said to characterise individuals with moderate learning difficulties. This debate became particularly heated when the US Interagency Committee on Learning Disabilities (1987) suggested that, since empirical data link social skills deficits so consistently with mild learning disability, such difficulties might be used as diagnostic criteria. Those against this position have argued that everyday adjustment for people with or without learning difficulties depends equally heavily upon motivational and personality variables and that cognitive ability is more important as a predictor of learning difficulties (Zigler and Hodapp, 1986).

Heterogeneity of MLD group

It has already been suggested that children with MLD do not constitute a homogeneous group. Korhonen (1991), using neuropsychological measures to examine a group of 9-year-old Finnish children with mild learning disabilities, identified at least five valid sub-groups which they described as normal, general language, visuo-motor, general deficiency and naming. It is also possible to distinguish between subgroups of children within the MLD category in other ways. For example, some children manifest behavioural disorders, others do not; some children with low IQ have one or both parents whose IQ is similarly low ('familial retardates'), others may have parents of average or even above average IQ ('polygenic isolates') and some may come from a background of extreme environmental deprivation. Zigler and Hodapp (1986) distinguish between retardation of known organic origin which they associate with IQ scores generally below 60. They estimate that this group accounts for about 25% of retardation, familial retardation for about 35%, polygenic isolates for a further 35% and environmental deprivation for about 5%. Although some recent research studies have paid attention to some of these variables, many have not. This is unfortunate since these variables pertain to the social context of children with learning difficulties and this social context provides much of the material which informs children's inner life including their expectations and memories of social interactions.

Large differences have been found between individuals with the same overall educational profiles, in motivation to succeed or overcome one's difficulties, in personality, in coping strategies and styles, and in family background and history of social interaction. Individual children with MLD may adopt a range of strategies to cope with their learning difficulties. Challenging and attention-seeking behaviours, for example, may be associated with attempts to protect from less controllable experiences of failure; the same underlying fear of failure in other children may give rise to over-dependency, over-compliance or premature task disengagement;

other children, though, may be able to persistently pursue more constructive strategies.

Such enormous variation must be expected to generate equally massive individual differences in respect of inner life or ways of making sense of one's experience. But, even given these variations, it seems that there may be differences which are uniquely associated with particular types of learning difficulty and individuals' experiences of coping with difficulties. It also seems important to ask whether there is any evidence that the inner life of children with MLD is characterised, for example, by more discomfort, more impoverished metacognitive structures or defence processes which are less adaptive than those of higher achieving children. These issues will be addressed through a review of research along a number of dimensions.

Self-concept, self-knowledge and social comparisons

Social cognitive theorists have described the self-concept as a collection of schemas or knowledge structures concerning the self which are constructed through memories and experiences of real-life interactions (Markus and Wurf, 1987). This set of scripts, event schemas or narratives governs the processing of incoming information and provides prescriptions for ongoing and future social interactions. It is generally accepted that the self-concept is a multi-factorial entity. Shavelson, Hubner and Stanton (1976), for example, have suggested that the self-concept can be divided into the academic (cognitive), emotional, social and physical self-concepts, whilst other theorists have suggested different divisions (e.g. Neisser, 1988; Damon and Hart, 1988). With regard to learning difficulties, these ideas are valuable, as they offer the possibility that negative self-concept in one area will not necessarily give rise to a negative general self-concept.

There has been much recent work on the development of the concept of self throughout childhood but still no satisfactory resolution of the point at which children can be said to have a concept of self. Many have maintained that pre-verbal children lack self awareness because they are unable to inspect mental representations of themselves. Cognitive developmental theory has suggested that the development of structures of the self begins during early to middle childhood (age 2 to 7): at first, children see things only from the perspective of self (unreflectively); gradually they become more able to conserve mental representations of themselves in interaction with others and, beginning to use social comparison processes to take account of other perspectives than their own, go through a phase of unquestioning conformity to the views of respected authority figures (adults or peers); finally, representations of oneself and others become more subject to scrutiny and mature self reflection is possible (Piaget, 1966; Kohlberg, 1969; Damon and Hart, 1988). Since, in this view, development depends upon cognitive maturational processes, it follows that cognitively challenged children may be delayed in attaining the early stages and may not reach the later stages of self-concept development.

Although, particularly more recently, there has been considerable interest in the question of the development of self-concepts in children generally, studies of children with learning difficulties are still rather sparse. The information below therefore is necessarily somewhat speculative but will hopefully give a picture of current knowledge in this area.

Self-knowledge

If, as mentioned above, children with learning difficulties fail to reach the later stages of self-concept development, what might be the consequences of this in terms of their inner life? Many workers have suggested that the ability to construct balanced, internally consistent and experience-related self-narratives has important links with the ability to form secure intimate relationships (Bowlby, 1969; Stern, 1985; Fonagy et al, 1993). These workers point to an important association between reflective self-awareness and the ability to be responsively aware of the feelings and needs of others. Fonagy et al (1993) have offered evidence for the possibility that more adaptive attachment patterns are associated with high scores on measures of Reflective Self capacity; further, they have argued that attachment patterns are consistent across mother-infant dyads with infant attachment type being fairly well predicted from mother's capacity for self-reflection. These arguments are strongly reminiscent of *cycle of abuse* fears and raise the question of whether children with MLD would be more likely than children without learning difficulties to achieve low scores on measures of Reflective Self ability.

There is not space here to do justice to the arguments concerning intergenerational transmission of abuse, the evidence for which appears to be slight (Kaufman and Zigler, 1987; Oliver, 1993). It does seem pertinent, though, to make two points. First, attachment classification in infancy has not been found to be significantly associated with cognitive ability. Hence, if capacity for self reflection is strongly associated with attachment, it would appear to follow that it is unlikely to be associated with cognitive ability alone. This does not, of course, preclude the possibility that there may be a subgroup of children with MLD who also have socio-emotional problems associated with the types of attachment which have been labelled by some workers as 'insecure' and/or abusive parenting (Svobodny, 1988). It also seems likely that intrafamilial pressures may make it difficult for children with MLD to achieve their potential, for example, there may be fear of outstripping a parent with MLD, awareness of a parent's envy, reluctance to compete with siblings, and so on. The second point concerns the gathering evidence of the value of teaching children with MLD to monitor their own learning. These findings suggest that children with MLD can benefit from extra encouragement to use any self-reflective capacities that they may have.

Social comparisons within the family

The first social group for most individuals is the immediate family. Psychoanalytic theorists such as Adler and Klein have suggested that social comparisons within the family are characterised by jealousy and envy for all children and that negative self-evaluations are often only avoided by aggressive devaluation of others. More recent research based on Festinger's Social Comparison Theory (Suls and Greenwald, 1983) supports the idea that social comparisons are a central source of information in self-concept formation which, if leading to lowered self-esteem, may be avoided or discounted.

In a study of fifty adolescents with a mild mental handicap (mean MA 9;4, CA 18;3, IQ 50.96), Szivos (1991) found that self comparison with non-disabled siblings did not yield negative self-evaluations, although students without siblings tended to feel more positive about themselves than students with siblings. When age and sex were taken into account, a more complex picture emerged: students saw themselves as most inferior to older same-sex siblings (who they selected most frequently as best-liked) and most superior to younger opposite-sex siblings (who were less often chosen as liked and more often derogated). Further, self-perception as stigmatised correlated highly with self-esteem and students who perceived themselves as stigmatised also considered themselves to be the most inferior to their siblings.

Szivos (1991) suggested that clear definition of the nature of a handicap can facilitate acceptance and understanding on the part of both disabled and non-disabled siblings. But she also warned that, if labels are used in a patronising way, they can limit expectations and lead the child to become a failure avoider (MacMillan, 1982) or to adopt a sick role.

Social comparisons within the larger social group

Research into the effects of integration has produced inconsistent findings. On the positive side, integration has been found to be associated with increased likelihood of socially adaptive behaviour (Gampel et al, 1974), the presence of 'enabling peers' (Russell, 1993) and similarities between observed playground behaviours (Roberts et al, 1991); in addition, segregation has been found to be associated with lower self-ratings on academic self-concept and global self-worth (Leondari, 1993). Alternatively, it has been suggested that, relative to the safer segregated setting, an integrated social context may increase the necessity to make negative self-evaluations and may encourage tendencies to deny consequently 'spoiled' identities (Edgerton, 1967; Coleman, 1983). Several workers, however, have failed to find differences associated with educational context on social comparison and self-esteem measures (Szivos-Bach, 1993).

Clearly, there are individual differences in this respect as much as in others but for many children with learning difficulties (LD) school presents challenges and repeated experiences of failure which, when they lead to negative self-evaluations, affect emotional, social and personality development. Chapman (1988), and other workers, describe a self-perpetuating cycle of failure which, established early in the lives of children with learning difficulties, diminishes motivation to succeed, discourages efforts to achieve, increases expectations of failure and leads to further failure. Numerous studies offer support for this negative view, showing that the self-perceptions of children with LD are more negative than those of non-LD children and that the discrepancy between real and ideal self is greater for children with than for children without learning difficulties. However, there appears to be some evidence that these strong associations may not apply to all subgroups of children with LD. In a study which controlled for the presence of behavioural disorders, Durrant et al (1990) showed that scores of children with LD but without behavioural disorders were as high as those of non-LD children in respect of cognitive, social and general self-concept. They argued that negative academic self-concept may be less influential than other socio-emotional and behavioural factors in determining how children cope with their difficulties. There appears also to be evidence that some adults and adolescents with moderate/mild learning difficulties identify disabled peers as inferior to themselves and that the ability to do this may make them less vulnerable to low self-esteem or feelings of being stigmatised (Szivos, 1991; Holmes, 1994).

Peer acceptance and bullying

It is well-established that bully-victims are often children who are in some way distinctive. Many children with MLD have reported being picked on, mocked and bullied, sometimes by teachers as well as by other children. The misery of being bullied can be gravely aggravated by inability to enlist assistance. This problem will be particularly serious if victims have communication difficulties, as many children with MLD have. For some children, low self-esteem and negative self-attributions will intensify this problem since they may feel that they are to blame for what happens to them.

Although several studies have found children with learning difficulties to be less well accepted by peers than children without difficulties (LaGreca and Stone, 1990; Bursuck, 1989), others have failed to find differences (Sater and French, 1989). Recent studies which have controlled for the co-presence of behavioural disorders suggest that it may be the combination of learning difficulties and conditions such as Attention Deficit Hyperactivity Disorder, attentional difficulties, anti-social tendencies, hostility, anxiety, depression/social withdrawal which make for decreased popularity rather than learning difficulties alone (Durrant *et al.*, 1990).

The perception of children with MLD of their own acceptance does not always tally with peer appraisals. Vaughn *et al.*, (1990) studied kindergarten children before they were formally identified as having learning difficulties. They found that, although these children received more negative and fewer positive peer nominations than low-achieving students, they rated themselves more highly than others on social acceptance. This finding led the authors to suggest that deficient social perception may render children with learning difficulties at greater risk than other children of peer rejection. However, this conclusion must be regarded with caution as the presence of problem behaviours in children later identified as having learning difficulties was not controlled for.

Research into social networks of children with learning difficulties suggests that for a substantial proportion there can be difficulties in making friends. The subsequent loneliness experienced can be severe (Margalit, 1991) and this lack of social support can make children with or without learning difficulties more vulnerable to developing ineffective coping behaviours.

Social perception and social skills

That children with learning difficulties are deficient in social skills has been found in numerous studies, whether based on teachers' perceptions, parents' perceptions, peer perceptions, self-perceptions or on observation of actual behaviour (Coleman *et al.*, 1992). Studies of social information processing in children with learning difficulties have highlighted problems at each stage of processing: failures at encoding due to inattention to appropriate cues or central details, failure to chunk bits of information effectively and inefficient use of mnemonic, rehearsal and matching devices for storage of information; at the next stage, information is often not represented mentally in a way that it can be linked meaningfully with past experiences and understood; subsequently, the search for the appropriate response is hampered both by misinformation and by failure to generate effective search processes; the fourth stage involves deciding which response might be best suited to the situation and this involves considering a wider range of possibilities than is usually considered; at the fifth stage, the child needs to monitor the impact of the chosen behaviour and this monitoring, too, is deficient (Tur-Kaspa and Bryan, 1994; Reiff and Gerber, 1990).

Faulty information processing of this nature may leave children with MLD feeling very unsure about themselves in social situations: being unable to gauge the effect of their participation in social interactions can leave children vulnerable to feelings of helplessness. A sense of non-contingency or meaninglessness may lead to unwittingly inappropriate behaviour which will have its own consequences. Poor assessment of risk, for example, may lead to social rule infringements and increased gullibility and susceptibility to victimisation or exploitation (Hewitt, 1987; Sinason, 1992). To cope with an inner sense of discomfort, embarrassment or unease, MLD children may develop any of a wide range of responses, such as internalising behaviours (for example, chronic anxiety, panic attacks, phobias, timidity, fearfulness, irritability, depression, tearfulness, etc.) or externalising behaviours (for example, temper tantrums, aggression, over-activity, restlessness, self-injurious behaviour, anti-social acting out, including lawbreaking, or reverting to developmentally earlier behaviours such as soiling or bed-wetting).

Self-esteem, learned helplessness, dependency and depression

It has been argued that a sense of helplessness may be associated with depression although there has been much debate over the precise nature of this link. The original 'learned helplessness' formulation has been modified several times. Essentially the reasoning is that early and repeated exposure to failure is likely to result in reduced motivation to use coping strategies in stressful situations. It is hypothesised that because they are less efficient than other children in problem-solving skills and in gaining control over the environment some MLD children develop an apathetic approach to new and seemingly challenging tasks. Experiences of failure may also result in the development of negative attributional styles which could trigger a spiral of low self-esteem and even depression. The explanation is similar to that put forward by Beck (1971) which characterised the depressive person's outlook in terms of faulty attributions belonging to a particular cognitive set or 'triad': negative conception of self, negative interpretation of experience and negative view of the future. However, in the case of MLD children the negative attributions of self would often be based on actual experiences.

To be called 'a stupid child' by teachers and others and to have few experiences of success would not surprisingly lead to negative views of self.

A wide array of psychiatric disorders has been associated with mental retardation (Menolascino, 1990). With respect to depression, there has been much interest in the notion that major depressive disorder in children may be associated with deficits in learning and cognition, and that right hemisphere dysfunction may underlie this condition (Brumback and Staton, 1983; Livingston, 1985). What is not yet clear is whether there is a causal relationship between depression and learning difficulties. But it is clear that carers need to be aware of the possibility that depression may play a role in exacerbating the difficulties of children with MLD.

Symptoms of depression are many and can include a sad appearance (facial expression, physical demeanour, lack of interest in self-care), lowered activity levels, failure to complete tasks, social withdrawal and isolation, uncharacteristic fighting and arguing, punishment or attention seeking, loss of self-confidence, verbal expressions such as 'No one likes me', 'I'm no good', 'I can't do it'. Children may also show tendencies towards paranoid ideation, shifting the locus of their sense of blameworthiness or damage to others and believing that everyone is against them: in this way they can make more problems for themselves by accusing neutral others of picking on them or angrily anticipating being deprived of fair opportunities. Other children soon get tired of being grumbled at and falsely accused and the unhappy MLD child may indeed become socially shunned.

Peter, youngest of three and due shortly to start at secondary school, has a history of family and learning difficulties. As a baby, his home environment was characterised by violent disputes between his drink-abusing father and his drink- and drug-abusing mother. By the time he was four, his mother, who also has moderate learning difficulties, had fled to a women's refuge with all three children. By this time, the children had already experienced the first of many spells in short-term local authority care, sometimes together, sometimes separated. At six, Peter's mother described him as looking too much like his father whom she hated. Until he was nine, he soiled during the day, often hiding his pants from his mother or other carers. Now, at 11, he is in long-term foster care and in the many times disrupted process of having a statement of educational needs drawn up. Recently, he was found to have been stealing from other children at school. Peter can read only a few words, has great difficulty with simple addition and subtraction and rarely persists with academic or other challenging tasks. It is noticeable that, after contact with his mother, his behaviour at school becomes particularly distractible and unfocused. He has also been through periods when he sleeps a great deal, shows very little interest in eating, feels that his siblings and stepsiblings are making fun of or cheating him, and generally seems lethargic and cast down.

Peter's case illustrates the immense complexity of untangling social, emotional, biological, cognitive and personality variables. In his experience of life, very little has been stable or predictable, his relationship with both parents has been characterised by separation, abandonment, rejection and inconsistency. Perhaps the only consistent threads have been woven by his own fantasy life. How important it must be for him to keep this separate from the many blows of reality if he is to maintain any sense of potency, but how difficult, too, to do this and to have any sense of meaningfulness in social relationships.

One day recently, Peter told a story. A big black poisonous snake was eating his mother. Why was it eating his mother? Because she kept trying to get away. As the snake ate his mother, she kept climbing out again. The snake ate his mother and then it died. His mother climbed out. How did the snake die? Peter killed it: 'I hate snakes'. Then the snake went up a hill. Did the snake come alive again? 'This is another episode.' Peter began to describe the snake on a hill with a man who was daddy. Suddenly, he changed the subject to football. His tenseness transformed into excitement. He became an eager little boy, keen to share his enjoyment. There seemed still to be an underlay of desperation. But he was battling on.

Children with MLD may often, like Peter, be battling on against a tide of frustrations, losses and failures. Many, like Peter, may go through periods of intense depression where nothing seems of interest and where anger is so profound that its expression is too terrifying to contemplate. Like Peter, they may even react to coming closer to expressing this anger by becoming fearful of and, sometimes, angry towards situations in which it is safe to begin to express it. This kind of behaviour can be as confusing for carers as it is for the children. Sometimes, all that can be done is to be ready to listen and to wait for the child to feel able to re-engage. This can take time. Unfortunately, for many children with MLD in our society, that time is not allowed and there is increasing recognition of and concern about the risk of suicide (Hayes and Sloat 1988, 1989).

Self-expression

Receiving and feeling that you receive unconditional positive regard has been thought by some to be a condition for healthy emotional development (Rogers, 1961). Not being valued or being expected to fail has also been associated with what has become known as the pygmalion effect. In educational settings where academic achievement and particularly written or verbal communication are valued, the positive contribution that children with MLD can make is often devalued. Shame about one's incompetence can lead to cheating or pretending to be untroubled and this can create a private world from which it is very difficult to communicate (Lee and Jackson, 1992). Children with MLD need to feel safe to make mistakes. They need to be faced with challenges appropriate to their abilities. They also need opportunities to relax, to escape from tensions and to use their sense of frustration creatively. Peter was able to express a little of his anger, if rather obliquely, in his fantasy about the snake. Such fantasies can be valuable vehicles for containing otherwise intolerable feelings and also for trying to make sense of experience.

For many children with MLD, being listened to appears to be as much of a problem as being able to communicate effectively. In one study of the communicative competence of 5- to 8-year-old children with or without mild or moderate learning difficulties, very few differences were found between children in terms of the nature of information exchanged. Differences were found, though, in the way children without difficulties communicated to the children with LD: they were more critical and directive in their speech; children with difficulties also tended to have less influence in decision-making and negotiating processes (Thomson 1993). This kind of research illustrates how early and easily the processes begin which serve to disempower people with learning difficulties and how important it is to pay attention to pressures which prevent people with learning difficulties having equal opportunities for self-expression. The assumtion that children with MLD do not understand or have no contribution to make can often deprive them of their right to be heard as well as the experience that they need as much, if not more, than other children to learn to communicate effectively (Hunt, 1967). This has particularly controversial poignance in relation to physical and sexual abuse. Children with learning difficulties, it is argued, are especially prone to being disbelieved (Craft, 1994).

Increasingly, particularly in this respect, the value of self advocacy for people with learning difficulties is being recognised (Craft and Brown, 1994). Care needs to be taken to ensure that children with MLD feel able to express their true feelings or knowledge. Sometimes, they may only feel able to express what they believe is wanted of them (and they may be very unsure about what exactly this is). Research on responses to different types of survey questions has shown that people with learning difficulties are more likely to give socially desirable responses, to answer yes/no questions inconsistently due to response set acquiescence and to misunderstand items (Zetlin *et al.*, 1985). This not only points to the need for caution in interpretation of research findings but also to the need to allow children with MLD to communicate as equals.

Thoughts and feelings

It has been suggested that people with learning difficulties do not have as complex an emotional (Webster, 1970) or as rich a fantasy life as other people. For children with MLD this seems unlikely but it is worth speculating on how their thought processes and inner world may be different from other children. There may be some differences associated with having a smaller vocabulary than other children of the same age. Associations between life events may sometimes not be noticed. There may be occasions when the points of view of other children are more likely to be overlooked. The qualities and failings of other people may be judged using a narrower range of constructs. At times others may be trusted too readily. Other children may seem better at doing things in school. Sometimes what the teacher says will not make much sense. It may be very hard to remember more than about three things at the same time. Reading may be difficult and not much fun because it takes such a long time. Abstract concepts like time, speed and the future may not make much sense. Perhaps, though this is much less clear, distinctions between reality and fantasy may be harder to make than they are for other children. As thinking adults we can imagine what each of these and other cognitive limitations would be like if they occurred singly. It is harder to evaluate the effect of most of them together. Might it result in an impoverished or even more frightening inner world?

As with other children, much will depend upon the quality of early social interactions. Those who have gained a sense of being wanted are more likely to feel content with themselves and to share their feelings with others. We know from contact with children with MLD in therapeutic contexts that they appear to experience the full range of emotions. Some, because of adverse life experiences, feel unhappy and isolated (Jones and Barrett, 1993). Others leave us in no doubt that they are capable of creative thinking in problem solving and that they may be perceptive judges of other people's characters and emotional states. The ways in which we all make sense of our experiences and respond to each other are influenced by automatic processes over which we often have little control or understanding. In this sense, children with MLD are similar to other children. But if children with MLD are using qualitatively different processes to many other people, then it may be more difficult for them to share their inner worlds and therefore to learn about themselves and others. Clearly, for many reasons, the inner lives of this very varied group of children merit further exploration.

References

American Psychiatric Association (1994). *Diagnostic and Statistical Manual of Mental Disorders* IV, Washington, DC: American Psychiatric Association.

Baumeister, A.A. (1987). Mental retardation: Some conceptions and dilemmas. *American Psychologist,* 42(8), 796-800.

Beck, A.T. (1971). Cognition, affect and psychopathology. *Archives of General Psychiatry,* 9, 295-302.

Bowlby, J. (1969). *Attachment and Loss, Vol. 2: Attachment.* Harmondsworth: Penguin.

Brennan, W.R. (1979). *Curricular needs of slow learners.* Working Paper no. 63. London: Evans/Methuen Educational.

Brumback, R.A. and Staton, R.D. (1983). Learning disability and childhood depression. *American Journal of Orthopsychiatry,* 53(2), 269-81.

Bursuck, W. (1989). A comparison of students with learning disabilities to low achieving and higher achieving students on three dimensions of social competence. *Journal of Learning Disabilities,* 22, 188-94.

Chapman, J.W. (1988). Cognitive-motivational characteristics and academic achievement of learning disabled children: A longitudinal study. *Journal of Educational Psychology,* 80(3), 357-65.

Coleman, J.M. (1983). Handicapped labels and instructional segregation: Influences on children's self concepts versus the perceptions of others. *Learning Disability Quarterly,* 6, 3-11.

Coleman, J.M., McHam, L.A. and Minnett, A.M. (1992). Similarities in the social competencies of learning disabled and low achieving elementary school children. *Journal of Learning Disabilities,* 25(10), 671-7.

Craft, A. (1994). *Practice issues in sexuality and learning disabilities.* London: Routledge.

Craft, A. and Brown, H. (1994). Personal relationships and sexuality. In Craft (1994), pp.1-22.

Damon, W. and Hart, D. (1988). *Self-understanding in childhood and adolescence.* Cambridge: Cambridge University Press.

DES (1981). *Education Act.* London: HMSO.

Durrant, J.E., Cunningham, C.E. and Voelker, S. (1990). Academic, social, and general self-concepts of behavioral subgroups of learning disabled children. *Journal of Educational Psychology,* 82(4),657-63.

Edgerton, R.B. (1967). *The cloak of competence: Stigma in the lives of the mentally retarded.* San Francisco: University of California Press.

Fonagy, P., Steele, M., Moran, G.S., Steele, H. and Higgitt, A. (1993). Measuring the ghost in the nursery: An empirical study of the relation between parents' mental representations of childhood experiences and their infants' security of attachment. *Journal of the American Psychoanalytic Association,* 41, 957-89.

Gampel, D.H., Gottlieb, J. and Harrison, R.H. (1974). Comparison of classroom behavior of special class EMR, integrated EMR, low IQ and non-retarded children. *American Journal of Mental Deficiency,* 79, 115-26.

Hayes, M.L. and Sloat, R.S. (1988). Learning disability and suicide. *Academic Therapy,* 23, 469-75.

Hayes, M.L. and Sloat, R.S. (1989). Preventing suicide in learning disabled children and adolescents. *Academic Therapy,* 24(2), 221-9.

Heber, R. (1970). *Epidemiology of mental retardation.* Springfield, IL: Thomas.

Hewitt, S.E.K. (1987). The abuse of deinstitutionalised people with mental handicaps. *Disability, Handicap and Society,* 2,127-35.

Holmes, L. (1994). *The relationships between community participation, self-esteem, perceptions of stigma and social comparison processes in adults with mild learning disabilities.* Unpublished dissertation: British Psychological Society Dip. Clin. Psychol.

Hunt, N. (1967). *The world of Nigel Hunt: The diary of a mongoloid youth.* New York: Garrett Publications.

Interagency Commission on Learning Disabilities (1987). *Learning disabilities: A report to Congress.* Washington, DC: Author. Cited in Coleman *et al.* (1992).

Itskowitz, R., Bar-El, Y. and Gross, Y. (1986). Thought processes in culturally deprived and learning disabled children. *Journal of Learning Disabilities,* **19**,432-7.

Jones, D. and Barrett, H. (1993). Coping with unhappy children who have learning difficulties. In V. Varma (Ed.), *Coping with unhappy children,* pp. 80-92. London: Cassell.

Kaufman, J. and Zigler, E.F. (1987). Do abused children become abusive parents? *American Journal of Orthopsychiatry,* **57(2)**,186-92.

Kohlberg, L. (1969). Stage and sequence: The cognitive-developmental approach to socialization. In D. Goslin (Ed.), *Handbook of socialization theory and research,* pp.325-480. Chicago: Rand-McNally.

Korhonen, T.T. (1991). An empirical subgrouping of Finnish learning-disabled children. *Journal of Clinical and Experimental Neuropsychology,* **13(2)**, 259-77.

LaGreca, A.M. and Stone, W.L. (1990). LD status and achievement: Confounding variables in the study of children's social status, self-esteem, and behavioural functioning. *Journal of Learning Disabilities,* **23**,483-90.

Lee, C.M. and Jackson, R.F. (1992). *Faking it: A look into the mind of a creative learner,* London: Cassell.

Leondari, A. (1993). Comparability of self-concept among normal achievers, low achievers and children with learning difficulties. *Educational Studies,* **19(3)**,357-71.

Livingston, R. (1985). Depressive illness and learning difficulties: Research needs and practical implications. *Journal of Learning Disabilities,* **18(9)**,518-20.

McCormack, B. (1991). Sexual abuse and learning disabilities: another iceberg. *British Medical Journal,* **303**,143-4.

MacMillan, D.L. (1982). *Mental retardation in school and society.* Boston, MA: Little Brown.

Margalit, M. (1991). Understanding loneliness among students with learning disabilities. *Behaviour Change,* **8(4)**, 167-73.

Markus, H. and Wurf, E. (1987). The dynamic self-concept: A social psychological perspective. *Annual Review of Psychology,* **38**,299-337.

Menolascino, F.J. (1990). Mental illness in the mentally retarded: diagnostic and treatment considerations. In A. Dosen, A. Van Gennep and G.J. Zwanikken (Eds.), *Treatment of mental illness and behavioral disorders in the mentally retarded: Proceedings of the International Congress, May 3-4, 1990, Amsterdam, The Netherlands,* pp. 21-35. Leiden: Logon.

Mercer, J.R. (1973). *Labelling the mentally retarded.* Berkeley, CA: University of California Press.

Montgomery, D. (1990). *Children with learning difficulties.* London: Cassell.

Neisser, U. (1988). Five kinds of self-knowledge. *Philosophical Psychology,* **1(1)**,35-59.

Oliver, J.E. (1993). Intergenerational transmission of child abuse: Rates, research, and clinical implications. *American Journal of Psychiatry,* **150(9)**,1315-24.

Piaget, J. (1966). *The construction of reality in the child.* New York: Basic Books.

Pihl, R.O. and McLarnon, L.D. (1984). Learning disabled children as adolescents. *Journal of Learning Disabilities,* **17**,96-100.

Reiff, H.B. and Gerber, P.J. (1990). Cognitive correlates of social perception in students with learning difficulties. *Journal of Learning Disabilities,* **23(4)**,260-2.

Roberts, C., Pratt, C. and Leach, D. (1991). Classroom and playground interaction of students with and without disabilities. *Exceptional Children,* **57(3)**,212-24.

Rogers, C. (1961). *On becoming a person: A therapist's view of psychotherapy.* London: Constable.

Russell, P. (1993). 'Unhappy children': A cause for concern? In V. Varma (Ed.), *Coping with unhappy children,* pp. 3-16. London: Cassell.

Rutter, M., Yule, B., Quinton, D., Rowlands, O., Yule, W. and Berger, M. (1975). Attainment and adjustment in two geographical areas: III. Some factors accounting for area differences. *British Journal of Psychiatry,* **126,**520-33.

Sater, G.M. and French, D.C. (1989). A comparison of the social competencies of learning disabled and low achieving elementary-aged children. *Journal of Special Education,* **23,** 29-42.

Scarr, S. and Yee, D. (1980). Heritability and educational policy: Genetic and environmental effects on IQ, aptitude and achievement. *Educational Psychologist,* **15,**1-22.

Shavelson, R.J., Hubner, J.J. and Stanton, G.C. (1976). Self-concept: Validation of construct interpretations. *Review of Educational Research,* **46,**407-41.

Sinason, V. (1986). Secondary mental handicap and its relationship to trauma. *Psychoanalytic Psychotherapy,* **2,** 131-54.

Sinason, V. (1992). *Mental handicap and the human condition: New approaches from the Tavistock.* London: Free Association Books.

Sinason, V. (1994). Working with sexually abused individuals who have a learning disability. In A. Craft (Ed.) (1994), pp. 156-175.

Stern, D. (1985). *The interpersonal world of the infant. A view from psychoanalysis and developmental psychology.* New York: Basic Books.

Suls, J.M. and Greenwald, A.C. (1983). *Psychological perspectives on the self,* **Vol.II.** London: Lawrence Erlbaum.

Svobodny, L.A. (1988). Adolescents with moderate learning difficulties: Are they 'at risk' for exhibiting abusive parenting interactions? *Maladjustment and Therapeutic Education,* **6**(1), 14-22.

Szivos, S.E. (1991). Social comparisons with siblings made by adolescents with a learning difficulty. *Journal of Community and Applied Social Psychology,* **1,**201-12.

Szivos-Bach, S.E. (1993). Social comparisons, stigma and mainstreaming: The self esteem of young adults with a mild mental handicap. *Mental Handicap Research,* **6**(3), 217-36.

Thomson, A. (1993). Communicative competence in 5- to 8-year-olds with mild or moderate learning difficulties and their classroom peers: referential and negotiation skills. *Social Development,* **2**(3), 260-78.

Toro, P.A., Weissberg, R.P., Guare, J. and Liebenstein, N.L. (1990). A comparison of children with and without learning disabilities on social problem-solving skill, school behaviour, and family background. *Journal of Learning Disabilities,* **23**(2), 115-20.

Tur-Kaspa, H. & Bryan, T. (1994). Social information-processing skills of students with learning disabilities. *Learning Disabilities Research and Practice,* **9**(1), 12-23.

Vaughn, S., Hogan, A., Kouzekanani, K. and Shapiro, S. (1990). Peer acceptance, self-perceptions, and social skills of learning disabled students prior to identification. *Journal of Educational Psychology,* **82**(1), 101-6.

Webster, T.G. (1970). Unique aspects of emotional development in mentally retarded children. In F.J. Menolascino (Ed.), *Psychiatric Approaches to Mental Retardation,* pp. 3-54. New York: Basic Books.

Zetlin, A.G., Heriot, M.J. and Turner, J.L. (1985). Self-concept measurement in mentally retarded adults: A micro-analysis of response styles. *Applied Research in Mental Retardation,* 6, 113-25.

Zigler, E. and Hodapp, R.M. (1986). *Understanding Mental Retardation.* Cambridge: Cambridge University Press.

Chapter 5
The Inner Life of Children with Profound and Multiple Learning Disabilities

PENNY LACEY

Introduction

To discover what constitutes the inner life of children who are at a very early stage of development is an extremely difficult and demanding activity. Most children with profound and multiple learning disabilities (PMLD) will be developing communication very slowly and perhaps unconventionally in that they are likely to make considerable use of non-verbal communication instead of spoken language. Adults working with children with PMLD need to be accomplished interpreters of the tiny and often inefficient indications of their thoughts and emotions and in this chapter an attempt will be made to indicate current thinking on how this can be achieved.

Endeavouring to understand the intellectual and emotional needs of the most profoundly disabled members of our society has only recently become a serious consideration, as for generations they have barely been afforded the basic dignity of being human, let alone considered to have thoughts and feelings. There are many harrowing stories of people with profound disabilities who were confined in large long-stay institutions who subsequently have revealed not only that they are able to understand much more than was thought possible, but that they have suppressed their thoughts and feelings under an aura of helplessness as a defence against an unbearable existence (Sinason, 1994). Today, children with PMLD are almost always found within families rather than in institutions and carers and educators have begun the long road towards recognising and developing their understanding and emotions.

What is profound and multiple disability?

In attempting to understand the inner thoughts and emotions of children with PMLD, it is necessary first to have some comprehension of the nature of the disabilities with which many of them have to contend. It is likely that they will have profound learning difficulties which in most cases will be compounded by at least one other severe disability, such as visual, hearing or physical impairment. Definitions of 'profound' vary, for instance the World Health Organisation (WHO) uses IQ of below 20 combined with adaptive behaviour and clinical judgements, whilst the American Association on Mental Retardation (AAMR) uses the amount of support that is needed by the individual (intermittent, limited, extensive or pervasive) (Ware, 1994). Children with profound disabilities would typically need pervasive support.

When the degree of learning disability is more severe or profound, there is an increase in the likelihood of other accompanying impairments. Over four-fifths of people with profound learning disabilities also have at least one other severe impairment (Kelleher and Mulcahy, 1986). This figure gives some indication of the complexity of difficulties faced by them. Each extra impairment compounds the problems and makes it incrementally more difficult for normal development to take place (McInnes and Treffry, 1982). An intellectually able blind child can make use of abstract contacts with the world to increase his or her understanding. This level of abstraction is not available to the child who also has profound learning disabilities; in consequence, he or she has multiple disabilities.

It is easy to become negative when cataloguing the difficulties faced by children with multiple disabilities. They may have restriction of movement, skeletal deformities, sensory disorders, seizures, lung and breathing difficulties and other medical problems as well as a lack of a formal communication system (Orelove and Sobsey, 1991). In the face of this it is tempting to view individuals as helpless and treat them accordingly. So much time is needed to fulfil the everyday caring tasks that it is easier to see children with PMLD as perpetual babies rather than as growing and developing people who have the potential to exhibit likes and dislikes and the right to express themselves. There is no doubt that enabling this development is a perplexing and arduous task for carers and educators but it brings untold rewards for both them and for their charges.

Understanding the inner life of children with PMLD

Cognition

In order to begin the uphill struggle of understanding the thoughts and feelings of children with PMLD, it is vital to have a good grasp of what is known concerning the early development of both normal and disabled children. It is not possible directly to equate infants in the first few months of life to older children who appear to be at the same stage of development because someone who has lived for, say, thirteen years has thirteen years of experience, however distorted and imperfect, upon which to draw for her or his interpretation of the world. It is also recognised that most children with PMLD have a very uneven development depending upon the complexity and severity of their disabilities (Goldbart, 1994). However, in the absence of evidence to the contrary, it seems sensible to use knowledge of normal development to guide the understanding of the development of children with PMLD (Hogg and Sebba, 1986).

It is helpful to consider Piaget's view of the development of very young children, despite the criticisms levelled at some of his research (Donaldson, 1978). The detail concerning the six substages of the sensorimotor period can offer much guidance on the way in which infants' thinking progresses. Table 5.1 summarises the stages.

There are several important aspects contained within this account of development which are useful to bear in mind. One is the progression from reflex activity through primary circular reaction to secondary circular reaction, building up the importance of objects in the life of the infant. The other is the next few stages where the infant is much more influenced by the social world around him or her. The growing importance of objects and people are crucial to cognitive development and to developing communication.

If this invariant developmental pattern is related to children with multiple disabilities, the extent of the interference to this progression can be appreciated. Imagine how difficult it must be to develop an understanding of simple cause and effect when the child, for instance, has impaired sight and physical ability compounding his or her profound learning disabilities. Developing understanding is dependent to a large extent on feedback from the environment and when this is so distorted, or even absent, it is not surprising that many children just give up and stop trying, sinking into *learned helplessness* (Seligman, 1975).

Alongside the work on developmental stages, it is helpful also to consider the work of researchers concerned with information processing. It is postulated that, rather like a computer, the brain processes information making use of both outside stimuli and internal procedures. However, children with multiple impairments and limited experience may not process information in quite the same way as those whose sensory, physical and perceptual systems are intact. It is known, for example, that children with Down's Syndrome use their visual memories more efficiently than their auditory memories, with the effect that learning to talk is considerably helped by the use of signs, symbols and the written word. Many children with Down's Syndrome learn to read before they demonstrate or use spontaneously the language contained in the text they can read (Buckley, 1990).

Table 5.1: Cognitive development in the sensorimotor period

	Age	Label	Description
1	0–1 month 6 weeks	reflex activity	Practice of innate reflexes e.g. looking, sucking and grasping.
2	1–4 months	primary circular reactions	Undifferentiated schemes e.g. visual inspection, holding, then the beginnings of scheme–scheme co-ordination. If babies do something interesting with their bodies, they have the strategies to keep it happening.
3	4–8 months	secondary circular reactions	Co-ordinated schemes e.g. banging, shaking,then differentiated schemes e.g. sliding,crumpling, tearing. Babies learn to keep interesting activities external to their own bodies happening, i.e. the beginnings of intentionality. Beginnings of object permanence.
4	8–12 months	co-ordination of secondary schemes	Socially instigated schemes e.g. drinks from a cup, brushes hair or teeth. Establishes goal prior to initiation activity i.e. intentionality fully established. Co-ordinates previously unrelated actions to produce interesting results or solve simple problems. Imitates unfamiliar visible actions.
5	12–18 months	tertiary circular reactions	Showing and giving of objects. Tools used. New means of achieving ends through experimentation. Exploration of container–contents relationships. Imitates unfamiliar invisible actions.
6	18–24 months	beginnings	Naming objects. Deferred imitation. New means of achieving ends through mental combinations. Predicts cause–effect relationships.

Ages are approximate but the sequence is invariant.

(from Goldbart, 1994a,p.21)

It is also known that many people with learning disabilities have specific problems with short-term memory which results in difficulties in remembering new information, in generalising what they have learned and in the speed with which they react or complete tasks (Dockrell and

McShane, 1993). Despite these observations concerning the way people with learning disabilities process information, understanding the main procedures can give considerable assistance to carers and educators of children with PMLD. If it is known that short-term memory is likely to be faulty, then adults can present new experiences many, many times before they can be expected to be assimilated. Working on simple routines to encourage anticipation can be a very useful precursor to encouraging the child to take more control over what is happening to him or her.

Building a clearer picture of the possible ways in which children with PMLD might be thinking and processing information contributes a large piece of the jigsaw which represents their inner life. The following brief pen picture demonstrates how this knowledge might be used.

> Clive is a six-year-old boy with quadriplegic cerebral palsy, asthma, eczema, profound intellectual impairment and slight visual impairment. He is unable to sit unsupported and is often struck by sudden muscular spasms. He has the stature of a twelve-month-old baby, a few sounds and a stunning smile.
>
> Assessment using Piaget's sensorimotor stages (see above) reveals Clive to be generally in substage 3 (4-6 months). His physical disabilities make it hard for him to differentiate actions but he certainly has the beginnings of object permanence as he looks fleetingly for things which go out of his reach. He also cries when his mother leaves him.
>
> Knowing the perceptual difficulties experienced by children with cerebral palsy, the short-term memory problems and the constant interruptions through muscular spasm faced by Clive, the most effective approach to attempting to interpret his thoughts is likely to be through constant repetition of simple meaningful routines. If a drink is given in exactly the same way, time after time, then it should be possible to pick up the signals Clive gives to indicate whether he wants that drink or not. When he turn his head away slightly he has had enough but when a spasm pulls his head away, it is unlikely that he has finished. It is a subtle difference and it is in the hands of his carers to interpret what he is thinking.

Communication and social development

Although many children with PMLD are functioning at a very early stage of development usually associated with a baby of a few months, it has already been suggested that the parallels are not exact. Normally developing babies are alert, eager to make sense of their world and anxious to begin to communicate with those around them. If Clive was a normally developing baby, not only would he be experimenting with objects but he would be engaging in simple turn-taking with an adult and moving rapidly towards using communication to achieve very simple ends.

Understanding the detail of this early stage of communication is as important as understanding the detail of cognitive development in the struggle to interpret the world of children with PMLD. Table 5.2 outlines the development of communication in normally developing infants.

Table 5.2: Social, cognitive and communicative development in infancy

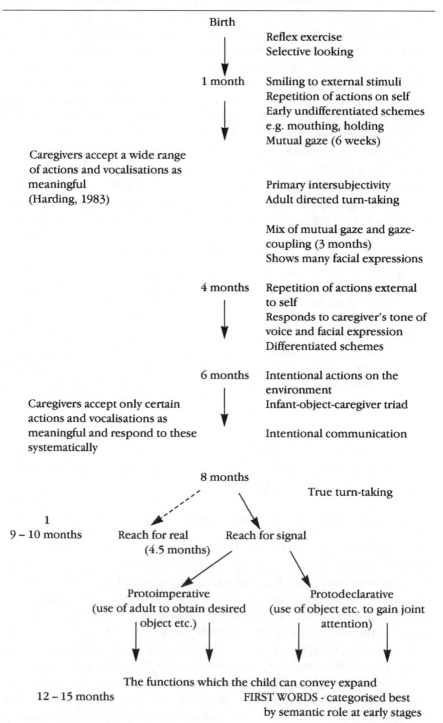

(from Goldbart, 1994b p5)

The major point of progression in this period is that between pre-intentional and intentional communication. Somewhere around six to eight months, infants make the step which demonstrates that they understand the communicative function of some of their actions. Parents, at this time, naturally shape the behaviour of their infants by only accepting as potentially communicative, some of their actions, such as vocalisations, facial expressions and gestures. Up to this time they treat almost anything the baby does as meaningful, whether it is intentional or not (Goldbart, 1994c).

At about the same time, babies become able to include objects in their communications, engaging in turn-taking and using objects to sustain joint attention. They begin to realise that their vocalisations and gestures have an effect on those around them. They can get more of that which they show they want, and have taken away that which they show they reject.

This is a stage which many children with PMLD fail to reach convincingly. Even if they do demonstrate preferences this is not always acted upon to encourage full development of intentional communication. Often their signals are weak or are unconventional, such as biting or hair pulling, so that caregivers either do not recognise them or are reluctant to accept them. Sometimes, the reaction of the child with PMLD can be very slow and the moment has long gone when communication might have been possible. One little boy with profound intellectual impairment who was also thought to be both deaf and blind could take several minutes before he reacted to stimuli. Caregivers had to learn to wait before moving on.

Understanding and shaping the communicative efforts of children with PMLD is both difficult and time consuming. Comprehensive assessment tools have been developed to help guide the intense observations needed to achieve the level of understanding needed by carers and educators. One such is the *Affective Communication Assessment* (Coupe *et al.*, 1985) which enables the assessor to build up a comprehensive picture of the responses of an individual to certain stimuli, indicate consistency and suggest how this knowledge can be used to encourage the development of intentional communication through systematic feedback (Goldbart, 1994c). Analysis of its use has shown that the most usual interpretations of responses have been *like* and *strong like, dislike* and *strong dislike, wants* or *rejects, more, puzzled* and *aware but neutral* (Coupe *et al.*, 1988).

Many children with PMLD seem to be locked into a world where they fail to see the advantage of communication with others. Nind and Hewett (1994, p8) describe these young people as 'experiencing extreme difficulty in learning and relating to others and . . . demonstrating ritualistic and challenging behaviours.' These two authors have developed an approach to unlocking this world called *intensive interaction*. It is based on the natural playfulness of early parent-child interactions and encourages the adult to join the world of the child on his or her own terms. One of their guidelines for assessing where to begin includes the words 'involve yourself warmly in behaviours which seem important to the client.' Encouraging this to happen enables the carer or educator to begin to see the world from the perspective of the child.

Personal and emotional development

Understanding the child's perspective in the light of profound disability is extremely difficult. Perceiving the feelings and emotions of very young, normally developing infants is far from a precise science. However, experiments have been carried out, the results of which suggest that infants can display distinct facial expressions, with gradations of intensity, from birth. From the experiments observers could tell that the newborns liked sweet tastes and disliked bitter tastes. They could also see differences in expressions according to the concentration or mildness of the tastes (Ganchrow, Steiner and Daher, 1983 cited in Harris, 1989). There is continuing argument concerning whether this is an innate ability or a learned response but the importance of this work for children with PMLD lies in the fact that it is possible for infants at a very young developmental age to display their emotions. Many adults who work with children with PMLD find it difficult to recognise these simple emotions, with the result that they are not encouraged to develop and become more sophisticated indicators of feelings.

It is very easy to dismiss the emotions of children with PMLD and assume that because they have difficulties in expressing them through spoken or body language that they do not exist, or if they do exist they should be modified or changed in some way. Consider the teenager who moans and cries and is generally miserable. It is much easier to use a scientifically devised behaviour modification programme to reward her for cheerful behaviour and ignore her sad behaviour than to attempt to discover the reasons for the sadness. One might want to argue that normally developing teenagers get 'the blues' for no apparent reason and the best way to deal with it is to ignore them, but the difference for them is that they usually have a network of friends, perhaps feeling similar emotions, with whom they can discuss the whole experience. Teenagers with PMLD do not.

Not only does Harris (1989) discuss the way very young infants can express emotions through facial expression, he also refers to experiments to demonstrate how they can respond to the facial expressions of those around them. One such experiment demonstrated that, as young as ten weeks, babies can respond appropriately to different facial expressions especially if they are accompanied by variations in tone of voice. From this it is very difficult to believe that children with PMLD at an early stage of development do not have a similar facility both to express and react to other people's emotions. But very often the way in which adults behave towards them belies this belief. It is not unusual to witness caretakers talking 'across' the children in their care, expressing emotions of which they plainly do not believe the child will be aware.

Because of the restrictions which accompany profound disability, it is extremely difficult for children with PMLD to express their emotions clearly and unambiguously. They often find it impossible to show the cause of the feeling and thus guide caretakers towards prolonging or removing that cause. As with a young baby, caretakers have to use trial and error to seek for the origins of discontent. Children with PMLD have so many possible frustrations which are compounded by their often complete reliance upon other people for their every need. Brudenell (1986) writes of the sheer horror of being watched all the time. Children with PMLD are virtually never left on their own. There is no chance of privacy, no possibility of taking 'time out' by removing themselves from a situation of which they have had enough. It is not surprising that sometimes this frustration is manifested in socially unacceptable behaviour.

Lack of control over one's life and surroundings can lead to difficulties which go beyond the primary disability. There is the possibility of emotional, psychological or psychiatric disorders accompanying the range of learning disabilities, for example depression, obsessional traits, anxiety and other more serious and specific mental illnesses. It is suggested that one in three people will suffer from some form of mental illness in their lifetime, so it seems sensible to expect people with profound disabilities to be equally at risk (Brudenell, 1986). In fact one might expect the multiplicity of disabilities to contribute more stress to their lives. Sinason (1994) suggests that psychiatric disturbances increase in proportion to the severity of multiple disability because the burden of the handicap depletes the resources the individual has, leaving him or her prey to what might be internally unresolved or disturbed. She goes on to paint a distressing picture of the kind of emotional messages parents can send to their babies who are disabled. She suggests that normally developing babies see uncritical love in their parents' faces but that often, with a baby who is disabled, parents are distressed and may be giving off messages that they wish the child had not been born. Remembering that even very young infants are aware of feelings (Harris, 1989), this could be a frighteningly strong influence on the child's development.

Not every child with PMLD is mentally disturbed but there are many examples of what could be described as depression, frustration or anxiety which, coupled with an undeveloped communication system can be manifested in behaviour that is considered challenging to caretakers. Because it is difficult to understand why children are self-injurious or violent towards others, it is easier to attribute the behaviour to their disabilities than to look for underlying causes. All of us, in the so-called 'normal' population, harbour stresses which we alleviate through drinking or smoking or through assertive encounters with colleagues, walking in the hills or listening to music. People with PMLD just do not have these remedies available without the help of other people. It is 'normal' to feel these emotions and caretakers of children with PMLD must be aware of this, recognise the signs and find ways of ameliorating the more debilitating of them. Arranging for quiet moments in a busy day, using physical touch through hand massage, making time for obsessive routines to be completed, accepting that food is not important today or just enjoying undemanding human contact can help produce an atmosphere of calm and well being instead of a continual battlefield.

Sexuality

In an effort to cope with the hurt of having a child who is seriously disabled, some parents and caretakers find it easier to keep the child as a permanent baby. Babies are expected to be dependent upon caretakers and it can put off the difficult day when the adulthood of that person must be faced. It also postpones or even denies the sexuality of that person. Some young people with PMLD may reach puberty later than is normally expected, especially if they are underweight and undernourished (Craft et al., 1990). This may contribute to the prolonging of childhood and the neglect of sex education.

By the time sexual maturity is reached, most normally developing people will be able to achieve a satisfactory sex life through a process of socialisation, sex education and self-knowledge. These goals are extremely difficult for young people with PMLD to achieve, partly because of the intellectual demand of the task but also because of the often accompanying physical and sensory impairments. It is, however, important that caregivers recognise this and offer every opportunity for children and young adults with PMLD to reach some understanding and knowledge of their own sexuality, enabling them to express their sexuality in ways that are appropriate and relevant to their level of understanding and need (Mallett, 1994).

One of the greatest difficulties for caregivers of young adults with PMLD is how to react to masturbation. Although this is recognised as normal and natural for the rest of the population, it is somehow unacceptable for those with learning disabilities. This is partly because privacy is so difficult to achieve for someone who is reliant on others for personal care and it is partly because many young people with PMLD who do masturbate tend to do it in socially unacceptable circumstances. Sinason (1994) suggests that masturbation in public may indicate that there has been sexual abuse of that person and she feels that it should always be investigated and not merely dismissed as the result of the learning disabilities of that person.

There are many dilemmas facing parents and caregivers of young people with PMLD and one that is most difficult to resolve surrounds masturbation. Questions include, under what circumstances should it be allowed or encouraged, should a satisfying technique be taught where there is obvious frustration, should caregivers actively help people with physical disabilities to achieve sexual satisfaction? There are still many more questions than answers but at least the questions are no longer ignored. It is no longer acceptable to see people with PMLD as non-sexual beings.

Relationships

Alongside the denial of sexual feelings can be found the failure to recognise the need to build up relationships of all kinds. Children with PMLD often have contact with an enormous number of people including teachers, nursery nurses, therapists, medics, bus escorts, dinner supervisors, as well as family and classmates. Many of these people will appear and disappear with little time to build up meaningful relationships. In addition, many children with PMLD appear to have little interest in making relationships. Some may not even really seem to be aware of people around them. Some seem to have an aversion to other people. Many need considerable help to understand the benefit to be gained from human contact.

It is recognised that young babies at an early stage of development need intense relationships with a small number of people, usually the parents. These are built upon the little routines of daily living and develop through reciprocal interactions in which both infant and parents are active participants (Nind and Hewett, 1994). If this knowledge is transferred to work with older children with profound disabilities, it could be concluded that sustained intense relationships within a small circle of adults will be the most productive in encouraging understanding of the benefits and the pleasure of human interaction. For a child at the pre-intentional stage of communication, it must be bewildering to be handled by a host of different people, probably all differently. How can he or she begin to build up relationships in those circumstances?

Forming friendships with peers is another area of difficulty. Young, normally developing infants have very little interest in other infants. They need 'superior interactors' (McConkey, 1987) with whom to communicate, people who can time their interactions, return their gaze, share their little games and interpret their responses. Many older children with profound disabilities show only fleeting interest in their classmates, especially if they too have profound disabilities. Expecting them all to join in a group activity is really not within their capabilities. This is a very good argument in favour of integrating children with PMLD into classes of children with less severe learning difficulties rather than gathering them all together in a group. Young, normally developing infants derive a lot of pleasure and appear to learn much from their older siblings who may not be as skilled as adults at interaction with them but who provide examples of life's routines and are often prepared to repeat little games over and over again. However, as was discussed in the communication section, children with PMLD have many difficulties which prevent them from learning naturally from their interactions with their parents and siblings. These difficulties mean that it can take many years of intensive work to accomplish the achievements that occupy a few months for those who are developing normally.

Turning to school, it appears that, in order to encourage children with PMLD to build up relationships with other people, they need a combination of a small number of adults (to simulate parents) and a small number of more able peers (to simulate siblings). There is also the necessity for the adults to work very slowly and sensitively and allow time for social relationships to be formed. Adults in schools are anxious to use every moment to its best effect and in consequence often hurry through daily routines such as eating and drinking and visiting the bathroom so that they can get quickly to the 'real teaching'. Spending more time on building up social contact and encouraging relationships is fundamentally crucial. Many theorists have expounded the importance of social interaction in the learning process. Bruner and Vygotsky are particularly well known in this field (Wood, 1988). They would maintain that effective learning is dependent upon relationships with adults who provide the mediation necessary for children to make sense of the world around them. Without social interaction, it is very difficult for children to learn.

Although building up relationships is of vital importance, it must also be remembered that there will be many times in the life of someone with profound disabilities when relationships will be broken. Because, in many cases, there may not be many manifestations of relationships, it may be assumed that people with PMLD will not notice when their caregivers change. Perhaps they have not been told that they are changing classes at school or given an adequate transition period before moving from school to social education centre. Some schools, in anticipation of avoiding the pain of separation, make sure that their pupils do not become too attached to one person and in consequence deny the possibility of building up any sustained relationships. As usual the answer is likely to lie between these two extremes. Taking the risk of allowing real human contact to take place is bound to engender moments of loss and grief, but as long as this is recognised and periods of sadness are expected and encouraged, greater fulfilment can be achieved through the increase of the repertoire of feelings and emotions.

Spiritual Development

In terms of attempting to explore the possible feelings and emotions of children with PMLD, the spiritual dimension is by far the most taxing. Very little has been written about spirituality in young children who can express their ideas and virtually nothing has been written about young babies. However, one might want to argue that for many adults spirituality is impossible to put into words. The communication between a person and his or her spirituality transcends spoken language and engages the emotions directly. It might be one of the world's great religions which gives a sense of wonder or perhaps the appreciation of the beauty of nature, or even the caring atmosphere of humans enjoying each other's company.

The possibility of experiencing spirituality is often denied to people with profound disabilities. It is thought that they cannot make sense of religious experiences or that taking them to the top of a hill and enabling them to wonder at the strength of the wind and rain is inappropriate. It is not possible to provide proof that they are in fact experiencing spiritual feelings. However, neither is it possible to prove that they are not. On a simple level, a quiet circle of people surrounding an aromatic candle, touching gently, perhaps swaying a little, can provide a profoundly comforting atmosphere and it may well also be providing a spiritual experience for those involved. Parents and caretakers can only encourage development, spiritual or otherwise, if there are lots of opportunities for children with profound disabilities to experience events that either comfort them or take their breath away, events that have the potential to stir the spirit.

The implications for education

Although it is an extremely difficult task to explore the inner life of children with profound and multiple learning disabilities, teasing through some of the possibilities has revealed that there is much for parents, caretakers and educators to undertake in the way of interpretation and to enable future development. In the past it was felt that children with PMLD were ineducable and they were shut away in large long-stay mental handicap hospitals. Many died as the result of their condition, although some lived into adulthood. In the past twenty years improved medical care has meant that more children with multiple disabilities are surviving and surviving for much longer. Since the 1970 Education (Handicapped Children's) Act, schooling has been available and educators have been endeavouring to find ways in which to enable learning to take place.

Sensitive assessment tools which probe the thinking and communicative patterns of the children are gradually becoming available. The

Uzgaris and Hunt (1975) *Scales of Infant Psychological Development* which was based on Piaget's sensorimotor stage of development were developed for use with profoundly disabled children by Dunst (1980). Using this alongside communication assessments such as *The Affective Communication Assessment* (Coupe *et al.*, 1985) and *The Pragmatics Profile of Early Communication* (Dewart and Summers, 1988) gives a workable picture of the developmental level of the child. *The Callier-Azusa Scale* (Stillman,1978) was developed particularly to assess the needs of children with multisensory impairments.

From instruments such as these, which encourage precise observation, it is possible to build up a picture of where to begin teaching. Educators are, however, aware that in the case of children who have multiple difficulties it is never wise to think that one set of assessments is sufficient to be used as more than a rough guide. Responses can vary from day to day and the multiplicity of difficulties can mask abilities that are hard to recognise.

Teaching approaches have been developing over the twenty-five years since the 1970 Act and present interest is in enabling children with PMLD to take some control over their own environment. This ranges from using microswitches to make toys work and offering simple choice of activity, to positioning children where they can be active explorers and letting them take the lead in communicative interactions (Coupe *et al.*, 1994; Nind and Hewett, 1994).

Intensive interaction

There is more and more interest in using *intensive interaction* to reach children with the most complex difficulties. This is a method of working, developed by Nind and Hewett (1994), which makes use of a range of interactive games used in the natural interactions between parents and infants. The emphasis is on pleasure and encouraging the child to enjoy human contact and often there is little structure to the games. They arise from facial expressions or tickles or 'blowing raspberries' or any other little action the child finds enjoyable.

The intention of *intensive interaction* is not to teach through mastery of tasks but to encourage the child to use meaningful communication where none has been apparent. As these methods were derived from working with normally developing infants and involved the use of games, the question arises as to whether this is an age appropriate manner in which to work with older children and teenagers with profound disabilities. Apart from wanting to answer this with retorts that playfulness is not age specific, there are very strong arguments for choosing activities which will make sense to the person involved. If learning is to take place, it is necessary to place activities within the *zone of next development* suggested by Vygotsky (Wood, 1988). Too difficult and the child cannot understand at all, too easy and the child becomes bored.

Age appropriateness is achieved through the value placed on the individual by the parent or educator. It has little to do with actual activities. It is quite possible for a make-up session to be both crass and undignified in the hands of someone who perceives the teenager with PMLD as a young baby, just as a simple turn-taking session with a favourite object can be respectful and dignified when conducted by someone who views that person as a young adult who is at an early stage of development. This is not an easy debate: it presents yet another dilemma faced by the educators of children with PMLD. It is similar to the question: *should Mary be allowed to explore her hands with her mouth because she is at the stage of development when this is usual or should we stop her because she is ten years old and it isn't appropriate at that age?* There is no simple answer. Hopefully, by engaging Mary in other exploratory play and in developing meaningful communication with people around her she will move on to more acceptable behaviour herself.

A team approach

Working with children with profound disabilities is difficult and demanding. The multiplicity of problems means that many people will be involved and, as was discussed earlier, this can potentially lead to confusion for the child and a waste of time and resources for the professionals. It has been suggested that the child, from a developmental point of view, needs a very small group of adults with whom to build relationships. How can this be achieved, bearing in mind the fact that there could be as many as thirty people involved in diagnosis, assessment and implementing programmes (RNIB, 1992)?

One way to manage such a situation is to adopt a team approach for the pooling and sharing of the work involved. The central figures in the child's life join together and agree on how they are going to work with him or her. One agrees to be the key person, through whom the rest of the team works. Prior to school, this is likely to be the mother or perhaps a therapist, during school years this role shifts to the teacher and post-school to a care worker or college lecturer, depending on where the young person is placed. There will be a small number of other key people involved at each stage depending on the particular needs of the child in question. For many these will include a physiotherapist, a speech therapist and perhaps a visiting teacher who is a specialist in sensory impairments.

In a school the team meets to discuss the next step forward. The team here may consist of parents, classroom staff, therapists and a visiting teacher. Programmes of work are devised between the members of the team but are mainly carried out by the key people, the parents at home and classroom staff at school. Other professionals take on the role of advisers who, together with the key people, assess needs, watch the children at work, demonstrate new techniques and evaluate progress. Occasionally other advisers are called in, such as the dietician or paediatrician but there is care to share the results of any such visits with the rest of the team. One set of records, to which everyone has access, is kept by the key person (Lacey and Lomas, 1993).

Working in this manner can avoid the problems which may be experienced through so many people trying to meet the needs of one child with multiple disabilities. If people do not work together in a team, much time and effort can be wasted through duplicated assessments and conflicting programmes. The child can get lost in a sea of barely familiar faces, all carrying out different tasks. Working in a collaborative manner can draw all this together and contribute considerably to the overall development of children with PMLD. It can only be achieved if time is set aside for discussion and mutual training. Realistically, an effective team approach is hard to achieve, but if professionals are prepared to invest time and resources and devise procedures and structures to enable it to happen, the benefits will be enormous, both in terms of the children's development and in terms of efficiency and staff training.

Conclusions

It is well recognised that people working together in a team can produce better results than one person working alone, especially when the task is complex (Lacey and Lomas, 1993). This chapter began with a suggestion that understanding and encouraging the expression of the inner life of children with profound and multiple learning disabilities is a difficult and taxing challenge. Collaborative work can enable parents and educators to tease out together what they understand to be the thoughts and feelings of the children in their care. It is incredibly difficult to interpret these and more than one brain on the subject can be of great practical help.

There is no doubt that improvements in sensitivity are being made constantly. Assessment instruments are being refined, approaches to communication development are being tested and generally caregivers have higher expectations of what children with profound disabilities can achieve. They realise that no assumptions can be made and refuse to place a ceiling on the possible levels of attainment. They offer interesting and exciting activities in which the children can be involved, but are careful not to overload someone who is at a very early level of development. There is no point, for instance, in taking a child who has not yet learned to fixate on objects into a multisensory room filled with flashing lights, moving images and musical sounds. What this child needs is one isolated light source on which to begin to learn to fix. Bombardment of the senses will not only be confusing but may actually encourage complete shut down of all sensory pathways. It would be worse than useless.

Sensitive adults spend time with children with profound disabilities. They observe carefully and listen hard to the tiny indicators of thoughts and feelings. They understand the implications of the very early stages of development as described by Piaget and the ways in which very young children begin to learn to take part in the world through the work of psychologists such as Bruner and Vygotsky. They desire to build up close relationships with their charges and encourage them to begin to take control over their own lives. They show them that communication is rewarding and that there are more positive alternatives to relating to people than through biting and scratching. They demonstrate unequivocally that they are people of worth and that their thoughts and feelings matter and deserve response.

References

Brudenell, P. (1986). *The Other Side of Profound Handicap*. Basingstoke: Macmillan.

Buckley, S. (1990).Teaching reading to teach language to children with Down's syndrome. In: Smith, B. (Ed.) *Interactive Approaches to Teaching the Core Subjects*. Bristol: Lame Duck Publications.

Coupe, J., Barber, M. and Murphy, D. (1988). Affective Communication. In: Coupe, J. and Goldbart, J. (Eds.) *Communication Before Speech*. Beckenham: Croom Helm.

Coupe, J., Barton, L., Barber, M., Collins, L., Levy, D. and Murphy, D. (1985) *Affective Communication Assessment*. Manchester: MEC.

Coupe, J., O'Kane, J. and Smith,B (1994). *Taking Control: Enabling People with Learning Difficulties*. London: David Fulton.

Craft, A., Andrews, E., Mallett, A. and Lewis, S. (1990). Sexual Development in Individuals with Profound and Multiple Impairments. In: Hogg, J., Sebba, J. and Lambe, L.(Eds.), *Profound and Multiple Impairments, Vol 3 Medical and Physical Care and Management*. London: Chapman & Hall.

Dewart, H. and Summers, S. (1988). *The Pragmatics Profile of Early Communication Skills*. Slough: NFER-Nelson.

Dockrell, J. and McShane, J. (1993). *Children's Learning Difficulties: A Cognitive Approach* Oxford: Blackwell.

Donaldson, M. (1978). *Children's Minds*. London: Fontana.

Dunst, C. (1980). *A Clinical and Educational Manual for use with the Uzgaris and Hunt Scales of Infant Psychological Development*. Austin, Texas: Pro-Ed.

Goldbart, J. (1994a). *Cognition and Learning.*A unit of the Distance Education Course 'Interdisciplinary Work with People with PMLD' Birmingham: The University of Birmingham.

Goldbart, J. (1994b). *Communication*. A unit of the Distance Education Course' Interdisciplinary Work with People with PMLD'. Birmingham: Birmingham University

Goldbart, J. (1994c). Opening the Communication Curriculum to Students with PMLDs. In: Ware, J.(Ed.) *Educating Children with Profound and Multiple Learning Difficulties*. London: David Fulton.

Harris, P. (1989). *Children and Emotion*. Oxford: Blackwell.

Hogg, J. and Sebba, J. (1986). *Profound Retardation and Multiple Impairment, Vol 1 Development and Learning.* Beckenham: Croom Helm.

Kelleher, A. and Mulcahy, M. (1986). Patterns of Disability in the Mentally Handicapped. In: Berg, J. and De Jong, J. (Eds.) *Science and Service in Mental Retardation.* London: Methuen.

Lacey, P. and Lomas, J. (1993). *Support Services and the Curriculum : A Practical Guide to Collaboration.* London: David Fulton.

Mallett, A. (1994). *Meeting Personal Needs.* A Unit of the Distance Education Course 'Interdisciplinary Work with People with PMLD'. Birmingham: Birmingham University.

McConkey, R. (1987). Interaction: The name of the game. In: Smith, B. (Ed.) *Interactive Approaches to Teaching Children with Severe Learning Difficulties* Birmingham: Westhill College.

McInnes, J. and Treffry, J. (1982). *Deaf-blind Infants and Children.* Milton Keynes: Open University Press.

Nind, M. and Hewett, D. (1994). *Access to Communication.* London: David Fulton.

Orelove, F. and Sobsey, D. (1991). *Educating Children with Multiple Disabilities.* Baltimore: Paul Brookes.

RNIB (1992). *Curriculum Materials used with Multihandicapped Visually Impaired Children and Young People.* London: RNIB.

Seligman, M. (1975). *Helplessness: On Depression, Development and Death.* San Fransisco: Freeman.

Sinason, V. (1994). *Mental Handicap and the Human Condition: New Approaches from the Tavistock.* London: Free Association Books.

Stillman, R. (Ed.) (1978). *The Callier-Azusa Scale.* Dallas: The University of Texas.

Uzgaris, I. and Hunt, J. (1975). *Assessment in Infancy: Ordinal Scales of Psychological Development.* Chicago: University of Illinois Press.

Ware, J. (1994). *Educating Children with Profound and Multiple Learning Difficulties.* London: David Fulton.

Wood, D. (1988). *How Children Think and Learn.* Oxford: Blackwell.

Chapter 6
The inner life of children with autistic difficulties

JILL BOUCHER

Introduction

> It is much easier to empathise with someone whose ways of experiencing the world are similar to one's own than to understand someone whose perceptions are very different . . . (It is inconceivable how) someone who has much better inherent communication abilities than I do but who has not even taken a close (enough) look at my perspective to notice the enormity of (the) chasm between us tells me that my failure to understand is because I lack empathy. ('Jim', quoted by Cesaroni and Garber, 1991)

> . . . nobody really understands what the emotional suffering of a person with autism is like, and there is no painkiller, injection or operation that can get rid of it or even at best relieve it even a little. ('TRC' - in Jolliffe *et al.*, 1992)

Autism is defined in terms of characteristic abnormalities of social, communicative, and imaginative behaviour. Recent authoritative definitions of autism emphasise the lack of reciprocal, or two-way, social interaction and lack of empathy, or sympathetic feeling. They also emphasise the inability to hold a normal conversation even in people who have large vocabularies and perfect grammar, conversation typically being egocentric and restricted in content. Concerning abnormal imaginative behaviour, recent definitions emphasise the restricted content of thought and interests, the lack of spontaneous pretend play in children, the insistence on sameness in the environment and the attachment to routine. Repetitive behaviour is also emphasised, especially the presence of odd repetitive movements, repetitive vocalisation, and sometimes impulsive actions such as sniffing or touching objects or people.

Autism is very commonly accompanied by general learning difficulty, and sometimes by other developmental difficulties such as visual impairment, clumsiness, or specific language disorder. Because the majority of people with autism have dual or multiple difficulties, it is easy to underemphasise the things which most autistic people *can* do, such as making bonded relationships with parents or primary caregivers, rote learning and remembering certain things in unusual detail, and seeing how things like jigsaws, or Lego, fit together. It is also easy to forget that the minority of people who do not have any other handicap except autism may develop good spoken and written language systems; do well at school, sometimes showing exceptional ability in one particular subject such as maths or music, and in occasional instances make important friendships and even life partnerships. Above all, it is all too easy to talk about people with autism as if they were a homogeneous group when they are, of course, just as different from each other as the people reading this book. The inner life of people with autism will reflect all these differences.

In this account of the inner life of children with autism I have drawn on first hand accounts of 'autism from the inside' written by some exceptional adults with autism, who are not only verbal and articulate, but also able to reflect on and analyse their own experience. In this they are not typical of the large majority of autistic people who have learning difficulties as well as autism. However, it is usual to argue that people with 'pure' autism can show us what is unique to the condition. The accounts of these able adults tells us, I believe, what it might feel like to be an autistic child.

The people whose published accounts I have drawn on are those of 'TRC' (as presented by Joliffe, Lansdown and Robinson), David Medzianik (DM) (as reported by himself), 'Tony W.' (as reported by Volkmar and Cohen), Temple Grandin (TG) (as reported by Sacks), and 'Jim' (whose verbatim account has been summarised by Cesaroni and Garber). I also quote extensively from John van Dalen's (JvD) personal account of autism which will be published in the near future. JvD is Dutch, but the quotes presented here are in his own written English with minimal stylistic corrections. Some of these people might be described as having Asperger's syndrome, which is generally considered to be a relatively mild, but typical, form of autism.

How the person with autism experiences the outside world

Sensation

People who are autistic have long been reported to be both over sensitive and under sensitive to sounds. So the same child at different times may hear a train coming long before anyone else can, but apparently not hear someone talking to them at close range. Autistic people themselves explain this in terms of being so sensitive to sound when they are young that traffic noises are terrifying or painful, and even the sound of their own blood in their ears makes an intolerable and ceaseless drumming (presumably as debilitating as severe tinnitus). Unexpected sounds are particularly unpleasant or frightening. Moreover, it seems that young children with autism cannot 'filter out', or attenuate, some sounds in order to attend to others: all sounds impinge on them equally, in what must be an unbearable cacophony. Even speech may be heard by the young autistic child as part of the overall jumble of noise to which he feels himself subject: it is not 'special' in the way that voices and speech are selectively attended to and perceived as meaningful by ordinary children. To escape this cacophony of undifferentiated sound, the autistic child may learn to cut out all sounds by shutting off the auditory channel completely by covering their ears, or by concentrating intensely on something else, such as a spinning object or their own rocking movement. This can produce the impression of deafness, or under sensitivity to sound, which contrasts so strangely with the acute hearing which is apparent at other times.

Young children with autism may also be hypersensitive to sights, smells, tastes and tactile sensations. Colours may be unbearably vivid, or appear to move or vibrate; visual stimuli which move, especially if movement is sudden or unexpected, can cause distress; eye contact is frightening and aversive (see TRC's account). Touch may be experienced as unpleasant or even painful, especially if unexpected, or not at the 'right' level of intensity. Everyday foods may be rejected because they taste too strong. People and places have powerful distinctive smells which may be experienced as unpleasant. One girl with autism is reported by her mother to have said 'Let's face it, nine out of ten people have halitosis. And their bodies smell too.' (Stehli, 1992). It seems likely that young children with autism shut their eyes, or sit with their eyes covered, in order to shut out the excessively stimulating visual environment, just as they may cover their ears to avoid sound, or move away from someone who touches them, or look away when looked at.

Some people with autism may experience a phenomenon known medically as synaesthesia, in which something seen is also experienced as something heard, or something felt is also experienced as something seen. The individual (Jim) who has reported this phenomenon also reports 'sounds in the head'. The occurrence of synaesthesia may explain why some children with autism cover their eyes when they hear loud sound, or cover their ears when there is a bright light.

Withdrawal from excessive, undifferentiated, and often *frightening* stimulation appears to underline what has been termed 'willed blindness', 'willed deafness' and 'willed isolation' (Park, 1972) in all the people with autism who have written or spoken about their early experiences. As these individuals with autism become older, it seems that they either learn to tolerate over stimulation, or become better at gating out excess stimulation. The fact that in a few cases systematic 'desensitisation' treatment appears to be helpful, at least to alleviate hypersensitivity to sound (Stehli, 1992.), could suggest that increased tolerance results from naturally occurring desensitisation.

Whether or not withdrawal can entirely explain the lack of responsivness to sound, sight and even pain which occurs in people with autism, remains an open question. Spinning objects, rocking, headbanging, and the host of other repetitive motor behaviours to which people with autism are prone might all be explained in terms of escape from over stimulation. However, sensory *deprivation* is known to cause repetitive, self-stimulatory behaviour in people who are not autistic. It may be, therefore, that many people with autism (though not those exceptionally able people who have reported their own experiences) have some degree of primary unresponsiveness to sensory experience. These children may self-stimulate to fill the vacuum, rather than to act as a barrier between them and the world.

Perception of the object world

It is one thing to hear sounds, or to see colours, shapes and movements, and quite another thing to perceive them as something which has familiarity and meaning. The difference between sensation and perception can be clearly illustrated by comparing hearing impairment with the phenomenon of speech imperception: someone with a hearing impairment hears the sounds of speech imperfectly; whereas someone with speech imperception hears the sounds of speech perfectly well, but cannot extract meaning from them.

From the first-hand accounts we have from people with autism, it is clear that even when the autistic person is looking and listening and seeking to learn and make sense of what they can see and hear, feel, taste and smell, there are obstacles which prevent them from building up a familiar and meaningful world picture in the way that other people do. These obstacles have a particularly devastating effect on the perception and understanding of people. However, they also affect the perception and understanding of objects.

JvD writes:

> I have discovered, during the years, that my way of perceiving things differs from that of other people. For instance, when I am confronted with a hammer, I am initially not confronted with a hammer at all but solely with a number of unrelated parts: I observe a cubical piece of iron near to a coincidental bar-like piece of wood. After that, I am struck by the coincidental nature of the iron and the wooden thing resulting in the unifying perception of a hammerlike configuration. The name 'hammer' is not immediately within reach but appears when the configuration has been sufficiently stabilised over time. Finally, the use of a tool becomes clear when I realise

that this perceptual configuration known as 'hammer' can be used to do carpenter's work. Each step of these successive integration-phases requires a considerable effort from me. It is a type of effort that can best be described as 'thinking in the background'. For me to perceive something is equivalent to constructing an object using explicit trains of thought, whereas it should all be done in a fully automatic way, without conscious effort and in rapid succession. (van Dalen, in press)

JvD's account of his own experience goes on to draw out the implications of perceiving the world in unconnected (or effortfully connected) parts. He points out that since object parts are the meaningful constituents of his world, an object (or, for example, a street) approached from an unfamiliar angle can strike him as completely unfamiliar. This is because his object concept has been laboriously constructed by relating the constituent parts from one particular point of view, and a different viewpoint requires a new construction of the constituent parts. From this he goes on to argue that:

The necessary thinking activities connected with everyday object-perception force autistic people to seek familiar settings where they can restrict and control their perceptual environment as much as possible. ...I think that for me a single room bears the same spatial perceptual characteristics as a whole house. That is why I can easily dwell in small areas while I do often feel quite lost in extended environments. (van Dalen, in press)

JvD also points out that:

In the eyes of a non-autistic person I seem to be slowed down. During a certain amount of time a non-autist can digest more perceptions with an object-like character than I, because I am forced to digest each object piece by piece. (van Dalen, in press)

Perception of social signals - faces and speech

JvD's experience of being able spontaneously to perceive parts, only, of objects, and of having to build up his perception of objects effortfully is echoed by TRC, who writes:

I have only just recently realised that when I look at people and pictures, I am not looking at the whole but rather just the outline or a part. I *can* look at a picture completely, but only a small section at a time. It is the same with people's faces: I cannot take in the whole face in one go . . . . A large part of my life is spent just trying to work out the pattern behind everything. Set routines, times, particular routes and rituals all help to get order into an unbearably chaotic life. (Jolliffe *et al.*, 1992)

An inability to perceive faces as wholes, added to the fact that eyes are 'frightening' or 'too penetrating', combine to produce poor memory for faces (see TRC and also TG) and, more catastrophically, great difficulty in comprehending the meaning of facial expression. Being able to 'read' non-verbal communication is particularly important in understanding the emotions and attitudes of others, and in synchronising conversation (think how much more difficult it is to gauge what another person is feeling, and turn-take smoothly, when communicating by telephone). Almost all first hand accounts of autism stress the difficulties which people with autism experience in interpreting the meaning of facial expression, and particularly in interpreting meaning signalled by the eyes. Jim, using the same kinds of phrases which JvD and TRC use to describe their efforts to understand the object world, points out that 'the autistic person spends enormous energy connecting with another person'. The implication is that the intelligent autistic person can learn to construct social meaning from the upturned mouth, crinkled lines round the eyes, and raised cheeks (for example), but that this is effortful and time consuming, and may be impossible if someone is seen from an unusual angle, or if facial expressions change rapidly or are fleeting.

If non-verbal communication conveys emotions and attitudes, speech is the pre-eminent medium for conveying other types of information. It appears that speech perception is no easier for autistic people than the comprehension of facial expression. TRC writes:

> When I was very young I can remember that speech seemed to be of no more significance than any other sound. For a time speech sounds seemed just to merge into one another without making any sense, a jumble of letters, hard to reproduce, let alone to understand. (Jolliffe *et al.*, 1992)

When he did begin to understand single words:

> Sentences still seemed to lack any clear definition . . . It is hard to reproduce and understand words that are similar in sound, like ball and bull, fend and vend . . . Although people pick me up on any mispronunciations, they do not seem to notice that when they speak there are in every sentence words that are hard to distinguish. . . . When someone talks to me I have to really try and listen carefully if I am going to stand any chance of working out what the words are . . . When I read books the problem of deciphering what the words actually are does not exist because I can see immediately what they are meant to be. (Jolliffe *et al.*, 1992)

As well as having difficulty in what linguists would call 'segmenting' heard speech into its component parts, and also in generalising across different pronunciations of words within different contexts, TRC describes the difficulty he has in remembering chunks of heard speech for long enough to decode them:

> When somebody starts to speak to me I have nearly always lost the first few words before I realise that I am actually being spoken to. This happens so much that I have called them the 'waking up words'. . . . At the end of a sentence the last few words seem to make a stronger impression and are on

occasions the only ones that can be meaningful. I often repeat what people are saying in my head, as if to try and get it clearer, and the last part always seems to stick, although the first part occasionally disappears... then I become completely lost. (Jolliffe *et al.*, 1992)

TG, also, describes how difficult it is to make sense of speech and to hold longer sentences in memory, especially if some interruption or brief distraction occurs between hearing something that has been said and responding to it. TG's solution appears to be to 'translate' what she hears into visual images. This may be a common solution amongst able people with autism, most of whom claim to think in pictures rather than in words (Hurlburt, Happe and Frith, 1994).

Feelings associated with the external world

Negative emotions

The most striking refrain running through autistic people's accounts of their inner experience is the word 'fear'. JvD writes:

I have discovered that my over-selective way of perceiving things is always accompanied by a sense of fear that is not specifically related to certain objects but originates in the fact that my first encounter with a physical object is a partial one. The experience of fear due to partial perception can best be understood by referring to a confrontation with a silhouette in the dark: one knows that something is there but it is not altogether immediately clear what it is. (van Dalen, in press)

TRC describes how, as a child, he was frightened by dogs because of their sudden movements and barking, and how this fear spread to the word 'dog' because when he heard the word he thought that a dog might suddenly appear. So 'language acquisition began to take on a horrible side'. As an adult, he is still sufficiently frightened by 'noisy crowded places, polystyrene being touched, balloons being touched, noisy cars, trains, motorbikes, lorries and aeroplanes, noisy vehicles on building sites, hammering and banging, electric tools being used, the sound of the sea, the sound of felt-tip or marker pens being used to colour in, and fireworks', to have to cover up his ears to avoid them. To look at people 'disturbs my quietness and is terribly frightening'. Later in his short article, he says, using terms similar to those used by JvD:

It may be because things that I see do not always make the right impression that I am frightened of so many things that can be seen: people, particularly their faces, very bright light, crowds, things moving suddenly, large machines and buildings that are unfamiliar, unfamiliar places, my own shadow, the dark, bridges, rivers, canals, streams and the sea. (Jolliffe *et al.*, 1992)

One has the feeling that the list is endless. TRC has suffered from stress-related stomach pain since he was a young child, and he now takes Beta-Blockers to 'reduce the physical symptoms of fear'.

Tony W. begins his account:

> I was living in a world of daydreaming and Fear . . . I was afraid of everything! I was terrified to go in the water swimming, (and of) loud noises; in the dark I had severe, repetitive Nightmares . . . I would wake up so terrified and disorientated I wasn't able to Find my way out of the room for a few miniuts. It felt like I was being draged to Hell. I was afraid of simple things such as going into the shower, getting my nails clipped, soap in my eyes, rides in the carnival . . . I was terrified to learn to ride the bybycle . . . And was verry Nervious about everything. And Feared People and Social Activity Greatly. (Volkmar and Cohen, 1985)

The use of capital letters expresses, one feels, Tony's strong emotion, since later he writes: 'I . . . FEARED People my age because of school.' Tony, like TRC, has at times taken prescribed drugs to calm his emotional feelings.

Certain sounds frightened Jim as a child. He recalls that when he was listening to a record, low-frequency notes in the background music became so terrifying that he refused to return to school. Jim's insights into the source of his fear have some similarity to, but are not quite the same as, the insights suggested by JvD and by TRC. Jim reportedly suggests that:

> . . . some stimuli act as 'triggers' for disorganisation of processing, not unlike epileptic seizures being triggered by light flashing at a certain frequency. 'I think the sounds on the record fell into this category. They didn't frighten me in themselves, but they triggered some loss of orientation that was unpleasant and frightening'. (Cesaroni and Garber, 1991)

TG's heightened emotionality took the form of anger when she was a child, and she describes the tantrums and rages of her early years. However, in her later childhood the heightened emotionality took the form of 'frenzied searches for the meaning of life, . . . fixations, and a feeling of being driven'. TG reports that these 'tore my body apart with stress-related health problems' and she eventually resorted to antidepressants to calm her.

Differences in the way in which individual people with autism react to their sensorially overwhelming and perceptually confusing environment probably reflect individual differences in personality and experience. JvD, TRC, and Tony all describe fear, though they react to it in different ways. TG describes anger turning into a furious attempt to conquer her confusion.

DM, whom I have not quoted up till now, appears to be a somewhat different character. DM's autobiography is a wonderfully detailed account of his day to day life, with comments on his achievements and hopes, as well as on the difficulties, frustrations and disappointments which he has encountered. In his autobiography DM does not analyse his experience of autism. However, his anxieties are patent in his writing, and he, like many other very able people with autism, takes medication to help to control the stress which he experiences on a daily basis.

Positive emotions

Although people with autism probably experience more negative emotions than ordinary people, it is also clear from the first-hand accounts that people with autism also have experiences which give them pleasure. Some of these experiences are the same as those which give pleasure to anyone. For example, TRC describes his pleasure in listening to music, and in cantering on horseback. All these able people with autism gain pleasure, just like everyone else, from the things they do well, whether this is reading, studying, writing poetry, making models, playing video games, drawing, playing a musical instrument, or writing a computer program.

However, some of the pleasurable experiences which people with autism describe are more idiosyncratic. A striking example is TG's now famous 'squeeze machine', designed to give her all-over body pressure of just the right intensity as to give her a sensation of relaxation and calm. Repetitious experience also appears to be pleasurable in a way which is unusual. For example, TRC reports that as a child he liked opening and closing the doors of a toy car and watching the wheels go round, or endlessly firing a cap gun in order to experience the predictable bang and the smell of the smoke. The pleasure experienced by people with autism from certain activities and occupations is also unusual in the extent to which it derives from the fact that the preferred activities are solitary (or shut out others) and from the fact that the activities give a sense of security and control. The two things are of course related in that most interpersonal interaction is painfully difficult for people with autism, and deprives them of a sense of control, whereas solitary, self-selected activities are under their control.

Can people with autism experience what is for most lucky people the greatest source of happiness, namely close and loving relationships with others? Autism certainly does not preclude a capacity to respond to being loved. Young autistic children experience security, comfort, closeness, and often - in special games or cuddles - fun with their parents, or those to whom they become most strongly attached; and they show this by their preference for their attachment figures, and by the increased security which is evident when with them. Nor does autism preclude the capacity to appreciate intellectually, to value, and to want more complex relationships, such as friendships, sexual relationships and life partnerships. However, the autistic person's communication difficulties, their difficulties in understanding the emotions and thoughts of others, combined with the fact that their experience of the world is so different from most people's, makes fully reciprocal relationships with ordinary people impossible.

Important relationships which are not fully reciprocal may be developed, such as DM's friendship with his adult education teacher. Similarly, important relationships with people who are not themselves ordinary may be developed. DM has a friendship with 'Peter', who himself has difficulties in coping with all the demands of normal life. Most intriguingly, in his account of TG, Oliver Sacks digresses to mention a family in which both parents and two children are autistic. He describes how the parents had met at college and had recognised each other's autism 'with a sense of such affinity and delight that it was inevitable that they would marry'. This family lives in its autistic world at home, but 'act normal' when in the outside world, without understanding what underlies the social conventions they have learned to 'ape'. Do children with autism in a special school or unit for children with autism feel a similar affinity, one wonders? And might this contrast with some of the negative feelings expressed in all the personal accounts concerning experiences at mainstream schools?

Being unable to make fully reciprocal relationships with ordinary people does not, of course, as TRC points out, mean that people with autism cannot love others. Nor does it mean, as both TRC and especially DM point out, that people with autism cannot feel desperately lonely and even despairing about their incapacity to relate. Nor does it, as Jim points out, necessarily mean that people with autism lack empathy. To use the explicit image of 'alien-ation' which recurs in these accounts, any one of us would be likely to fail to make a reciprocal relationship with a Martian, but we would not on that account expect to be charged with lacking empathy.

The autistic person's knowledge and their mental activities

Knowledge representation, narrow interests and repetitive behaviour

JvD points out that the autistic person's perceptual knowledge consists of wholes effortfully constructed out of many parts, rather than consisting of abstractions or Gestalts. He also points out that the autistic person's effortfully assembled wholes are always constructed from a particular point of view, which may then be compared mentally with the whole constructed from other points of view. He suggests that this abnormal way of perceiving the object world and storing knowledge about it can explain the autistic person's restricted range of interests and some of their repetitive behaviour. Concerning the former he writes:

The autistic 'narrow field of interest'... should in reality be interpreted as an inability to spread attention across a large number of different objects. Autistics have an ability to delve deep into many aspects (points of view) all related to the same topic ('object'). That is, they have the ability to become deeply involved in a certain field of interest thereby being inevitably forced to drop everything else that does not belong to it. It should also be clear why they can talk incessantly about one topic: they can perceive many subtle parts of an object, normally called details, but they can hardly perceive many different objects. As non-autistics do their talking mainly using object-ingredients, quickly jumping between a large variety of subjects, autistical conversation is based on pieces of talk all more or less related to a single object of interest. (van Dalen, in press)

Concerning repetitive behaviour JvD writes:

Before acting, autistic people must go through a number of separate stages in perception by making 'decisions'. It is very important to realise that, if this long decision-chain is interrupted, the autistic person must start all over again . . . In other words, an interruption effectively wipes away any intermediate result . . . The long autistical process towards meaning generation of the complex situation restarts from scratch. (van Dalen, in press)

TG describes how, when she is solving a problem related to the work she does designing systems for herding animals, she is able to visualise and manipulate the component parts of possible systems in her mind. This tends to suggest that TG, like JvD, perceives and stores objects in memory as assemblies of parts, enabling her to mentally deconstruct and reconstruct complex objects with ease. However, TG also describes how her personal experience is stored visually (in 'prodigious detail' and with 'pathological fixity', according to Sacks) just as if it were recorded on videotape. If she wants to recall a component part of a past experience, or event, she is specifically *not* able to break the tape into its component parts in order to recall some detail of it. The tape has to be played through memory at real-time speed until she gets to the exact incident, or visual image, which she wants to think or talk about. This suggest that events, like objects, are stored as unique items in memory rather than being entered into abstract representations of related events. However, events are *involuntarily* stored as unbreakable sequences of component parts, whereas objects are *effortfully* stored in terms of particular points of view.

Imagination, dreams and thinking

Almost all the personal accounts of people with autism mention dreams and sometimes nightmares. TW's nightmares have already been mentioned. TRC writes:

(A)utism . . . will not even leave you while you are asleep. It affects your

dreams and when they wake you up, you have to cope not only with what
seemed a very real dream but a dark bedroom. (Jolliffe *et al.*, 1992)

Some of the accounts also describe daydreaming, fantasising, or other
conscious use of visual imagery. For example, TG describes how, when
she is trying to solve a problem about a new stockherding design, she
runs 'simulations' through her mind, in which she visualises an animal
passing through a particular design:

> I visualise the animal entering the chute, from different angles, different
> distances, zooming in or wide angle, even from a helicopter view - or I turn
> myself into an animal, and feel what it would feel entering the chute. (Sacks,
> 1995)

Even more strikingly, she reports how she originally learnt to draw by
pretending to be someone whom she had observed drawing out
designs. Sacks reports TG as follows:

> 'I saw how he did it', she told me. 'I went and got exactly the same instru-
> ments and pencils as he used - a point-five-millimetre HB Pental - and then I
> started pretending I was him. The drawing did itself, and when it was all done
> I couldn't believe I'd done it. I didn't have to learn how to draw or design, I
> pretended I was David - I appropriated him, drawing and all'. (Sacks, 1995)

This account conflicts directly with the recent theoretical suggestion that
people with autism cannot generate mental models, or cannot imagina-
tively enter into the role of another person. However, it may be significant
that TG enacted David drawing *exactly*. There is a suggestion here, again,
that what runs through the mind of a person with autism, perhaps in
dreams, or which may be used by them to solve problems or to
daydream, are precise, almost photographic reruns of experience. The
capacity to take a bit from here and a bit from there may be missing, since
to do this one must be able to break the remembered chunk into its
component parts. And this, perhaps, is something which even able
people with autism, such as those quoted from here, find it difficult to do.

Conclusion

How much more difficult, then, for the large majority of people with
autism whose inner experience is only partially captured by the accounts
which have been considered above. These are the children, and adults,
who are learning impaired as well as autistic; and those who are multiply
handicapped, with autism being a part, only, of their developmental
difficulties. These people constitute 75-80% of all people who are autistic. The personal accounts which have been quoted above may therefore
represent something of the essence of what it feels like to be autistic, but
they do not represent what the majority of people with autism must
experience, which is beyond current imagination or understanding.

Postcript

Every Day Seems Not Much Fun - by DM (Medzianik, undated)

I walk past the railings.
I kick the odd tin can down the street,
I walk around town till I have pains in my feet.
I sit in the same old cafe every time I go to town.
I look in the mirror and my face wears a constant frown.

That was the case until you came along to brighten my day.
You used to meet me outside the cafe.
You then would hold my hand.
Until you came along I didn't know that being with someone could be so pleasant.
Now you don't want me any more and things are back to what they were before.

I go in the same old cafe and put some coins in the juke box.
They are the same records that I used to play when I knew you,
only they seem sadder somehow.
I wish I could die and be reborn as you,
You get a lot of friends.
I have never had the friends you have, people don't want to talk to me now I am sad.

You were the girl that made me feel wanted again,
Now the same old juke box plays in that same cafe.
A year has gone by since I knew you, the records on the Juke Box have now changed too.
But music doesn't take away the pain of not knowing you.

The Bridge - by Jim (Cesaroni and Garber, 1991)

I built a bridge
out of nowhere, across nothingness
and wondered if there would be something on the other side.
I built a bridge
out of fog, across darkness
and hoped that there would be light on the other side.
I built a bridge
out of despair, across oblivion
and knew that there would be hope on the other side.
I built a bridge
out of helplessness, across chaos
and trusted that there would be strength on the other side.
I built a bridge
out of hell, across terror
and it was a good bridge, a strong bridge,
a beautiful bridge.
It was a bridge I built myself,

with only my hands for tools, my obstinacy for supports,
my faith for spans, and my blood for rivets.
    I built a bridge, and crossed it,
    but there was no one there to meet me on the other side.

References

Cesaroni, L. and Garber, M. (1991). Exploring the experience of autism through first-hand accounts. *Journal of Autism and Developmental Disorders,* **21**,303-14.

Hurlburt, R.T., Happe, F. and Frith, U. (1994) Sampling the form of inner experience. in three adults with Asperger syndrome. *Psychological Medicine,* **24**,385-95.

Joliffe, T., Lansdown, R. and Robinson, C. (1992). Autism: A personal account. *Communication,* **26**,12-19.

Medzianik, D. (undated). *My Autobiography.* University of Nottingham: Child Development Research Unit

Park, C.C. (1972). *The Siege: The First Eight Years of an Autistic Child.* London: Little, Brown.

Sacks, O. (1995). *An Anthropologist on Mars: Seven Paradoxical Tales.* (Chapter 7) London: Picador.

Stehli, A. (1992). *The Miracle of Silence.* Doubleday.

Van Dalen, J. (in press). Autism seen from the inside. *Communication.*

Volkmar, F.R. and Cohen, D.J. (1985). The experience of infantile autism: A first-person account by Tony W. *Journal of Autism and Developmental Disorders,* **15**,47-54.

Chapter 7
The Inner Life of Children with Emotional and Behavioural Difficulties

PAUL COOPER

This chapter deals with the inner lives of children with Emotional and Behavioural Difficulties (EBD). The chapter is based on the premiss that children's perceptions of themselves and their circumstances are crucial factors in helping us to understand the nature of emotional and behavioural problems, and vital in our endeavours to find ways of overcoming such problems. For too long emotional and behavioural difficulties have been equated in the minds of too many people with behavioural problems alone. This chapter attempts to take us beyond this view and goes on to indicate some of the ways in which we might incorporate the internal lives of pupils more fully in our schools, in ways that will benefit not only those children who exhibit or experience EBD, but all children.

A note on gender

A significant limitation of this chapter is the fact that it focuses exclusively on evidence from interviews with boys. On the one hand this could be justified on the grounds that the EBD label is overwhelmingly applied to boys. A survey of special facilities for children with EBD in England and Wales (Cooper, Smith and Upton, 1991) recently found that boys made up 85% of the total pupil population (8,556). This is not to say, however, that girls are not as likely as boys to experience emotional and behavioural difficulties. Knox (1988), for example, points to the alarming five-fold rise in female suicides, between 1950 and 1980. Davies (1979, 1984) gives us some clues as to why fewer girls become officially labelled as deviant or 'EBD'. She indicates, on the basis of interviews with girls and boys, that girls, whilst on the one hand tending to have a more positive view of school than boys, also, when they do behave in a deviant manner express their deviance in different ways to boys, and at the same time have their deviance interpreted by teachers in different ways from boys' deviance. Girls, by and large, tend to internalise their difficulties, whilst boys are prone to 'acting out' behaviour. In short, girls' difficulties can often be less disruptive to classroom processes than boys'. This tends to underline the point made earlier, that the 'emotional' aspects of EBD are often relegated to second place behind the 'behavioural' aspects.

The dearth of literature on girls' perceptions of schooling needs to be addressed, and it is a limitation of this chapter that girls' views are not included. Even if the population of EBD facilities is overwhelmingly male, there is still a need for the minority female voice to be heard. Since these data are not here, however, the present chapter should be offered as a piece in the as yet incomplete larger picture.

What is EBD?

Among descriptors for problems presented by children with special educational needs, EBD is one of the more problematic and unsatisfactory. Children who find their way into this category exhibit behavioural and/or emotional characteristics that appear to interfere with their own learning, and in some cases the learning and security of their peers. In many cases, though not all, this problem is experienced by teachers and other adults as disturbing and disruptive. These problems can take the form of disruptive and/or aggressive behaviours, or withdrawn uncommunicative behaviour. Such children are often nervous and anxious in demeanour, and sometimes considered to be 'anti-social' or 'asocial'. There is a wide range of factors that can influence the development of EBD, ranging through organic, congenital and psycho-social factors, such as: birth complications, inappropriate parenting, childhood emotional trauma, and factors associated with schooling. It is rare for a single cause to be implicated; in most cases children's difficulties are influenced by a range of interacting factors.

EBD and ADHD

Recently, the term Attention Deficit Hyperactivity Disorder (referred to by the acronyms ADHD or ADD) has begun to be widely used in the UK as a descriptor for children exhibiting severe behavioural problems in classrooms (see Cooper and Ideus, 1995a, 1995b). This is a more narrowly prescribed diagnosis than the EBD label, that some argue (e.g. Kewley, 1995) should replace the EBD label for many children in the UK. ADHD is a psycho-medical diagnosis devised by the American Psychiatric Association, applying to children and adults, that identifies marked dysfunctions in children's abilities to control their impulsivity, maintain sustained attention, and control their motor activity (i.e. hyperactivity). Difficulties with organisational tasks and a tendency toward socially inappropriate behaviour are common aspects of this condition. Hyperactivity is not present in all cases, a small number of people are diag-nosed with a condition known as 'Undifferentiated ADD' or ADD with-out H (i.e. hyperactivity). The bearers of this diagnosis tend to exhibit withdrawn behaviour, to appear listless and to daydream in situations where they are required to attend and concentrate. The disorder is believed to be related to neurological impairment that is in turn associ-ated with genetic and other psycho-social factors (Hinshaw, 1994; Barkley, 1992).

There is considerable overlap between the kinds of problems that are associated with ADHD and EBD in the classroom. It is not appropri-ate in this chapter to debate the pros and cons of the two labels. For the purposes of the rest of this chapter the term EBD will be used, but much of what will be said will have relevance for our understanding of ADHD as well. What is important to note, however, is that the kinds of problems associated with EBD and ADHD can be highly influenced by the kind of demands that schools in our society make on pupils. Whether or not a child's difficulties in concentrating, or emotional withdrawal, are associated with a psychological problem or neurologi-cal impairment, the response of the school culture is critical in influenc-ing the extent to which the problems are alleviated or exacerbated. Where the school is punishing and rejecting, the school environment becomes a factor conducive to the development, maintenance and esca-lation of EBD. Where the school is supportive and nurturing, the prob-lems will possibly be alleviated or at least not worsened by the school experience.

The personal consequences of EBD

Like all children who have special educational needs, the fact that chil-dren with EBD reveal themselves to be different from the majority of their peers creates problems. They are different because they display emotional and/or behavioural characteristics that make it difficult for them to engage in effective learning in the classroom and school. They are different because the difficulties they have will often lead to relation-ship problems that mean they are shunned or ridiculed by peers. After all, it is understandable that people will not seek to interact with some-one who is aggressive and oppositional. Similarly, the highly withdrawn and uncommunicative person will either be overlooked by others, or 'given up on' as being socially unrewarding. The fact is that EBD is often associated with patterns of behaviour that are socially undesirable and simply not likeable.

A further distinctive aspect of emotional and behavioural difficulties lies in the emotional responses that people often have towards chil-dren who present these difficulties. The child who exhibits emotional and behavioural difficulties is often *blamed* for having those difficulties. In these circumstances, the child can be accused of simply not trying hard enough to control himself or herself, or of having an insufficient regard for the feelings and needs of others that is based on some form of social and emotional laziness. The powerful effect of others' images of us is such that children with EBD who are subjected to such blaming responses can often come to adopt the idea that they are indeed to blame for their problems. This in turn inflicts damage on an often already battered self-esteem, filling the child with a sense of demoralisation and helplessness that is often characteristic of the child with EBD.

It is a normal, and often necessary, human and animal trait to make judgements about our fellow creatures on the basis of their behaviour. It is argued in this chapter, however, that our responses to emotional and behavioural difficulties in children – if we are seeking to limit the negative effects of those difficulties – must go beyond the external manifestations of the difficulties, and be informed by an understanding of the human interior. Not only will an understanding of the interior help us to identify possible solutions to problems, but such understanding will also help us to move beyond the hindrance of our own emotional reaction. It is a major underlying contention of this chapter that an understanding of the inner lives of children with EBD is essential if we are to develop a reasoned and professional response to EBD in schools. It is further suggested that the most valuable source of information on 'the inner lives' of children with EBD is the children themselves.

This chapter is based on evidence drawn from pupils' first hand accounts of the experience of being officially categorised as having 'Emotional and Behavioural Difficulties'. These accounts are valuable for a number of reasons:

• First, they suggests that children can be highly insightful and articulate about their own circumstances and the nature of the difficulties they face. Recent legislation – such as the Children Act (1989) and the Education Act (1993) and the non-statutory Code of Practice on the identification and assessment of pupils with special educational needs (DFE, 1994) – places great emphasis on the need to consult pupils about their problems and potential solutions. These pupil accounts reveal that such consultation is highly desirable and likely to be very fruitful.

• Second, many of the most useful ways of thinking about EBD in relation to school children involve a recognition of the central importance of children's perceptions. The reference here is to approaches such as the psychodynamic, humanistic, cognitive and eco-systemic (see Cooper, Smith and Upton, 1994). An underlying principle shared by these approaches is that EBDs are often embedded in the ways in which people perceive themselves and their environment; this refers to both the perspectives of the EBD pupils themselves and the perceptions of them held by others. In these circumstances emotional and behavioural change stems from the articulation and analysis of these perceptions. The principle at work here is that people must own their problems before they can solve them. The pupils' accounts presented here show some of the ways in which these kinds of approaches might work.

- Third, these accounts show how pupils' perceptions might help us to understand the effects of and thus evaluate the effectiveness of provision and intervention. This is particularly important in an educational and political climate that is dominated by notions of 'market forces'. In markets we have service providers and customers. The problem with education is that there are many customers for its services. There are employers, parents, the government and, of course, pupils. Between and even within some of these constituencies there is not always consensus about what 'good' education looks like. A powerless and often neglected *expert* voice in this area is that of the pupil. Although the Code of Practice and OFSTED (1994) stress the importance of pupil consultation, it is difficult to ascertain just how rigorous the actual consultation is, since the *process* by which the consultation is to be carried out is not made explicit. The accounts provided by pupils in this chapter were elicited with the help of a systematic interview approach and as part of a carefully developed research process, which is described in detail elsewhere (see Cooper, 1989; 1992; 1993). This chapter offers an insight into the value of pupils as expert witnesses in the education process.
- Fourth, what is clear from listening to the accounts of children with EBD is that these children are often particularly vulnerable to environmental factors that are generally aversive to the educational process of ALL children. It is suggested that many of the problems experienced by children with EBD are the result of their hypersensitivity to these generally undesirable environmental circumstances. By listening to these pupils, therefore, we can learn about some of the dysfunctions of institutions for children that affect *all* children, and so begin to identify areas for reform that will benefit *all* children.

The rest of the chapter will be devoted to describing the thoughts and feelings of children with EBD as they describe them. The bulk of the information in this chapter is based on interviews with 24 boys, aged between 13 and 17, who were referred to two residential schools for boys with EBD. For a full account of this research see Cooper (1992; 1993). The chapter will conclude with a brief discussion of some of the implications of that can be drawn from such a treatment of the pupil perspective for the running of schools.

On becoming 'EBD': from objectification to rejection

Susman (1994) has pointed out how labels of social or physical handicap that in the past were seen as marginalising and stigmatising are increasingly being embraced by individuals and pressure groups as a means of gaining access to scarce resources. It might be speculated that the increased interest in the ADHD diagnosis owes something to this process. The young people in this study do not portray EBD as one of these labels. To be given the EBD label is not experienced in terms of being defined as an individual who has difficulties that require help and understanding. The EBD label is more often a sign of disgrace and deficit. It is often experienced as a recognition of badness. For many of these pupils, once they were assigned the EBD label they believed themselves to be EBD people, rather than people with EBD. It became their defining characteristic, central to their identity.

When these boys spoke about their understanding of why they had been given the EBD label, their responses ranged from ones of bewilderment to ones of anger and frustration. A common pattern in their reasoning, however, often portrayed them as victims of external forces to which they reacted in ways that led them into difficulties. This is not to say that they always saw themselves in the victim role. It was not uncommon for the boys to consider themselves to have been at fault. A common picture, therefore, was of the blameworthy victim, which represents a fairly comprehensive indication of low self-esteem. A graphic example of this is provided by Colin, 16-year-old boy who had been first referred to residential schooling whilst in infant school.

PC: Did you ever go to an ordinary day primary school?

Colin: Well only for a few weeks. That's all . . . I don't know, but something happened and they put me in one of these (residential EBD) schools.

PC: Do you know why?

Colin: No. I think it was about my education. I don't know. I'm confused, you see, because some kids from my old school . . . told me: 'it all happened when . . . we was all in the playground. Someone pulled up a rose bush; put it in your hand. The headmistress came out, took you in, told you off.' And all this. Then a couple of days later I was sent off to the (residential) school. . . . I think it was through that. 'Cos I was bullying, at my age, y'know, small. You couldn't believe it, but that's what I've been told. . . . I used to swear at the teachers . . . Then I got put away in a school, as far as I remember. I can't remember that far back, 'cos I was only a little toddler then. . . . I was a little brute at (infant) school. Y'know, they couldn't stand me. I was that vicious when I was small. I was like a wild dog . . . I was really foul mouthed . . . I used to start: 'o, fucking hell!' and all this crap. y'know. And the teachers used to come in and say: 'Stop that! Stop that! You're only young! Stop it!' I dunno where I picked it up. I don't know if it was when I was in the flat, at my other school, when my mum and dad broke up. (I don't want them to know I've told you . . . That's nothing to do with the school like. That's personal like.) They broke up when I was little, and a load of swearing went on. I probably picked it up then. When I came to school I had a mouth, y'know. And anyway, the teacher used to say, 'stop swearing!' And I'd shout foul-mouthly to her to high heavens . . . They'd stand there, mouths shut . . . They used to give me the slipper, like, and a clip round the ear. I used to carry on and on. They probably got that sick of me. They must have gone to the authorities and said: 'Sorry, we can't have him with us. You've got to put him somewhere where he'll be tamed down.'

Colin's construction of the events leading to his being 'put away' in a residential school reads like the account of a criminal who has been convicted of a crime and sentenced to a period of penal servitude. This does not sound like the story of a child who was referred to a special school in order to meet his special educational needs. He appears to have only sympathy for his teachers, who failed to prevent this 'vicious' 'brute' from behaving like a 'wild dog'. It appears to have been for their benefit that he was removed, under the direction of faceless 'authorities', so that he could be 'tamed down'. Colin seems to sympathise with them that 'they couldn't stand me'. For him, the brutality of his teachers' attempts to deal with him through corporal punishment seems incidental to his animal like behaviour. And although he sees some link between his bad behaviour and his parents' marital difficulties, again, this is part of the background, rather than an important focus in his personal drama.

Whether or not this is an accurate account of events that really happened is less important than what it tells us about the way in which Colin *understands* his situation. The whole tenor of his account has the effect of portraying him as a villainous and, at times, inhuman character.

Colin stands out among this group of boys for the fluency and graphic quality of his accounts. The tendency to self-blame, and self-objectification, however, recurs in many other interviews. For the overwhelming majority of these boys it is their badness that brought them into the EBD realm, as these quotations from two other boys illustrate:

I was naughty to get myself here like. I ran away from school and that.

(I'm here) because I've been bad. A trouble maker at school. Bad to my mum. You know. About every bad thing.

These are, by and large, children and young persons who believe themselves to have failed as people. It is their shortcomings that they believe to have been responsible for their being 'chucked out', 'kicked out', 'put away', 'sent away', and all the other expressions that the vast majority of these boys used to describe their experience of being rejected by their previous schools and, in some cases, their families.

Perceptions of the roles of family, school and peer group

A major theme in the pupil interviews was the way in which the residential setting gave them respite from the distressing situations which many encountered in their home settings, in the form of negative family relationships, delinquent peer group associations, and disturbed schooling. These problems can be summarised in terms of personally distressing circumstances in:

the family
the school
the peer group

The pupils' reflections on each of these issues will now be illustrated. In the family, the major problems identified by pupils were:

economic and social disadvantage
severe emotional tension and discord
the presence of delinquent influences

The following quotations give a flavour of the value which pupils in these schools placed on simply being free from family stresses:

'It's usually horrible (at home) . . . when our dad's there. He spoils all the fun . . . Some kids love being at home I can't stand it . . . I'm always glad to get back to (the residential school). . . . If I had been at home, and hadn't come here, I'd probably be in the same place where our brother is at the moment (i.e. prison). (Jock, aged 17)

'I've settled down with my mum a bit. And I think I've improved a bit . . . (as a result of) me being away from home. (Jim, 14)

'I think it's got better (his relationship with his mother) because we've spent longer apart.' (Ryan, 15)

At their former, mainstream school and other schools, major problems identified by pupils were:

unsatisfactory relationships with school staff
belief that they had been victims of inconsistent and unfair treatment by school staff
belief that they received insufficient personal and academic support from staff
perceived inability to tolerate institutional demands of schools

Many boys provided accounts of their prior school experience which emphasise intolerance and a sense of being victimised:

'I got kicked out (of a comprehensive school) because I didn't fit in to normal schools . . . I was messing around in my old school. Like in lessons, I'd start playing around and that in lessons. They was trying to make out that I was worse than I was. Half the time, I was just shouting things out; talking; standing up. Things like that. Just walking around like. They'd tell you to get out. Sometimes they'd tell you to get out for a little reason, and I'd say, 'I ain't getting out!' And there starts a fight, with me and a member of staff . . . Them just dragging me out. They was trying to make out I was worse than I am. (Tom, 15)

'The staff at Lakeside are a lot better. They're more like people! When I was at (day special school), they were more like robots really. You do something wrong, the first thing they do is grab 'em, and stick 'em in a room, and just lock them up!' (Arthur, 15)

They commonly described difficulties in their relationships they had with teachers, and made the following list of complaints about the ways in which teachers behaved in class: teachers were often described as being:

too formal in their behaviour towards pupils
too strict
'stuck up'
unfriendly
intolerant
humourless
uninterested in pupils' personal welfare
not prepared/able to give pupils individual attention
guilty of labelling some pupils with negative identities
guilty of treating some pupils unfairly
guilty of conducting boring lessons
insufficiently helpful to pupils with learning difficulties

These pupils felt marginalised and rejected by their schools. Far from being supported, nurtured or helped to achieve personal autonomy and the skills for active and constructive participation in society, these children felt disempowered and helpless. They believed themselves to be victims of forces beyond their control: forces that not only failed to help and support them, but actively undermined and in some cases abused them, leaving them with low self-esteem and not only a sense of failure, but a fear of being unable to face the challenges they must meet in order to develop positively.

Problems within the neighbourhood peer group were essentially related to peer pressure to engage in delinquent activity, as the following quotations illustrate:

'(being at this residential school has) changed me a lot. If I was at home now, I'd probably be inside or something . . . I know there's a bunch of kids, some

old mates, who, if I hang around with (them)], I'll get nicked . . . But I don't
bother hanging around with them no more, because I know it will bodge up
my life with the army. Before, I wouldn't have thought of it.' (Ryan, 15)

. . . I haven't got any good mates (at home). They all gets in trouble. (Ian, 14)

It is interesting to note that this range of problems is reflected in the
research literature on deviant and disturbed young people (e.g. West
and Farrington, 1973; Dunlop, 1974; Pringle, 1975; Hoghughi, 1978;
Tattum, 1982; Rutter and Giller, 1983). Whilst few pupils experience all
of these problems (though some do), all of the interviewees in this study
experienced a combination of some of them. Particularly prominent
were school and family difficulties. Whilst it would be over-simplistic to
think of these problems as causes of their EBD, it seems to be the case
that for these pupils the experience of having to cope with these circumstances occupied their energies to the exclusion of all else. And often,
although the boys themselves were seen by others as contributing to
some of these difficulties, the boys felt powerless to change their behaviour, whilst feeling responsible for it (see above). The respite provided
by the residential situation was experienced by these boys as enabling
them simply to break the cycle of their involvement in these distressing
circumstances. Respite in itself was believed by these pupils to be a
necessary starting point for their positive development, since it gave
them relief from circumstances which sometimes exacerbated or helped
maintain their problems.

Pupils' concerns about the importance of relationships

For these pupils relationships of a high quality with staff and fellow
pupils in the residential community contributed to the development of
more positive self-images by giving pupils a sense of being valued and
cared for by significant others whom they came to learn to trust. When
these pupils talked about their residential experience and its positive
effects, relationships came out as the single most important mechanism
at work. This refers especially to relationships with particular members
of staff. It was through these relationships that pupils were often first
exposed to an image of themselves which challenged their own low
opinion of themselves as bad and worthless individuals. It was the reflection of themselves that they saw in others' responses to them that
enabled them to develop a positive self-image. This in turn gave them
the confidence to take on new challenges (educational, social,
emotional, etc.) in the knowledge that they would be accepted and
valued by others, even if they failed in mastering those challenges. The
following quotation indicates the significance to one pupil of the

relationship he shared with his teacher and its perceived effects on his progress:

> 'I think he's (my teacher) helped me quite a bit. He's helped me with my work, talked to me quite a bit. Like I never used to like to go anywhere to do anything. Now I feel quite happy to go to snooker clubs. John (the teacher) takes quite a few of us there. We save our pocket money from the weekend and go there.' (Stan, 15)

Another pupil provided a graphic account of how his relationship with a residential social worker (RSW) influenced his decision making processes in a way that challenged, in a positive sense, his delinquent tendencies:

> Mr Brown (the RSW) I know I can trust . . . Cos a while ago I got in a lot of shit – I didn't exactly get in shit –. But I got a lot of clothes hot (i.e. stolen), right? And I brought them back to school, and Mr Brown sussed on. And he could've had me done, really bad. Y'know, fucked me up going home for a long time; got me in shit with the geezer (the principal of the school) . . . everyone. But he didn't say a word, and everything turned out alright. Cos I got rid of the clothes, and nothing happened. And I promised I wouldn't get no more stuff, and that was it . . . he trusted me . . . Cos I promised him I wouldn't do it no more, and I'd get rid of the stuff, and I did.

Further probing revealed that this apparent change of heart had not been a simple matter, but had come about as a resolution to a dilemma which involved a conflict between his desire for the spoils of a delinquent act and his sense of respect and value for the relationship he shared with the RSW:

> When he (the RSW) sussed out that I'd got these clothes he got slightly worried about it. Cos he knows my old dear can't afford all this stuff. So he come to me, and I give him two stories, right. The first time it didn't work; the second time: 'this is the honest truth, sir. You got to believe me now.' The third time, I let it out. Cos he made me feel so bad when he said, 'right Ryan, I believe you, but if I find out it's a lie, just don't bother talking to me again.' And I knew, if he found out it was a lie, I wouldn't be talking to him now. It was then I thought: 'Shit! I've had it, haven't I? I suppose I've got to tell him now, and get it all cleared up. And if I get nicked, I get nicked.' So I told him. And he said he wouldn't say nothing to (the principal) so long as I didn't get no more, right, and I got rid of the stuff.
>
> PC: Is that one of the ways the school helps?
>
> Ryan: I suppose so, cos I couldn't have talked to my mum about it.

Here we see, portrayed graphically, the value that this boy placed on the quality of the relationship he shared with the RSW, and how this influenced him in his way of dealing with a difficult moral challenge that ultimately placed him in a highly exposed position. He accepts the challenge and is ultimately rewarded in an unexpected way for bravery. Clearly, however, without the involvement of the highly valued RSW he would not have experienced this moral dilemma; he would have had no reason to avoid handling stolen goods.

The importance of re-signification or positive signification

The term 'signification' has been employed by Hargreaves et al. (1975) to describe a key component of the process by which pupils come to be labelled as 'deviant'. The term is used by Matza (1976) to describe the point at which an individual's persona becomes identified with a particular form of deviance. It is the process by which a pupil becomes objectified as a 'truant', 'yob', 'bully' or 'EBD'. Signification is when the pupil's deviant acts are taken to be his or her most representative acts. *Positive* signification, on the other hand, occurs when the pupil is labelled with a *positive* identity. In both cases, the labelling is likely to have the effect of a self-fulfilling prophecy, whereby the pupil comes to internalise the image of himself or herself that is projected by others. *Re-signification*, it is suggested, describes the process that many of the boys in the present study appeared to undergo in their residential schools. Re-signification involves the development of new and positive identities as a consequence of relationships and experiences which undermine the pupil's original negative view of self, by revealing evidence of desirable, positive qualities. Re-signification was achieved, for the boys in this study, through the availability in their schools of opportunities for them to take on new challenges, learn new skills, develop a deeper knowledge of themselves and move toward a more willing acceptance of themselves as people with positive characteristics. To succeed, this process depends upon the supportive structure of good quality staff-pupil relationships, and a secure environment, as well as the provision of carefully controlled but challenging situations in which effort and success are rewarded and community involvement is encouraged and acknowledged. In its early stages, positive signification for these pupils involved the rewarding and highlighting of positive attributes that they already possessed. Its success, however, depended on its being progressive, by providing an impetus for pupils to take on new challenges and thus reveal new or previously hidden qualities.

According to many of the pupils in this study a significant factor in their rehabilitation was the experience of involvement in the schools to which they were referred. Of particular note was the contrast identified between their experience of powerlessness and victimisation in their mainstream schools and their sense of being valued members of residential communities. In these particular schools shared responsibility and self-government were important aspects of school organisation. Mechanisms for these features, identified by pupils, involved group meetings with staff and pupils as well as more informal systems by which staff consulted pupils on their concerns. Pupils also had access to formal and informal channels which enabled them to express personal and other concerns with a view to influencing the running of their schools.

The issues and concerns that these pupils were able to raise in these circumstances were very wide ranging. Routine institutional matters included the identification of perceived needs for repair and maintenance activities to the fabric of the schools, discussion of decoration requirements, discussion of bed and meal time arrangements, and other rules. Other matters included the discussion of particular incidents of concern to the school community: these ranged from incidents of individual conflict between pupils to problems of theft and vandalism and the needs of individuals for particular dispensations or privileges. In some cases decisions on expenditure were delegated to pupils, for example in relation to the purchase of leisure equipment, and the planned development of some disused buildings on the school site.

Conclusion: why should we be interested in the inner lives of children with EBD

Whilst we should not think of the views of pupils with EBD as being necessarily representative of the views of all children, we should think of these views as being of special significance. Such pupils often react to aspects of the school environment that other pupils find aversive, but are able to 'put up with'. Rather like the canaries that 19th century miners employed to test the toxicity of the mining environment, pupils with EBD can be seen as being particularly sensitive to those aspects of the school environment that are socially and personally 'toxic'[1].

Children who attract the EBD label often experience a wide range of difficulties of a social and personal nature, particularly in their family situations. These difficulties make them especially vulnerable and sensitive to aversive aspects of their school environments. Children with EBD simply react more graphically than the majority of their peers to environmental circumstances that are experienced as negative by all pupils. They can, therefore, be seen as markers for such negative environmental circumstances. These circumstances need to be brought to light because they contribute to the development and maintenance of pupil deviance in schools. Furthermore, we find that their complaints about school are echoed in the views of a much wider range of pupils, as illustrated in

[1] I am indebted to Dr Katherine Ideus for this analogy with regard to pupils with emotional and behavioural difficulties.

research by Schostak (1983) and Keys and Fernandes (1993). Both of these studies chart the growing disaffection of pupils as they progress through schooling, indicating that such disaffection is not simply the province of a disgruntled failing minority, but rather is far more widespread and systemic than this.

Pupils, then, should be seen as a source of knowledge and expertise that should be harnessed in the service of schools and the educational enterprise in general. The particular expertise of pupils lies in their unique knowledge of what it is like to be a pupil in a particular school environment, and inside knowledge of the factors that are experienced as motivators and demotivators.

The involvement of pupils in decision making processes has for many years been a common feature of special schools for pupils with EBD (Bridgeland, 1971). This is perhaps ironic when we consider that pupils who find their way into such schools are often considered to be uncooperative and a threat to the school communities from whence they came. What these pupils tell us, however, is that they value the powerful therapeutic effect of self-government and shared responsibility offered to them by the residential schools they attended. The schools achieved this outcome by helping pupils to develop a sense of belonging and personal value in relation to the school community. They demonstrate that formal and informal arrangements which enable pupils' voices to be heard (and be influential in the running of their schools) have the effect of promoting a sense of involvement and commitment to the community: in short, they help to promote the very *sense of community* referred to earlier as being of such importance.

Pupils, learning and governance

Clearly practices which result in the enhancement of pupils' levels of self-esteem are in themselves valuable. Pupils, however, are not the only beneficiaries of the outcome of pupil involvement. Increasingly, the pupil perspective on the educational process is being seen as a source of expert knowledge that needs to be drawn on in order to maximise effective teaching. Socio-cultural theories of learning, such as those proposed by Bruner (Bruner and Haste, 1987) and Vygotsky (1987) stress the importance of pupil involvement in the learning process, and the need for teachers to construct learning situations that are based on the specific characteristics of learners. Recent research by Cooper and McIntyre (1993, 1994, 1995) reveals the possibility that pupils are in possession of a specific form of 'craft knowledge' which they employ in the learning process. The research also indicates that they are able to offer clear and persuasive accounts of their own learning processes and the ways in which these can be aided by particular teaching strategies. It is unclear at the present time the extent to which opportunities exist for pupils to share these insights with staff. Clearly one such vehicle might be school governance and related processes.

A more pressing reason why pupil knowledge and expertise should be allowed to feed directly into the governance process relates to the particular pressures that governing bodies face in the current market economy approach to education. Recent research (Deem et al. 1994) suggests that governing bodies, in response to market forces, are neglecting the interests of their current pupils. The researchers conclude:

> Governors, even those closest to the collective rather than the consumer interest end of the value spectrum, spent a great deal of their time considering pupil numbers, school image and marketing strategies . . . The major emphasis (of governors in their study) was often on who (i.e. pupils) might attend in the future, rather than the quality of schooling offered to existing pupils. Indeed, . . . existing pupils were often subjected to criticism (e.g. for lack of exam success, behaviour, social class, haircuts). (p.547)

In these circumstances pupils have little opportunity to defend themselves from such 'criticism'. Currently they rely on others to state their case for them (e.g. teachers, parent governors). This is in spite of the fact that they possess a distinctive perspective on the educational process that is directly related to the central aim of schooling, namely that of education. Something of the nature of this perspective has been illustrated above, and from this it should be clear that there are times when the pupil perspective may be in conflict with the interests of other parties whose concerns may not serve the needs of effective education. Where such conflicts exist, their negative effects on the life of the school community will be exacerbated by the feelings of powerlessness that naturally flow from the lack of involvement in the governance process that pupils, by law, experience.

To look at the issue of conflict from a slightly different perspective, it might well be asserted that the commitment that flows from formal involvement in school life brings with it responsibilities. Where pupils (or anyone else for that matter) have no power, they also have no responsibility for outcomes: they can, in fact, blame those with the power for whatever negative outcomes arise, even when they themselves contribute to such outcomes. The responsibility that comes with power can help give the empowered individual a vested interest in making things work effectively. This can lead to a situation in which a high value is placed on compromise, conciliation and cooperation in place of opposition, hostility and entrenchment. This point is illustrated negatively by a statement given by a pupil in one of the residential schools referred to earlier. The powerlessness that this boy perceived himself to experience in the school, made it possible for him to make completely unreasonable demands on the school community, and allowed him to avoid taking responsibility for his own behaviour:

> I think they should be more stricter. But if they get it more strict, I'm going to be the one that's breaking all the rules.

This boy's refusal to accept responsibility points to the heart of the problem of ignoring the pupil perspective. Only by raising the status of the pupil perspective and thus giving pupils access to power in schools can we help them to develop and demonstrate the sense of responsibility that is necessary to enable our schools, and ultimately our society, to run effectively.

References

Barkley, R. (1992). *Attention Deficit Hyperactivity Disorder: a Handbook for Diagnosis and Treatment.* New York: Guilford.

Bridgeland, M. (1971). *Pioneer Work with Maladjusted Children.* Crosby: Staples.

Bruner, J. and Haste, H. (1987). *Making Sense: the Child's Construction of the World.* London: Methuen.

Cooper, P. (1989). *Respite, Relationships and Resignification: a study of the effects of residential schooling on pupils with emotional and behavioural difficulties, with particular references to the pupil perspective.* Unpublished PhD thesis: University of Birmingham.

Cooper, P. (1992). 'Pupils' perceptions of the effect of residential schooling on children with emotional and behavioural difficulties'. *Therapeutic Care and Education* 10,1.

Cooper, P. (1993). *Effective Schools for Disaffected Students: Integration and Segregation.* London: Routledge.

Cooper, P. and Ideus, K. (1995a).'Is ADHD a Trojan Horse?'. *Support for Learning,* 10,1.

Cooper, P. and Ideus, K. (1995b). *Attention Deficit Hyperactivity Disorder: educational, medical and cultural issues.* East Sutton: AWCEBD

Cooper, P. and McIntyre, D. (1993). 'Commonality in teachers' and pupils' perceptions of effective learning'. *British Journal of Educational Psychology,* 63.

Cooper, P. and McIntyre, D. (1994). 'Patterns of interaction between teachers' and students' classroom thinking, and their implications for the provision of learning opportunities'. *Teaching and Teacher Education,* 10,6.

Cooper, P. and McIntyre, D.(1995). *Effective Teaching and Learning: Teacher and Pupil Perspectives.* Buckingham: Open University.

Cooper, P., Smith, C.J. and Upton, G. (1991). 'Ethnic minority and gender distribution among staff and pupils in facilities for pupils with emotional and behavioural difficulties in England and Wales'. *British Journal of Sociology of Education* 121.

Cooper, P., Smith, C.J. and Upton, G.(1994). *Emotional and Behavioural Difficulties: from theory to practice.* London:Routledge.

Davies, L. (1979). 'Deadlier than the male? Girls' conformity and deviance in school'. In: L. Barton and R. Meighan, *Schools, Pupils and Deviance.* Driffield: Nafferton.

Davies, L. (1984). *Pupil Power.* London: Falmer.

Deem, R. Brehony,K. and Heath, S. (1994). 'Governers, schools and the miasma of the market'. *British Educational Research Journal* 20 (5), 535–550.

DFE (1994). *Code of Practice on the Identification and Assessment of Children with SEN.* London, HMSO.

Dunlop, A. (1974). *The Approved School Experience*. London: HMSO.

Hargreaves, D., Hestor, D. and Mellor, F. (1975). *Deviance in Classroom*. London: Routledge.

Hinshaw, S. (1994). *Attention Deficits and Hyperactivity in Children*. London: Sage.

Hoghughi, M. (1978). *Troubled and Troublesome: coping with severely disordered children*. London: Burnet.

Kewley, G. (1995). 'Medical aspects of assessment and treatment of children with Attention Deficit Disorders'. Paper presented at the 4th International Special Education Congress, Birmingham, UK, April.

Keys, W. and Fernandes, C. (1993). *What do Students Think About School?* Slough: NFER.

Knox, P. (1988). *Troubled Children: a fresh look at school phobia*. Upton upon Severn: The Self Publishing Association/P. Knox.

Matza, D. (1976). 'Signification'. In: M. Hammersley and P. Woods (Eds.) *The Process of Schooling*. Milton Keynes: Open University.

OFSTED (1994 3rd edn). *Handbook for the Inspection of Schools*. London: HMSO .

Pringle, M. (1975). *The Needs of Children*. London: Hutchinson.

Rutter, M. and Giller, H. (1983). *Juvenile Delinquency: trends and perspectives*. Harmondsworth: Penguin.

Schostak, J. (1983). *Maladjusted Schooling*. Lewes: Falmer.

Susman, J. (1994). 'Disability, stigma and deviance'. *Social Science and Medicine* **38**, 1, 15-22.

Tattum, D. (1982). *Disruptive Pupils in Schools and Units*. Chichester: Wiley.

Vygotsky, L. (1987). *The Collected Works of L.S. Vygotsky vol. 1*. Edited by R. Reiber and A. Carton. London: Plenum.

West, D. and Farrington, D. (1973). *Who Becomes Delinquent?* London: Heinemann.

Chapter 8
The Inner Life of the Dyslexic Child

TIM MILES

Introduction

There is reason to think that, because of the circumstances in which dyslexic children find themselves, an important characteristic of their inner life is that they feel *frightened*. This is the aspect of their inner life which will be emphasised in the present chapter.

In the first section evidence will be cited which points to the origins of these fears and shows some of the different ways in which different individuals have tried to deal with them. In the second section some suggestions will be made as to how the damaging effects of fear can be reduced.

Source material will be quoted in italics. This material will be of different kinds. In some cases there will be records of actual behaviour, in some cases inferences drawn from behaviour over a period of time (note 1). For convenience the different sources will be numbered.

No attempt will be made to justify the claim that the individuals concerned were dyslexic. Those looking for further evidence on dyslexia may wish to consult Fenwick Stuart (1988), Thomson (1991), Miles (1993a; 1993b), Fawcett and Nicolson (1994), Miles (1995), Miles and Varma (1995). The method adopted in the present chapter is basically similar to that of Fenwick Stuart (1988) in that it is 'personal', i.e. based on the experiences of individuals, rather than one involving systematic comparison of dyslexics and controls. It is my belief that many different approaches to dyslexia are legitimate, of which the 'personal' is one.

What the 'personal' approach lacks is conclusive demonstration. In the words of Aristotle (*Nichomachean Ethics*, I,3), 'We must be content if we can attain to so much precision . . . as the subject before us admits of . . . It is equally absurd to accept probable reasoning from a mathematician, and to demand scientific proof from an orator'. In accordance with this principle, the extracts which follow are not intended to be a *proof* of any particular generalisation about the inner life of dyslexics, nor do they tell us, for instance, what percentage of a precisely specified population of dyslexics have excessive feelings of fear. Rather they are an invitation to the reader to consider what the individuals referred to may have been feeling or thinking when they behaved in a particular way. This procedure is in line with the current trend to consider the 'human' aspects of dyslexia (Hales, 1994). It is a necessary part of the total picture, despite the price to be paid in terms of lack of experimental rigour.

Types of fear

For convenience, the different types of fear will be discussed under four heads, viz. fear of failure, fear of being different, fear of words, and fear of social 'gaffes'.

Fear of failure

> Source 1. *(Children) are afraid, above all else, of failing, of disappointing or displeasing the many anxious adults round them, whose limitless hopes and expectations hang over them like a cloud.* (Holt, 1969, p.9)

This was an observation made by Holt about children in general. In the case of dyslexic children I suspect that the pressures can often be of a very subtle kind. I have in fact met many parents who, with total genuineness, were concerned not to 'pressurise' their dyslexic children. However, as Holt rightly observes, we should not overlook the extent to which any child – including the dyslexic child – is anxious to please. This means that, even when their parents show full sympathy and under-standing, many dyslexic children feel that they are letting their parents down whenever they fail. In this connection there is one particular experience which I remember from some years ago. I was visiting a fee-paying school which gave special tuition to dyslexics; and one of the boys there, in the course of a conversation with me, made clear (I forget his exact words) that the fact that his father was making considerable financial sacrifices to send him to this expensive school put additional pressure on him to succeed. There is a very thin line between doing one's best in the knowledge that one's family will be pleased if one is successful and feeling, in Holt's words, that the pressures 'hang like a cloud' and that one will be 'shown up' if one fails.

It is interesting in this connection that in their study of families where there was a dyslexic child Kappers and Veerman 1995 found more 'control and discipline' on the part of the parents than in the case of non-dyslexic families, arguably, they suggest, because this was an appro-priate way of dealing with the dyslexia.

Here is an account by a dyslexic adult of his experiences at primary school:

Source 2. *It was a private school and I used to hate it there because they were all bloody clever and I was stupid. They all passed their 11-plus and I couldn't even read the bloody questions. I hated all of them.* (Edwards, 1994, p.27)

One obvious strategy is that of avoidance.

Source 3. *I started acting ill and trying to miss the bus, but my mum always knew when I was faking, and always made me go, even when I was ill, 'cos she never knew if I was faking or not.* (Edwards, 1994, p.103)

A possible way of retaining one's self-respect is not to try. This is because it is less humiliating to fail when one has made little effort than to fail after one has tried one's hardest.

Source 4. *When I tested his reading and spelling levels I was surprised and disappointed at his low scores. The boy subsequently explained that he had intentionally done badly, 'because then neither you nor I will ever know how well I would have done if I had tried.'* (Thomson, 1988, p.9)

Here is the same point, made by another teenager:

Source 5. *I get stressed when I have failed and people say, 'Never mind, you did your best'. I don't want to fail when I have done my best. If I think I am going to fail then I won't do my best so when I do fail I can think, 'Well, I didn't try'.* (Chinn and Crossman, 1995, p.49)

It is interesting that both these teenagers were able to express their fear of failure in words. One may surmise that there are many others who have not given of their best without being fully aware why they were doing so.

Failure to try is not the best of strategies because it involves an element of self-deception. However the situation is one which needs to be handled with extreme sensitivity by counsellors, since for a particular child self-deception may be a lesser evil than losing his or her self-respect. To allow the child to believe that he 'ought not' to be afraid of failure may therefore aggravate the situation rather than ease it.

Occasionally the stress caused by failure is so great that something 'gives way'.

Source 6. *Margaret's frustration finally snapped whilst doing a national curriculum test. She couldn't do it, but could have no help and she had an outburst in which she threw the textbook, chair and desk at the headmaster who was taking the class.* (Dodd, 1995, p.2)

Moreover, as the child grows older, feelings of failure may be intensified.

Source 7. *So I would like to tell you about my school years. I think I was about seven years old when I became awair that I wasn't learning very much. My reading was very poor untill I was about 11 years and my spelling was awful and my maths were poor....We had a nasty and old head-*

mistress....She always picked me out and when I couldn't give the right answers she would shout at me and when she was angry she would spit the words at me. She always made me cry and I was so frightened of her. She tried to bully me into getting it right and I really wanted to please her.
(Letter from an adult; Thomson, 1995, pp.43-44)

There is reason to think that dyslexic children may be aware that they are failing even before the time when difficulty with reading and spelling begins to show itself. For instance they may forget oral instructions; they may have a poor sense of direction and be dependent on following others, or they may be clumsy and knock things over or bump into their teachers or classmates (Thomson, 1995, p.38). As they grow older this sense of failure is likely to increase.

Source 8. *(At Junior School) children were, if anything, becoming increasingly aware of their failings as they fell further behind other children. Mothers reported that children made a number of negative comments about themselves such as 'I'll never be able to do the same as other children'.*
(Riddick, 1995)

This comment points the way to another common source of fear: children do not like to be different.

Fear of being 'different'

Source 9. *Out of the 22 children 15 said that before they were told they were dyslexic they had thought they were 'thick', 'stupid', or an 'idiot'.* (Riddick, 1995)

This fear may well be the more oppressive because the child will almost certainly not have worked out what 'being different' means. Clearly there is no need to worry about being 'different' if this means being more successful than others. Nor is there the same kind of worry if the child is physically handicapped: this is an obvious fact which parents, teachers, and other children recognise and make allowance for. For the undiagnosed dyslexic, however, it is the uncertainty which is often the source of the problem. This uncertainty may generate fears and fantasies which the child may recognise are irrational but which are still threatening because their nature is not understood.

Above all, there may be the fear that one is mad.

Source 10. *A 10-year-old whom I assessed some years ago at one point produced the lighthearted remark, 'They seemed bonkers'. His mother then said, 'He often uses the word "bonkers"'* (Case notes, TRM).

This was a lighthearted conversation, but I could not help wondering if there was not some serious underlying worry. Might it not be that this 10-year-old was genuinely *afraid* that he was 'bonkers' and that the lightheartedness was something of a cover up? I do not know, but it is possible. In this connection I should like to quote the following:

> Source 11. *John was nine years old when his parents decided that they needed to know why he was not progressing at school. A full diagnostic assessment was carried out, and dyslexia was established. John's mother, a teacher, explained to him in suitable fashion the details of the problem: John listened carefully, and then asked: 'Do you mean I've got something?' His mother thought that this was by no means a bad description for a small boy, and so she answered in the affirmative. John replied, 'That's OK then. If I've got something I can cope. I thought I was going round the bend'.* (Hales, 1994, p. 182)

It can fairly be said that this boy had a realistic appraisal of what needed to be done. This outcome is likely to be much more satisfactory than self-deception.

Fear of words

> Source 12. *I can think OK, but what's wrong is my words. I forget them and I can't manage them.* (Rawson, 1981, p.15)

I suspect that fear of words can sometimes influence dyslexic children at very young ages. There is evidence for this from my experiences with Daniel.

I first met Daniel when he was aged 2;5. His father and two elder brothers had all been diagnosed as dyslexic, and his parents offered to bring him to see me at regular intervals. The following are extracts from my notes.

> Source 13. *I could not get any response from him over any of the 'saying to command' items in the Merrill Palmer test. When I gave him a second object he said 'two' spontaneously. Mother reported that any number more than one is called 'two'. I do not know, however, whether one should say he* couldn't *repeat words to command or* wouldn't. *From his performance items I think we may conclude that at this age he is above average in intelligence.*
>
> *He was particularly good with the Seguin Form Board* (note 2) *which he enjoyed. However, when he had to answer orally ('What runs?' 'What sleeps?' 'What scratches?)' he made no answer. On the second visit, at age 2;11, he still did not reply when asked a verbal question.*
>
> *(Age 4;3): he does not know his letters, and there is reason to think that he does not always answer questions about letters in case he gets them wrong. When I tested him on the ability to recognise rhymes the results were:*

Stimulus	His response
bat bat	*yes*
bat cat	*no*
cat dog	*no*
big pig	*no*

(Age 8): his difficulties over reading and spelling are clear confirmation of his dyslexia.

It is arguable that a boy of Daniel's age would not put his fears into words. It is surely significant, however, that over several different sessions he showed a reluctance to answer orally and that this was in marked contrast with his ability to handle objects, which was clearly something which he enjoyed. Even at this age he was already showing what would now be called 'right hemisphere' skills (Springer and Deutsch, 1984). Since such a large amount of interpersonal communication is through words the child who is *afraid* of words is particularly at a disadvantage.

> Source 14. *Arthur, who was aged 14, had been asked, along with other members of his class, to write a poem. He declared himself unable to do so, on the grounds that 'words terrify me'. His teacher said, 'Well, why not make that the first line of your poem?' He proceeded to write a very effective poem.* (Source: Lynn Lewis, personal communication)

In this case it was possible to confront the fear head-on. Surprising as it may seem, older dyslexics sometimes have considerable sensitivity to the meanings of words, and to write a poem about his fears must in this case have been a therapeutic experience.

That tests and examinations often generate fear in dyslexics is so well known that detailed documentation is unnecessary. (For further discussion, however, see Thomson, 1995; Chinn and Crossman, 1995). The important point is that when dyslexics have to operate through the medium of words there is *additional* cause for worry quite apart from the strains which many people feel when they are being 'tested' or 'examined'. It is entirely understandable if dyslexics worry over examination results. The facile advice 'Don't worry' is unlikely to achieve much; an important task for parents and counsellors is to ensure that the feelings of worry do not get out of hand.

Fear of social 'gaffes'

Some years ago I listened to a dyslexic adult who was talking to a group of teachers about her childhood. She said that both then, and even recently, she was continually afraid that she would somehow manage to 'put her foot in it'.

Here is some evidence from the USA:

> Source 15. *There were four brothers. One was dyslexic but not the other three. When I visited the family this boy said to me, 'Why does Mom always have to pick on me?' I noticed that all four brothers regularly romped around and got into healthy mischief. The difference was that the dyslexic one failed to 'read the signs'; unlike the other three, who stopped what they were doing in time, he did not spot when Mom was about to 'blow up'.* (Dr Sylvia Richardson, personal communication)

This ability to 'read the signs' is sometimes lacking in dyslexics. In particular they do not always pick up is the significance of body language (cf. Chinn and Crossman, 1995). Yet they may find that unwittingly they have 'committed a gaffe' or 'done the wrong thing'.

It is possible that this kind of fear was at work in the case of the dyslexic children studied by Williams and Miles (1985). These children were aged between 8 and 16 years and were given the Rorschach ink-blot test. In this test the subject has to say what he can 'see' in a series of 10 specially made ink-blots. The tester permits several responses per card if the subject wishes to give them; and the 12 control subjects in this study ranged in the number of responses from 14 to 30. In contrast, the numbers of responses given by the 15 dyslexics were: 10, 12, 10, 10, 15, 10, 10, 10, 9, 11, 5, 10, 10, 11, 10. For many of them this in effect meant one response per card. The authors suggest various reasons for this restricted kind of responding, an important one being the wish to deal with an unusual social situation by keeping things simple.

Source 16. *By the strategy of keeping things simple, they were able to meet the social demands of the situation without mishap . . . At the risk of being over-speculative one might perhaps describe their thoughts as being some-what as follows: 'At all costs let us keep things simple; letting oneself go is too dangerous and is liable to have punishing consequences'. Then would follow a kind of defiant determination, as though, presented with a particu-lar card, they said to themselves, 'It's a bat – and that is all I am prepared to tell you about it'.* (Williams and Miles, 1985)

One consequence of 'getting it wrong' is, of course, punishment. The following poem (quoted in Miles, 1993, pp.19-20) is an expression by a 10-year-old of his fears in this respect. He entitled the poem, *'What punishment is next?'*

Source 17

I am tortured every day
My hands or feet are blown away
A rook's nest in my head, feathers in my shirt
Handed down from farmers' wives.
What punishment is next?

I am lonely and the birds won't come near me
Unless to take a grain of straw
But me – I am hung on a frame
And cannot fight the evil world.

When gale force winds whistle past my ear –
That will be my dying day.
Me, a scarecrow, dead, nothing left.
No punishment is left.

Some years later this boy reached university, being far more gifted than some of his teachers realised. It is sad that fear of punishment plays the part that it does in the lives of young dyslexics.

Ways of coping

Some of the ways of coping with these fears are less than satisfactory. This applies in particular to those methods which involve self-deception – 'if I deny it is there it will go away'.

> Source 18. *When he started school he became withdrawn and introverted . . . In spite of his assurances that life had never been so good it soon became clear that something was badly wrong . . . The need to hide his difficulties and appear the same as the other children in its turn increased his feelings of anxiety and fear of failure.* (Fawcett, 1995, p.6)

Similarly, the boy described in Source 4 was reacting by means of denial; and, as has already been said, counselling in such cases calls for extreme sensitivity. The truth about dyslexia need not in fact be all that alarming, but it is no kindness to force people to recognise the truth before they are ready to do so.

> Source 19. *Of course, not all children react to stress by becoming withdrawn and introverted . . . It is possibly just as common . . . to adopt a 'devil may care' response to failure . . . Dominic . . . threw mud in the playground. When his teacher asked him to stop this, Dominic responded by throwing mud at her and was subsequently expelled. In Dominic's case, his school had been unable to identify the real cause of the problem, because he had used bad behaviour as a smoke screen to hide his inability to cope with literacy skills.* (Fawcett, 1995, pp.17-18)

The situation is sometimes compounded by accusations of laziness.

> Source 20. *Half way through the junior school my mum realised my reading and spelling was going wrong and my reports were getting bad. I was called lazy all the time and I said I wasn't to my parents. I thought, right, they say I'm lazy; I bloody well will be.* (Edwards, 1994, p.93)

Children who think, 'If I am different I may as well be different in a big way' may resort to defying their teachers, to bullying or to being disruptive.

> Source 21. *He seemed to feel he had a running vendetta with the staff. 'I got my own back though, it was only fair – sneaked in and blocked the staff loos. I remember feeling really chuffed. They was all women, I couldn't see them using the men's'.* (Edwards, 1994 p.33)

If a child has got into serious trouble a counsellor can sometimes be of help by saying, for instance, 'You did this because of your worries over your dyslexia'; and in the right context this can provide the opportunity for a fresh start.

In some cases it is possible for dyslexics to find outlets for their frustration which are socially harmless.

Source 22. *Donald had been assessed at age 7 as having an IQ of 72 and had been sent to a school for the mentally handicapped. At age 13 a further assessment showed him to be dyslexic and to have a Performance IQ on the Wechsler Scale of 118. I immediately asked myself how a boy of that ability coped among the mentally handicapped. I was told that he had in fact acquired a reputation for 'acting the clown'.* (case notes, TRM)

Donald received special help with his reading and spelling and eventually ended up in the army. Clowning may not always be a realistic way of responding to stress, but in this case one is amazed that he discovered an outlet which caused so little harm.

Finally, there is the situation where there is no need to resort to denial, bad behaviour, or even clowning. I myself have been lucky in that the great majority of dyslexic children whom I have seen were referred to me by concerned parents (Miles, 1993a). The emphasis in such cases can be on helping both child and parents to a realistic appraisal of the child's strengths and weaknesses. (For further suggestions in this area see Miles, 1988.) It is essential to warn of possible disappointments and to make clear to the child that it will not be at all surprising if he or she experiences moments of self-doubt. Unless, however, there are extraneous complicating factors, dyslexics who are in an environment where their dyslexia is understood and taken into account are likely to thrive; and there is no reason why their thoughts and feelings should be other than happy ones.

One of the most exciting developments in the last decade has been the recognition that dyslexia involves a distinctive balance of skills. There are physiological reasons for this (Galaburda et al., 1989), and it is now recognised that there have been many highly gifted and creative individuals (for instance Michael Faraday, Albert Einstein, and Thomas Alva Edison) who, in spite of their talents, had some degree of difficulty with literacy and language (West, 1991). This does not mean that every dyslexic person has special talents, but it underlines how mistaken it is to focus simply on the weaknesses of dyslexics rather than recognising both their weaknesses and their strengths.

Here, to end, are two brief studies which illustrate how, despite poor spelling, the creative imaginations of dyslexics can flourish provided the environment is a sympathetic one.

Source 23. *Terence had three sisters two of whom were also dyslexic. Among samples of his written work I found the following:*

My Thee Wises
(1) I wisce that I gode haF a stamp awden to geeq (changed to 'keeq') my stamps in

(2) I wisce That I gode hepe The reF you jes to Find homes For Them
(3) I wisce That I was a powem riter and bese OF all I that I could read.
(I wish that I could have a stamp album to keep my stamps in. I wish that I could help the refugees to find homes for them. I wish that I was a poem writer and best of all I wish that I could read). (Miles, 1993b, p.96)

In Terence's case the family knew, from their experience of his sisters, what kind of support was needed; and even a cruel verbal assault by a Remedial Teacher which accused him of not making sufficient effort (ibid. p.97) did little damage.

Susan, too, came from a very caring family. She was diagnosed as dyslexic at the age of 9 and immediately was able to accept herself as she was and to view her dyslexia positively. The following is a letter from her mother, written just over a year after she had been assessed.

Source 24. *As soon as she was told what the nature of the problem was Susan began to regain confidence and to blossom again into the child she'd been until the age of 5 or 6. It was really quite dramatic, and because I now understood much better what her strengths and weaknesses were I began to treat her appropriately and to give her more freedom and responsibility, which she now enjoys.* (Letter to TRM from Susan's mother)

Here are two compositions by Susan, one an essay, one a poem. The following are extracts from the essay. Its title was 'I am special because...' (Words in brackets are taken from her mother's transcription)

Source 25. *Many of her friends know her as Susan. But many know her as Dielixe woman ever alert to the cry of dielexer zooming of to give prive lessens to children everywhere with the help of Afig to Omig (note 3). . . . This story is about Tim. One sunny morning in March Susan (crossed out and changed to 'Tim') walked along with her (crossed out and changed to 'his') mum and siter they were walking fast because he was late . . . 'So your late again' said his teacher . . . Tim he blewed (bellowed) a bit later Come here your book a desres (disgrace) spelling worng afer I told you to look in a dictor' (illegible but = 'dictionary'). 'No buts you will stat in tilll it finished. Tim finised it looking in a dictonary (but want helps that if you dont now how to spell it in the first place. Nexted paly (playtime) the boys were all canting (chanting) rams (rhymes) like . . . Tim dose not know spell cat, bat or hat ha ha ha Tim ran as fast as he could out on to hill lane Then from no were can (came) bright light that nearly blindid his it was Dielixe woman zoom down and took his hand a took him to Bagor and Tim Miles said in his kind voice you are diexleic And that is way (why) Im special because I am diexlie Woman.* (case notes, TRM)

Here is the poem, which was spoken by Susan as she painted wine bottles. It was transcribed by her mother.

Source 26 *I am dyslexic*
I know you didn't expect it!
I spell a bit differently

My words are all jumbled
My reading is mumbled
But that's what makes me me!
I'll tell you what I'm good at
and I'd like you to look at - the things I make artistically
I make miniature wine bottles that I paint by hand - I'm doing it now, and
isn't it grand? (Case notes, TRM)

These writings by Terence and by Susan speak for themselves. Special mention, however, should be made of their concern for helping others. In Terence's case there was a sensitivity to the plight of refugees; in Susan's case the fact that she had discovered that she was dyslexic encouraged her to indulge in the fantasy of being a grown-up woman who helps other dyslexics. In addition, in Susan's case in particular, the evidence suggests that she had come to terms with her dyslexia in a very positive way: there is self-acceptance, a willingness to call attention to the things which she can do well, and, above all, the recognition of her own self- worth – 'My reading is mumbled but that's what makes me me'. If dyslexics are in the right environment and understand the nature of their dyslexia a happy inner life is entirely possible.

Note 1.

There is a notorious philosophical problem which centres on the theme of 'knowledge of other minds' (see, for instance, Wisdom, 1952). However, it is not a problem which need concern us here. One may sometimes be *unsure in practice* what other people are thinking or feeling but there is no logical absurdity in attempting to put those thoughts or feelings into words.

Note 2.

When presented with the Seguin form board the child is required to place objects of various shapes – star, circle, square, etc. – into the correct spaces, i.e. those of the same shape.

Note 3.

The reference is to *From Alpha to Omega* (Hornsby and Shear, 1977).

References

Chinn, S.J. and Crossman, M. (1995). Stress factors in the dyslexic adolescent. In: Miles, T.R. and Varma, V.P. (Eds.) *Dyslexia and Stress*. London: Whurr.
Edwards, J. (1994). *The Scars of Dyslexia*. London: Cassell.
Fawcett, A.J. (1995). Case studies and some recent research. In: Miles, T.R. and Varma, V.P. (Eds.) *Dyslexia and Stress*. London: Whurr.

Fawcett, A.J. and Nicolson R.I.(1994) (Eds.). *Dyslexia in Children.* London: Harvester Wheatsheaf.

Fenwick Stuart, M. (1988). *Personal Insights into the World of Dyslexia.* Cambridge, Mass.: Educators Publishing Service.

Galaburda, A.M., Rosen, G.D. and Sherman, G.F. (1989). The neural origin of developmental dyslexia: implications for medicine, neurology, and cognition. In: Galaburda, A.M. (Ed.) *From Reading to Neurons.* Cambridge, Mass.: MIT Press.

Hales, G. (1994). The human aspects of dyslexia. In: Hales, G.(Ed.) *Dyslexia Matters.* London: Whurr.

Holt, J. (1969). *How Children Fail.* Harmondsworth: Penguin.

Hornsby, B. and Shear, F. (1977). *Alpha to Omega.* London: Heinemann.

Kappers, J. and Veerman, J.W. (1995). *Dyslexia: An International Journal of Research and Practice* 1 (2),108–119.

Miles, T.R. (1988). Counselling in dyslexia. *Counselling Psychology Quarterly,* 1,97-107.

Miles, T.R. (1993a). *Dyslexia: The Pattern of Difficulties.* London: Whurr.

Miles, T.R. (1993b). *Understanding Dyslexia.* Bath: Amethyst Books.

Miles, T.R. (1995). Dyslexia: the current status of the term, II. *Child language Teaching and Therapy,* **11**(1)23-33.

Miles, T.R. and Varma, V.P. (Eds.) (1995). *Dyslexia and Stress.* London: Whurr.

Rawson, M.B. (1981). A diversity model for dyslexia. In: Pavlidis, G.T. and Miles, T.R. (Eds.) *Dyslexia Research and Its Applications to Education.* Chichester: Wiley.

Riddick, B. (1995). Dyslexia and development: an interview study. *Dyslexia: An International Journal of Research and Practice* 1(2), 63–74.

Thomson, M.E. (1991). *Developmental Dyslexia.* London: Whurr.

Thomson, P.M. (1988). *Treatment of Intransigent Reading Failure: An Evaluation of Interactive Criticism as an Effective Strategy in Teaching Dyslexic Children with Persistent Reading Difficulties.* M.Ed.Dissertation, University of Wales.

Thomson, P.M. (1995). Stress factors in early education. In: Miles, T.R. and Varma, V.P. (Eds.). *Dyslexia and Stress.* London: Whurr.

West, T.G. (1991). *In the Mind's Eye.* Buffalo, NY: Prometheus Books.

Williams, A.L. and Miles, T.R. (1985). Rorschach responses of dyslexic children. *Annals of Dyslexia,* **35**,51-66.

Wisdom, J. (1952). *Other Minds.* Oxford: Blackwell.

Chapter 9
The Inner Life of Youngsters with Specific Developmental Language Disorder

WENDY RINALDI

Introduction

Language impairments have been associated with a number of aetiologies including hearing impairment, learning difficulties, emotional disturbance and physical structural abnormality (Emerick and Hatton, 1978; Lees and Urwin, 1989).

Language impairment thus frequently forms part of the picture of special needs within a number of groups, such as autism, hearing impairment, physical disability and learning difficulty, which are considered in other chapters of this publication. Some of the content of the present chapter will, therefore, be relevant to these groups. The focus here, however, is on a group of children who have been described as having Specific Developmental Language Disorder. This diagnosis is applied to youngsters where, in relation to other developmental skills, their language is significantly impaired and where, although there may be some associated factors, such as a history of hearing loss, learning or emotional difficulty, the language impairment can not be attributed to any one of these alone nor to the sum of these effects (Lees and Urwin, 1989).

This chapter will first provide a review of the literature to introduce the notion of language disorder, to describe in more detail how the diagnosis of Specific Developmental Language Disorder (SDLD) is reached and to summarise research findings on the kinds of difficulties that SDLD youngsters have. I will then draw on my own experiences and observations from my work as a speech and language therapist with school-aged SDLD youngsters, looking particularly at the aspects of language which impinge upon learning, social development and behaviour. These observations and those outlined in the literature review will then be used as a basis to reflect upon aspects of 'inner lives' of youngsters with Specific Developmental Language Disorder. Finally, the chapter will outline how aspects relating to youngsters' inner lives can be considered in developing educational programmes in order to enable them to progress to their maximum potential.

Literature review: Understanding the concept of language disorder

Introduction

A useful starting point in understanding the concept of disordered language development is by looking at models of human communication, because in understanding the different aspects which make up the communication process, it is then possible to analyse the breakdown of language when development is delayed or disordered.

The big picture. Understanding the communication process

The model outlined in Figure 9.1 is an extension of the 'speech chain' model, first outlined by Denes and Pinson in 1978. This model shows communication as a chain of events which takes place in communicating both verbal messages (containing words) and non-verbal messages (containing gestures, tones of voice, facial expression and other forms of body-language).

At the language or linguistic level, the content of the message is first encoded by **the speaker** into language form. In the verbal route of communication this encoding involves selection and combination of phonemes (sound units), morphemes (including words and grammatical markers), phrases, sentences and clauses; in the non-verbal route it may involve selection and combination of, for example, gestures, facial expressions and tones of voice.

The language is then communicated, at the physiological level, by voice and speech musculature (verbal and non-verbal (tone of voice) route) and facial/body musculature (non-verbal route). At the acoustic level the sound is transmitted in the form of pressure changes in the air (sound waves). **The listener** then perceives the sound or visual communication at the physiological level and understands or interprets the communication at the linguistic level. The communication process therefore involves language (encoding and understanding thoughts, feelings and ideas, conveyed verbally and non-verbally), speech (the physical process of uttering sound, including articulation and tone of voice), vision and hearing.

There is also, essentially, a two-way process in communication, involving speakers and listeners, which makes communication a social enterprise. It should be noted that although much of language is used as

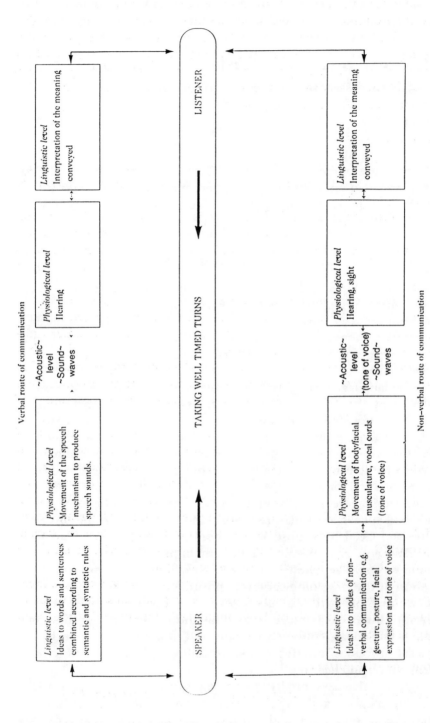

Figure 9.1 The interactive process of communication (Rinadi, 1992)

a part of communication, it may also be used in a 'non-communicative' way, for example, to enable an individual to organise their thoughts more effectively in a learning task. There are a number of ways in which language and/or communication development may be delayed or disordered and in understanding these different kinds of language impairments it is necessary to take a closer look at the component parts which interact to create 'human language'.

A closer look at language

Crystal's 1987 linguistic model for organising and analysing language discusses three different levels or components – phonology, grammar and semantics.

The **phonological level** of language is concerned with the organisation of sound, including how sound units may be contrasted to signal meaning. For example, in minimal pairs such as 'pin' and 'bin' the voicing component of the initial phoneme provides contrast and signals a change in meaning.

The **grammar** of language involves the study of word structure and sequence, that is, the way in which words and grammatical markers signalling meaning (morphemes) are combined to form larger units such as phrases, sentences and clauses.

Semantics is the study of the way in which meaning is organised in language. There is also an aspect of meaning that practitioners and researchers are increasingly discussing as a separate component of language called pragmatics.

Pragmatics is particularly concerned with contextual aspects of language, involving both understanding and use. For example, in understanding ambiguous language such as 'plays' on words, sarcasm etc., the listener uses the context in which the communication is made to sort out the speaker's intended meaning. Similarly, speakers can make use of context to convey particular meanings and to make their language easier to follow, for example by introducing a conversational topic or 'theme' appropriately, by extending themes with an appropriate amount of detail and by indicating a shift to a different topic.

Difficulties with language can occur in any one or more of the areas outlined above and this chapter will now explain these difficulties in relation to the diagnosis of 'language delay', 'language disorder' and 'specific language disorder'.

Language difficulties

The difference between language delay and language disorder

One method of describing or diagnosing language impairment has been to make comparisons with reference to developmental norms. For example, Ingram (1976) outlined a developmental sequence in the acquisition of phonology, comprising different simplifying processes occurring at different ages between eighteen months and six years. Crystal, Fletcher and Garman (1976) outline stages in the development of syntax up to the age of five years. Carol Chomsky (1969) outlines a further five aspects of syntax acquired between the ages of six and ten years. Bloom and Lahey (1978) noted common features in children's development of language content.

Considering receptive language, the standardisation of a number of language comprehension assessments has proposed developmental norms, for example, on the understanding of grammar (Bishop, 1983) and word meaning (Dunn *et al.*, 1982). Normative guidelines have also been proposed for aspects of perceptual and cognitive development which are seen as prerequisite for language. Cooper, Moodley and Reynell (1979), for example, outline stages during the pre-school years in the development of attention control, concept formation and symbolic understanding.

In making comparisons to developmental norms, some have attempted to differentiate language impairments in terms of delayed and disordered development. Cooper, Moodley and Reynell (1979), for example, outline language delay as a slowing in the rate of language development and they note that in this kind of impairment the language follows a developmental pattern along the lines of recognised normative stages, with verbal comprehension developing prior to verbal expression. When language development is disordered, however, it develops in an uneven and a typical way in terms of normative trends. A child with language disorder, therefore, may show linguistic features not found in the course of normal development (Bishop and Rosenbloom, 1987). Bishop and Edmonson (1986) also noted that deficits within a language disorder are more persistent than those of a language delay.

It should be noted that the distinction between delay and disorder outlined above is not always clear. Ingram (1989) for example, believes that knowledge with regards to normal acquisition is not sufficient to allow accurate judgement here. Further, reported case studies (for example, Rinaldi, 1992) show that Bishop and Edmunson's claim for delayed language development to be less persistent may not always be so. Youngsters may continue to simplify their language in ways usually seen in the speech of preschool children into the secondary school years, despite specialist teaching/therapy in their primary school years.

Other descriptions of language disorder have focused entirely on the language itself as opposed to considering age related observations. Lees and Urwin (1989) for example, emphasise mismatches in the development of the various subsystems of language as being a feature of language disorder as opposed to language delay.

Such mismatches were also evident in Bloom and Lahey's (1978) observations of language disordered children. For example, they outline instances where ideas about the world of events and objects (concerning language content or semantics) are more intact than their knowledge of the linguistic system for representing and communicating these ideas (concerning language form). Youngsters with this kind of problem are able to formulate ideas, but may be unable to communicate them, because they have insufficient phonological or syntactic skills. This kind of problem clearly indicates communication as a frustrating experience, on the part of the youngster and on the part of those attempting to communicate with him or her. Bloom and Lahey observed that other children have a good knowledge of the linguistic system but are weakest in developing ideas that make up the content of language. Youngsters with this kind of problem are able to produce well formulated sentences but there are large gaps in conceptual/vocabulary knowledge.

Bloom and Lahey also note another kind of difficulty, where language use is more impaired than content or form. They suggest that when there is a relatively strong weakness in language use, or 'pragmatics', compared with language form and content, difficulties are not as obvious to detect and may require continual interaction with the child before the nature of the disruption becomes apparent. They describe children who have this latter kind of language difficulty as appearing 'intrapersonal' rather than 'interpersonal'; 'they talk about something that is out of context and ramble repetitively or tangentially associate ideas without regard for the listener' (Bloom and Lahey, 1978). This chapter will now consider these kinds of language difficulties in relation to the diagnosis 'Specific Developmental Language Disorder'.

The concept of Specific Language Disorder

The concept of language disorder has already been associated with i) a developmental pattern which deviates from common developmental patterns, ii) mismatches in the child's language profile and iii) identifiable aetiology. The diagnosis of specific developmental language disorder (that is a problem specific to language development) appears to have been applied where there is no identifiable aetiology. Lees and Urwin (1989), for example, summarise attempts to define specific language disorder as having been reached at by exclusion. Therefore, a child is said to have a specific language disorder if there is an absence of the predisposing or precipitating factors outlined in the introduction to this chapter. This kind of definition was first applied in the 1960s to the diagnosis of 'childhood aphasia' (Zangwill, 1987).

Lees and Urwin note this kind of definition as unsatisfactory, since their observation is that in the vast majority of children with specific language disorder, predisposing or precipitating factors have been or are present. Bishop (1987) also suggests a multifactorial aetiology, where specific language disorder is the final common pathway for a number of factors which interrupt development. Lees and Urwin therefore propose a definition that acknowledges that a specific language disorder may be associated with a history of hearing, learning, environmental or emotional difficulty, but cannot be attributed to any one of these alone or even to the sum of these effects. That is, the predisposing factors are not of a degree sufficient to bring about the degree of language disorder.

Lees and Urwin also summarise four other common findings which may be seen in a child with specific language disorder. These are i) a family history of specific difficulty in language development, ii) evidence of cerebral dysfunction, for example, presence of neurological signs such as clumsiness or epilepsy (Robinson, 1987), iii) mismatch in the subsystems of language in relation to aspects of cognitive development, and iv) a failure to catch up these differences with 'generalised' language stimulation.

The theoretical framework for disordered language development presented by Kirchner and Skarakis-Doyle (1987) also assumes a genetic or lesion based disruption in the growth of component language skills required for the development of normal communication. Lees and Urwin note however that despite their findings outlined in their points i) and ii) above, as yet it has not proved possible to isolate a genetic marker for developmental language disorder nor to find evidence of clear cerebral lesions (Robinson, 1992).

Richard Cromer (1987) highlights the importance of underlying perceptual and cognitive impairments to account for the observed language behaviour of children with specific developmental language disorder, in particular that affecting auditory processing and memory. Menyuk's (1978) study indicated that a memory deficit could account for some language deficits. In an imitation task, SDLD children performed differently from non-language disordered children in that they omitted the first part of the sentence and could not retain strings greater than three to five morphemes in length.

Tallal and Piercy (1978) found SDLD children's ability to process the order of auditory signals was particularly affected by the rate of presentation. They also found that the children had difficulty making distinctions between and remembering sequences of auditory events when a chunk of that event was too short in duration. Therefore, although it has been found that children with specific language disorders may attain values equivalent to average or above average intelligence on performance IQ subtests, it is not true that these children are, except for language, cognitively intact (Menyuk, 1978).

Case studies of language disordered children (Lees and Urwin, 1989; Bloom and Lahey, 1978) have shown that specific developmental language disorder is not a unitary condition. Language disorder can affect any one or more of the language components (phonology, syntax, semantics, pragmatics) and/or their interactions. Further, language profiles of language disordered children may show discrepancies between their comprehension and expression of any one or more of the language components.

Kirchner and Skarakis-Doyle's (1983) theoretical framework explains some of the heterogeneity within the language disorder population as occurring because of the different compensatory strategies children use to adapt to communication demands. These strategies involve behaviour processes which are relative strengths in the child's communicative system, such as gesture to aid word finding and simplification of syntax to increase intelligibility. The use of these kinds of strategies will be discussed later in this chapter, in reflecting on the inner lives of SDLD youngsters.

Summary

Impaired language may involve a delay or disorder in language development which may be linked to one or more of a number of predisposing or precipitating factors and may affect one or more language areas (phonology, syntax, semantics, pragmatics) in terms of comprehension and/or expression. Differential diagnosis between delayed and disordered development is determined by comparison to normative stages or by the presence of mismatches in the child's language profile. Children with specific language disorder have particular difficulties with language in comparison to other developmental skills, although the type of language difficulties shown may vary considerably from individual to individual.

This chapter will now provide a more personal account, focusing on my observations as a speech and language therapist working with school aged SDLD youngsters.

Some observations on the effects of having a language difficulty

Language difficulties relating to the learning situation

Learning Styles

Because of the difficulties SDLD youngsters have with auditory processing and auditory memory, the auditory channel is usually the weakest in terms of learning. Teaching which includes information presented auditorially only, therefore, presents the most difficult learning environment and is the least motivating. My experience is that language impaired youngsters learn much better when auditory information is supplemented with visual and tactile/kinaesthetic learning in 'seeing and doing' tasks. My findings are that this kind of learning is frequently used within primary education, but as children become older, the emphasis is placed more on auditory learning and the expectation is for youngsters not to need additional kinaesthetic and visual cues to support the auditory channel. One of the challenges of working with the secondary school age group is, therefore, to provide age appropriate visual/kinaesthetic 'support' materials. I will address this issue again later in the chapter in discussing appropriate educational programmes.

Difficulties with language comprehension

Children with receptive language difficulties and/or auditory processing difficulties are reliant upon the speaker limiting or simplifying their language to a level where they are able to follow. Their ability to listen and understand may also be enhanced if the speaker uses gesture (or a signing system) to supplement auditory information. Clearly SDLD children can be placed at a disadvantage if those communicating with them are not aware of their level of understanding with regard to, for example, vocabulary or grammatical structure. Unfortunately, as Lees and Urwin (1989) note, receptive language difficulties are more likely to go undetected in comparison with expressive language difficulties which are more readily observable. This problem is exacerbated by the tendency for language impaired children not to show their confusion, either because they do not have the verbal or non-verbal language to do so (for example a puzzled facial expression, a request for clarification) or because they are not aware that there is a possibility that they may not understand. This latter skill, referred to as comprehension monitoring, normally develops around 7 to 8 years in non-language impaired youngsters (Bonitatibus, 1988), but is often not evident in language impaired youngsters, even at secondary age.

Difficulties with attention control are also frequently evident in youngsters with specific language disorder. Even in later years, they may be easily distracted, finding it difficult to attend to key information and not be 'side tracked' by environmental factors such as noise, interruption etc., or by extraneous factors intrinsic in a task, such as irrelevant information.

Expressive language difficulties

The difficulties that SDLD youngsters have in communicating their ideas can occur as a result of one or more or a number of factors. I have outlined below three common areas of difficulty.

1. **Phonological problems** may result in the youngster simplifying or leaving out sounds so that their speech is difficult to understand. If they

are consistent in the way they substitute sounds, their teacher, and possibly other youngsters, will be able to 'tune in' to their talking and work out their meaning. If, however, they do not make consistent errors, their speech may be very difficult, perhaps impossible, to follow.

2. **Word finding difficulties.** Youngsters who have word finding difficulties have a knowledge of the vocabulary but are unable to access the words they want at the time of communication. In these instances, they may become very dysfluent as they struggle to find the words they wish to use to convey their ideas. Their speech may be filled with hesitations, 'starters' such as 'um' and 'er' and 'revisions'. In this latter feature, the youngster begins a sentence but gets 'stuck' at a word and therefore attempts to express the idea in a different way

3. **Organisational difficulties.** When asked an open question, or in a task which requires the youngster to organise a number of different pieces of information, the youngster may have difficulty in the following ways:

i. They may not be able to identify the key information and thus not be able to introduce the topic or theme. In such instances youngsters may say 'don't know' or abandon a task because they are simply unable to formulate a response.
ii. They may give irrelevant or very detailed, specific information, without having introduced the theme, so that the listener is unable to link what they are saying into any frame of reference.

Clearly, language difficulties such as those outlined above also have implications for how well language impaired youngsters are able to talk with their peers. Since conversation becomes an increasingly important part of youngsters' leisure time as they grow older, this has further implications for the development of friendship. The chapter will now focus on this and other aspects of social development in relation to language difficulties.

Language difficulties relating to social development

Although research in this area has been limited, a longitudinal study by Haynes and Naidoo (1991) which examined the progress of 34 SDLD youngsters into adulthood, found that many of the youngsters had difficulty socially. For example, although 20 of the 34 subjects reported going out socially with friends of their own age, 14 of the 20 did so only rarely.

This finding supports my own observations outlined below on areas of language difficulty which relate to the development of friendship and the use of language in social contexts.

Difficulties with the interactive process of communication

Difficulties here can involve a number of aspects including i) the ability to give and respond to listener feedback appropriately (for example, eye contact, facial expression, questions, interjections); ii) the timing of turns so as not to interrupt the speaker; iii) the 'repair' of conversation on occasions when two people start to talk at the same time; iv) the ability to signal intention to initiate a communication (for example with eye contact, gesture, body posture) and v) the ability to terminate or 'hand over' the conversation.

In my opinion, these skills form the basis of all social communication; it is very difficult, for example, to deal effectively with any social context, such as taking a message for someone, joining a club, requesting a refund for an unwanted gift etc. unless these skills are established. Furthermore, impaired interactive communication skills may give the impression that the youngster isn't interested in his or her peers and has no desire for friendship.

Difficulty understanding and using non-verbal communication to express/interpret emotion

Language impaired youngsters can appear 'uncaring' or lacking in empathy to their peers, because they do not tend to perceive the more subtle forms of emotional expression such as tone of voice/facial expression and may not enquire upon the feelings of others. They also frequently have difficulty in understanding non-verbal cues to distinguish humour from serious comment and can, therefore, respond inappropriately. Their own attempts to express emotion can be inappropriate and socially unacceptable; if they are unaware of the more subtle verbal and non- verbal forms of emotional expression, they can resort to more gross forms of non-verbal expression, such as hitting to convey anger or hugging to convey pleasure.

Low awareness of self and others

When asked questions about themselves and their friends, language impaired children are often unable to answer, or they give inaccurate information. This inaccuracy or lack of awareness indicates that in fact they have a very poor concept of friendship even though they may talk about having 'friends'. In addition, I have found that many language impaired youngsters are unaware of basic strategies for making friends, such as finding out and pursuing common interests, sharing/swapping possessions and so on.

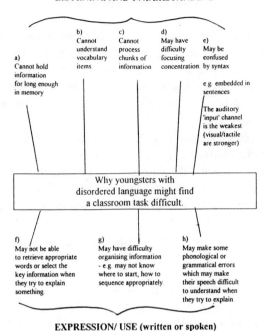

Figure 9.2 Why youngsters with disordered language might find classroom talk difficult

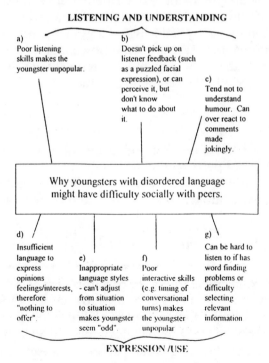

Figure 9.3 why youngsters with disordered language might have difficulty socially

Avoidance of social communicative contexts

A common finding from interviews with parents and SDLD youngsters themselves, is that they avoid situations where social communication is required, other than in familiar settings or with familiar people at school and home. Observation has shown that frequently, the difficulties that youngsters experience in these less familiar social contexts arise because of their poor non-verbal communication skills. For example, a commonly observed feature is that SDLD youngsters do not indicate their desire to communicate, for example, by making eye contact and using appropriate posture. The language difficulties outlined above are summarised in Figures 9.2 and 9.3. These figures explore why SDLD children i) may find a classroom activity difficult and ii) have difficulty socially.

How language difficulties can create behaviour which is difficult to manage

Strategies for resolving conflict

Studies of non-language impaired pre-school children (for example, Tyneside Child Films, 1988) show how they are able to use a range of verbal and non-verbal communication skills to resolve conflicts, caused, for example, by disagreement and accidental hurt. These skills include negotiating compromise, validating opinion, suggesting alternatives, facial expression to convey sadness, apology and gentle touch. Observations of language impaired youngsters show that they do not have these strategies; rather their conflicts more often escalate to a point where they can only be resolved by adult intervention.

The tendency to overreact

Language impaired youngsters can give the impression of 'overreacting' because they do not perceive the more subtle non-verbal cues such as a gentle tone of voice or a 'fun' facial expression. Therefore, for example, they may perceive a 'fun tease' as an insult and respond accordingly.

Thinking/perceiving in a narrow frame of reference

Language impaired youngsters appear particularly vulnerable to a rigidity in their thinking and learning. In part, this may be related to the fact that learning is generally a very effortful experience for them because of their difficulties with, for example, auditory processing, auditory memory, attention control and verbal comprehension. In basic terms, it may be that because learning is such an effortful experience, challenge to learning, requiring a flexibility of thought, is resisted and could be responded to with anger. This aspect of the 'inner life' of the language impaired youngster may also be related to the type of language difficulty affecting the pragmatic area, since here, there is a tendency to understand in a very literal inflexible way.

Distinguishing opinion and fact

The difficulties language impaired youngsters have in differentiating opinion from fact is apparent from observing their spontaneous talk. My observation here is that much of their language relates to factual, descriptive information and very little, if any, focuses on their thoughts and feelings. My belief is that this lack of awareness, relating to the notion of 'opinion' as distinct from fact, creates difficulties in accepting differences in opinion, which are seen as a challenge to learning and, relating back to the point I made in my previous paragraph, met with anger.

Low tolerance to making mistakes

This fifth area of difficulty, I believe, may be linked to past experience of failures, associated with the communication difficulty as a whole, which is such a central part to the youngster's life both at home and at school. The development of this type of problem will be discussed more fully in considering the inner lives of SDLD children. At this point, however, it is worth noting that low tolerance in making mistakes can relate to a range of behaviours which can be hard to manage.

This includes outbursts of anger, refusal to participate, tears and techniques the youngster uses to distract attention away from their learning or communication difficulty. This latter behaviour may include 'clowning' around, claims that the work is 'too easy' or 'boring', late arrival to lessons and so on. This kind of behaviour clearly provides an enormous barrier to the youngster's learning. The acceptability (and, indeed, inevitability) of making mistakes or having weakness, therefore, needs to be addressed in the educational programme in order to allow learning to take place. Ways of implementing this kind of work are discussed later in this chapter.

From observation to speculation. A closer look at the inner lives of children with specific language disorders

Within the field of speech and language disorder, observation from research study and practice are developing our knowledge relating to the 'outer lives' of language impaired youngsters although, because of the heterogeneous nature of the disorder, it is clear that there is a considerable degree of variability here.

In general, what we see on the surface are youngsters who

i)   do better on performance IQ subtests than verbal IQ subtests, with performance scores within or around the average range
ii)   have difficulty in expressing their ideas
iii) tend to have difficulty with language or tasks requiring the processing and organisation of a number of instructions
iv)   can learn better if a multisensory approach is taken
v)   may appear to have little interest in their peers
vi)   have difficulty 'reading the signs' if communication goes beyond a literal sense
vii) may appear to 'overreact' in their behaviour
viii) may have difficulties with gross and/or fine motor co-ordination and appear 'clumsy'.

But what is it like below the surface, in the inner life of the youngster with specific language disorder?

First, the indication is that there must be a good deal of confusion. So much of everyday language involves, for example, processing chunks of information, understanding 'plays' on words, drawing inferences from what's not said as much as what is said; all of which are likely to present difficulty to the majority of language impaired children of all ages.

It is apparent that at some age, my observations suggest 9 to 10 years, language impaired youngsters become increasingly aware of their difficulties in relation to their peers. At the same time, the onus on communication for socialisation and learning becomes increasingly greater. For example, research studies by Robinson (1978), Ackerman (1981; 1982) and Rinaldi (unpublished) have shown that non-language impaired youngsters develop an understanding of figurative language, including sarcasm and appreciation of jokes, around the age of 7 to 9 years. The expectation of those talking with youngsters at this age is, therefore, that they will understand this kind of language.

Therefore, alongside the language impaired youngster's growing awareness of their difficulties in relation to peers (and also, perhaps, younger children) there occurs a growing demand upon the youngster as to what is expected of them in terms of communication. It is little wonder that low self-esteem appears a fairly common denominator for teenagers with specific language disorders. Since communication is such a central part of work and leisure and because the past experience of learning may have been somewhat of a struggle, it is possible that fear of failing and low motivation may also form part of the SDLD youngster's inner life.

Having identified areas of potential difficulty for language disordered youngsters, I will now focus on outlining ways of developing educational programmes to enable youngsters with these kinds of difficulties to make progress. Before doing so, however, I would like to emphasise the very positive aspects of working with youngsters with specific language disorder. I have tended in this chapter, so far, to focus on youngsters' difficulties and may have created a rather negative picture. However, I must emphasise that by taking an educational approach based on an understanding of the difficulties, it is possible to prevent development of the more negative aspects of inner lives that I have outlined in this chapter, to alleviate the 'struggle' of learning and to help youngsters to do well socially with their peers.

In order to do this, early intervention is essential, but of equal importance is **continued** intervention and support into the teenage years, as language impaired youngsters begin to face new communicative demands both in the social and learning contexts.

Developing educational programmes

Why we need to consider youngsters' inner lives

Although exploring inner lives necessarily involves some speculation, albeit drawing upon observation, my belief is that it is an invaluable exercise which i) gives further insight into youngsters' difficulties, allowing a more positive view of what may be seen as negative behaviours and attitudes on the part of the youngster, and ii) enables an important focus for education. The aspects relating to inner life discussed above, create barriers to progress which need to be prevented or removed. The following paragraphs give suggestions on how this can be achieved through the educational process.

Allocating time for more focused language work to enable access to broader curricular areas and more effective participation in social communicative contexts

In order to develop the range of language/communication skills, outlined in this chapter as problematic to language impaired youngsters, I have found it necessary to use educational programmes specifically focusing on these skills. These programmes have included organisational language skills, vocabulary/ word finding and 'hidden meaning', (Rinaldi, 1992) and the Social Use of Language (Rinaldi 1992, 1993). Other programmes I have found to be of value to SDLD youngsters focus on aspects relating to the language/communication difficulty, for example, memory and thinking skills (De Bono, 1986). The skills taught in this focused language work can then be applied to broader curricular areas including National Curriculum attainment targets for Maths,

English, Science, Geography and History and to a range of social contexts, including the ability to resolve conflicts, to express and respond to opinions/feelings appropriately, to request clarification and so on.

There is no space for detailed descriptions here, but reference is made to published language educational programmes, in the appendix of this chapter. The following aspects of these programmes have been found to be of particular value to youngsters with specific developmental language disorder.

1. The use of activities which allow multisensory learning.
2. The use of activities to initially raise youngsters' awareness /comprehension (for example by using modelling, video material and stories), to precede youngsters' practise/use.
3. The ordering of activities to allow a building of learning in gradual steps.

Such programmes also provide an excellent opportunity for joint working between teachers and speech/language therapists.

Helping youngsters to see the significance of the learning.

I believe this aspect is key in developing educational programmes which will enhance youngsters' motivation. Youngsters need to know how working on quite specific aspects of their language/communication will enable them to make gains in other areas of school and home life. To this end, on starting a programme of work, I outline the 'big picture' or the purpose for learning, so that the youngsters are clear about the overall learning target. Time is also allocated after each activity to enable youngsters to locate the learning point and to relate the activity to the long term learning target.

For example, one aspect of the Social Use of Language Programme, is designed to enable youngsters to develop and maintain friendship more effectively and this is stated at the beginning of the course. Youngsters are encouraged to think about themselves and each other around a number of topics, through a range of activities, and then to remember and make use of this information in a further set of activities. Discussion after each activity focuses on points relating to friendship, for example, the effects of forgetting information about others, how to pursue common interests and so on.

Developing a 'making mistakes is O.K.' policy

If youngsters can be encouraged to see the acceptability, and indeed the value of making mistakes as an inevitable part of learning, this prevents or reduces the kinds of barriers to learning, including 'problematic' behaviour, that have already been outlined in this chapter as being linked to low self-esteem. This can be achieved in a number of ways.

1. Adopting a general ethos or approach where i) areas of weakness are acknowledged as an inevitable part of any individual; ii) areas of strength are equally acknowledged and iii) the emphasis is placed on capitalising upon strengths whilst improving weaknesses. This incorporates verbal reinforcers as responses to mistakes, such as 'well, you didn't do too well there, but you're learning' (or to simplify 'you're learning') and attitudes to one's own errors, for example 'yes, I got that wrong, but I shall remember next time' (or to simplify 'I'm wrong, I shall do better next time').

The making mistakes policy can be agreed on a formal contract within a group or a whole school population.

2. More focused activity relating to strengths and weaknesses. A number of more focused activities have been outlined, for example, in The social Use of Language Programme (Rinaldi 1992, 1993) to enable youngsters to view their weaknesses more positively. Other activities include discussion about video or television programmes, such as 'It will be Alright on the Night', which show TV and sports personalities, held in high regard by the youngsters, making mistakes. Drama sketches can also be developed to show the positives of openly accepting weaknesses as opposed to developing 'cover up strategies'. These can be presented to individual groups or as part of a whole school assemblies.

Helping youngsters to develop compensatory strategies

The work of Kirchner and Skarakis-Doyle (1983), outlined on page 130 of this chapter, emphasises a positive aspect of SDLD youngsters' inner lives. Their observation that some SDLD youngsters can develop compensatory strategies to enable more effective communication indicates that some SDLD youngsters are able to call upon a number of very useful 'inner resources'. The development of successful compensatory strategies would imply, for example, the ability to be aware of the communication partners needs, to self monitor, to problem solve (including lateral thinking), to action a 'solution', adjust as necessary and to persevere in adjusting! Unfortunately a number of SDLD youngsters appear not to have these kinds of inner resources and rather than developing useful compensatory strategies, resort to the kinds of 'cover up' strategies which have already been described. Therefore, a useful focus in educational programmes is to enable youngsters to develop some of the skills outlined above, thus enabling them to replace unproductive and potentially damaging strategies with strategies which will be of value to them.

Monitoring your language; revising and extending

When talking to youngsters with specific language disorders, the first step is to identify their level of comprehension in terms of, for example, vocabulary and grammatical components. This can be done by requesting speech and language comprehension assessment, which is usually completed by a speech and language therapist. Having identified the youngster's level of language comprehension, the next step is for the person talking to the language impaired youngster to carefully self monitor and to simplify their language, if necessary, in a second attempt at conveying the communication. This simplification may include, for example, emphasising 'key' words, the use of additional visual cues such as a gesture or pictorial representation and extension by example or description. It should be realised that the SDLD youngster may not be able to give appropriate listener feedback (such as a puzzled facial expression) to show that they are not understanding.

Summary and concluding points

This chapter has attempted to build a picture relating to youngsters who have Specific Developmental Language Disorder. This picture has included description of observations relating to communication, social development, behaviour and learning and the possible links between them. Attempting to explore inner lives has shed light on our understanding of why SDLD youngsters show these kinds of difficulties and on how the educational process can be developed to best serve their needs.

There is a need for early intervention to prevent the development of the kinds of barriers to learning and social development outlined in the chapter, but continued intervention into the secondary years is also important.

Teenagers with specific language disorders are particularly vulnerable to the more negative aspects of inner lives such as poor self-esteem, low self-expectation, lack of self-confidence and so on, because at the same time as the learning and social communicative demands upon them increase, they begin to develop a heightened awareness of their difficulties in relation to their peers and, with the onset of adolescence, a strong desire for peer conformity. The indication is, therefore, that without intervention and support of the kinds outlined in this chapter, and particularly the focus on understanding weaknesses or difficulties as an acceptable and inevitable part of any individual, the youngsters may attempt to develop 'cover up strategies' which may include avoidance, disruption and pretence.

This chapter has attempted to provide an overview of the ways in which youngsters with specific developmental language disorders can be encouraged to progress in educational settings to meet the demands of everyday living. It is hoped that the appendix will now point the reader in the direction of more focused, practical teaching and assessment material.

Appendix

A selection of Assessment and Teaching Materials

Bishop, D.V.M. (1983). The Test for Reception of Grammar. Published by the author c/o Age and Cognitive, Performance Research Centre, University of Manchester, M13 9PL

Boehm, A. (1986). The Boehm Test of Basic Concepts (revised) London: Psychological Corporation, Harcourt, Brace & Jovanovich.

Bracken, B.A. (1984). Bracken Basic Concepts Scale. London: Psychological Corporation, Harcourt, Brace & Jovanovich.

Bracken, B.A and. Myers, D.K. (1986). Bracken Concept Development Programme. London: Psychological Corporation, Harcourt, Brace & Jovanovich.

Dean, E., Howell, J., Hill, A. and Waters, D. (1990). Metaphor Resource Pack, Windsor: NFER Nelson.

Goldsworthy, C. and Secord, W. (1982). Multilevel Informal Language Inventory. Bell and Howell Publishing Company.

Rinaldi, W. (1992). Working with Teenagers with Language Impairment and Moderate Learning Difficulties. London: I CAN.

Rinaldi, W. (1992). Social Use of Language Programme.Windsor: NFER Nelson.

Rinaldi, W. (1993), (1995). Social Use of Language Programme Primary/Preschool packs.

Rinaldi, W. (in press) Understanding Ambiguity; An assessment of pragmatic meaning comprehension. Windsor: NFER Nelson.

Semel, E., Wiig, E. and Secord, W. (1987). Clinical Evaluation of Language Functions. (revised). London: Psychological Corporation, Harcourt, Brace & Jovanovich.

Wiig, E. (1989). Test of Language Competence. London: Psychological Corporation. Harcourt, Brace & Jovanovich.

Wiig, E.H. and Secord, A. (1990). Test of Word Knowledge. London: Psychological Corporation, Harcourt, Brace & Jovanovich

Wiig, E. (1990). Criterion referenced Inventory of Language. London: Psychological Corporation, Harcourt, Brace & Jovanovich.

References

Ackerman, B.(1981). Young children's understanding of a speaker's intentional use of a false utterance. *Developmental Psychology* 17,472-80.

Ackerman, B.(1982). On comprehending idioms: Do children get the picture? *Journal of Experimental Psychology,* 33,439-54.

Bishop, D. and Rosenbloom, L.(1987). Classification of childhood language disorders. In: W.Yule and M.Rutter (eds.) *Language Development and Disorders.* Oxford: MacKeith Press.

Bishop, D. and Edmunson, A.(1986). Is Otitis media a major cause of specific developmental language disorder? *British Journal of Disorders of Communication,* 21, 321-38.

Bonitatibus, G. (1988). Comprehension monitoring and the apprehension of literal meaning. *Child Development,* **59,**60-70.

Cromer, R. (1987). Language acquisition, language disorder and cognitive development. In: W.Rule and M.Rutter (eds.) *Language development and language disorders.*Oxford: Mackeith Press.

Crystal, D. (1987). Concept of language development a realistic perspective. In: W.Rule and M. Rutter (Eds.), *Language development and language disorders.* Oxford:Mackeith Press.

Crystal, D., Fletcher, P. and Garman, M. (1976). *The Grammatical Analysis of Language Disability and Remediation.* London: Edward Arnold.

De Bono, E. (1986) *The CORT Thinking Programme.*2nd edn. Henley-upon-Thames: Science Research Associates.

Denes, P. and Pinson, E. (1973). *The Speech Chain. The Physics and Biology of Speech.* New York: Anchor Press/Doubleday.

Dunn, L., Dunn, L., Whetton, C. and Pintillie, D. (1982). *British Picture Vocabulary Scale.*Windsor: NFER Nelson.

Emerick, L. and Hatton, J. (1978). *Diagnosis and evaluation in speech pathology.* USA: Prentice Hall.

Haynes. C. and Naidoo, S. (1991). Children with specific speech and language impairment. *Clinics in Developmental Medicine* 119,. London: Mackeith Press.

Ingram, D. (1976). *Phonological disability in children.*London: Edward Arnold.

Lees, J. and Urwin, S. (1989). *Children with language disorders.* London: Whurr Publishers.

Rinaldi, W.(1992). *Working with language impaired teenagers with moderate learning difficulties.*London:I CAN.

Rinaldi, W. (1992) *The Social Use of Language Programme,* Windsor: NFER Nelson

Robinson, R. (1992). Brain imaging and language. In: P.Fletcher and D. Hall (Eds.) *Specific speech and language disorders in children,* London: Whurr Publishers.

Tallal, P. and Piercy, M. (1978) Defects of auditory perception in children with developmental dysphasia. In: Wyke (Ed.), *Developmental Dysphasia.*London: Academic Press.

Tyneside Child Films (1988) 'Falling Out'. Available from Tyneside Child Films Tel. 01642 221298.

Zangwill, O. (1978). The concept of developmental dysphasia. In: Wyke (Ed.), *Developmental dysphasia.*London:Academic Press.

Chapter 10
Diagnosing and treating the problems of able maladjusted children

LUDWIG F. LOWENSTEIN

Current research demonstrates that maladjusted children can be treated successfully if skilled and timely help is brought to bear on their needs. The methods used to assist in this programme of rehabilitation and sometimes prevention of maladjustment are delineated in the paper. Of the 100 children treated to date, 90% achieved higher levels of performance in school and later in society and, most especially, vocationally. Of the 100 able children who acted as a control group, only 20% achieved such success. Many became maladjusted adults and in some areas also suffered from difficulties with personal relationships, including a lack of success in their marriage and in parenting.

The identification of maladjusted children has not always proved to be an easy matter. Frequently it has been left either to parents or teachers to identify such youngsters, usually by their performance or appearance. Much of the judgement is subjective and frequently is not based on an intellectual diagnosis of the child. Lowenstein (1972) noted the difficulties teachers frequently had in identifying gifted children. This was due to the fact that the bright child or bright looking child who had some particular ability in the area of reading or writing was often deemed to be advanced for his or her age when, in fact, this was due to excessive coaching at home or resulted from a specific area of ability which did not necessarily match with other intellectual functions.

Another booklet by Lowenstein (1976) noted that there were certain personality characteristics likely to be influential in whether a child achieved or not. Intellectual ability as measured by intelligence tests was naturally one of these. Other aspects identified through the literature as well as through observations of able children were:

Reprinted from the European Journal for High Ability, 1993, 4, 142–151

1. Reducing the likelihood of depression;

2. Parental attitudes;

3. Removing the need for immediate gratification and hence seeking long term goals;

4. Developing perseverance, reducing emotional and psychological problems;

5. Reducing hostility towards others;

6. Receiving effective teaching for a particular ability;

7. Developing the capacity to conform to school discipline and rules;

8. Developing powers of concentration;

9. Developing general motivation towards learning.

Giftedness or high intellectual ability is of special importance in less technologically developed countries in promoting these nations and their human resources to the maximum. Lowenstein (1979) identified numerous children as gifted in the Sudan, this being the largest country in Africa and tenth largest in the world. He suggested that it was important to do the following in these particular countries, where the development of ability was of paramount value:

1. Organise courses for teachers to develop an understanding of the psychology of child development.

2. Set up a School Psychological Service to deal with emotional and educational needs of problem children.

3. Promote the growth of special education for the educationally handicapped and disadvantaged as well as those of high ability.

4. Develop an assessment technique whereby the intellectually able were identified as early as possible so that their education could be promoted in every way. It was of course vital to gear the intellectual assessment techniques to the culture, and current methods being used in the West were unlikely to be altogether relevant for such populations.

More recent studies (e.g., Hollinger, 1985) indicated that self-esteem was an important factor in gifted children. Emotional problems also affected the development of gifted children and their potential, according to Roedell (1986). Typical problems included myths surrounding giftedness, unrealistic expectations, pressure to perform, constant criticism or praise, and difficulties in finding friends.

Underachievement, especially with able children, frequently resulted in internal conflicts as reported by Janos, Sanfilippo and Robinson (1986). These symptoms in turn affected further academic achievement. The fact that able children engaged in abstract thinking early (Thornburg, Adey & Finnis, 1986) indicated that special approaches at an early age may well be required, to cater for such development. As was frequently pointed out, it is vital to identify gifted children as early as possible in order to develop educational strategies which are in line with their needs (Heller, 1986). Among the methods frequently considered were an enriched or accelerated programme, opportunities for individualisation, and introduction of some degree of structure and flexibility in the programme (Kitano, 1986). Lowenstein (1980) emphasized the importance of segregation as an additional measure for very able children in order to provide them with a programme which was tailor made for their personal needs.

The parenting of able children must also be relatively specialised. Such children are often difficult to treat as ordinary children in the home. They are often quite active, require little sleep, and need a great deal of individual attention, especially in connection with learning. Failure to provide such individual care and learning experiences leads to pressures on gifted children (Silverman, 1986). Needless to say both parents of such children and the gifted children themselves suffer from the stressfulness of life unless their individual needs are somehow met. The fact that such children are labelled as gifted should not lead to greater stress for them (Karnes & Oehler-Stinnett, 1986). Parents of gifted children need a considerable amount of information on how best to deal with such youngsters, but first of all there is a need for psychological assessment and an increased understanding of giftedness (Freeman, 1986).

Much research still needs to be done to examine giftedness in its sociocultural context. Most common approaches, as already mentioned, use enrichment and acceleration as a model (Horowitz & O'Brien, 1986). Many investigators who have worked with able children agree with Lowenstein (1982), that there should be education for the intellectually and emotionally different.

Despite the fact that intelligence tests are not the only way of assessing able children, or anyone for that matter, there are positive features to such an objective assessment (Kaufman & Harrison, 1986). Indeed it is important to use such tests and other measures as early as possible in order to identify such young persons, as there are many benefits to be derived from early identification (Edwards & Edwards, 1986; Robinson & Chamrad, 1986).

The social and emotional adjustment of talented adolescents was studied by Brody and Benbow (1986). They investigated self-esteem, locus of control, popularity, depression and discipline problems in 300 highly verbally or mathematically talented adolescents with a mean age of 13.7 years. Compared to a group of 111 students of approximately the same age, who were much less gifted, the highly gifted youngsters perceived themselves as less popular, but no differences were found in self-esteem, depression or the incidence of discipline problems. The gifted youngsters reported greater internal locus of control. Comparisons between the highly mathematically talented and the highly verbally talented children suggested that the latter group perceived themselves as less popular. Within both groups there were slight indications that higher verbal ability was related to social and emotional problems. Naturally much depended on the type of environment in which the able children resided, as did their signs of adequacy. Providing for the special needs of gifted youngsters, for instance by providing diversity of reading matter, was likely to make them feel more adjusted, as they could learn and practise larger vocabularies and their heightened curiosity and sensitivity was also likely to be satisfied (Greenlaw & McIntosh, 1986).

The speed of learning of able children makes it possible for them to learn complex materials. Lajoie and Shore (1986) found this speed to be both a handicap and an asset, depending on the type of teaching that was provided. It was likely to be a handicap rather than an asset when ordinary teaching in the classroom was available, but an asset when more advanced and speedier teaching was available. Despite this fact, gifted children frequently suffered from certain deficits which made it almost impossible to identify them through the teaching process. Warkany (1986) presented examples of precocious and slow children who became outstanding scientists such as Blaise Pascal, Albert Einstein and others. The inability of some of these children to express themselves despite high intelligence suggested that researchers and practitioners were perhaps failing to recognise faculties that existed beneath the superficial surface of academic performance in the classroom. Certain characteristics of mathematically and verbally precocious students were studied by Benbow (1986) using the College Board Scholastic Aptitude Test. Three physiological characteristics were found with high frequencies: left or mixed handedness, asthma and other allergies, and myopia.

Gifted children were described as a heterogeneous group with its own set of strengths and weaknesses by Hillyer (1989). She noted that different societies had contradictory treatments for gifted children. This gave rise to a number of crises facing gifted children, especially when there were gaps between intellectual and social skills or when unrealistic goals and expectations or perfectionism were stressed, leading to anxiety and possible depression when there was a failure in achieving success. One of the major problems that gifted children have, according to Gross (1989), is the dilemma concerning interaction of psychosocial drives towards intimacy with desire for achievement. If the gifted child chooses to satisfy the drive for excellence, she or he risks forfeiting the attainment of intimacy with age peers; if the choice is intimacy, she or he is forced into a pattern of deliberate underachievement to retain membership in a social group. It was for this reason that homogeneous grouping of gifted pupils was suggested as a partial solution to this dilemma.

Gifted pupils, despite their ability, sometimes suffer from suicidal ideation, according to Farrell (1989). He reviewed the literature on incidents and causes of suicide in gifted pupils. The incidence of suicide and suicide attempts among youth in the United States increased every year during the past decade. While evidence of giftedness among suicide victims was difficult to document in the literature, it was likely that there would be a corresponding increase in that subgroup. In addition to the usual stressors, gifted teenagers also confronted such issues as perfectionism, societal expectations to achieve, differential development of intellectual and social skills, and impotence to effect real world change. For this reason it was recommended that a preventive counselling intervention strategy was necessary as part of every programme, to address these issues and others.

The present study

The research to be reported here is a 16 year study of 200 consecutively referred boys who were diagnosed via the Wechsler Intelligence Test for Children (Short Form) (WISC) as able or gifted with an intelligence level of 125 - 135+. The children ranged in chronological age from 7-14+ when first referred and assessed. Those below that age or above it, for various reasons, were not included in the study. Children suffering from specific learning difficulties such as those commonly termed dyslexia, dysgraphia or mathematics blocks were also excluded from the study. Many of the youngsters were underachieving academically. There were also problems in such categories as behaviour and emotional problems and withdrawing from the educational system (see Table 1 on the page after the next). Academic underachievement was diagnosed on the basis of whether a child's attainments in reading, spelling or mathematics were at least two years behind chronological age and intellectual ability. The question which needed to be answered was, "Do able malajusted children benefit from treatment and/or alternative forms of education including an enriched programme, acceleration or segregation?"

Of the highly able youngsters, 100 were placed into a control group on the basis of their not being able or willing to receive therapeutic input or education commensurate with their ability or needs. The study concerned itself with boys only, as these appeared to present themselves more often than girls, although there were numerous girls but an insufficient number for this study. A number of problems in school, at home or in both settings were manifested among these high ability boys, who, on the whole, appeared to be frustrated by their inappropriate earlier and later learning experiences. They had frequently attended a number of schools, and were referred to the psychologist from a number of sources with the following general problems:

1. Poor academic achievement.
2. Behaviour/emotional problems.
3. An apparent wish to withdraw from the educational setting.

In addition to the WISC, the children were assessed on the following:

1. Standardised tests of reading, spelling and mathematics;
2. The Mooney Problem Checklist (Junior);
3. The MPI (The Maudsley Personality Inventory), and later
4. The EPQ (Eysenck Personality Questionnaire).

The objective was to verify both the severity and number of symptoms related to maladaptive behaviour and emotional problems as measured through the neuroticism and psychoticism scales of the tests. In order to validate observed behaviour by teachers and parents, the objective personality testing was supplemented by:

5. The Sentence Completion Test;
6. Selected cards from the Thematic Apperception Test (TAT).

Both the experimental and the control groups were followed up 10 years later.

In the case of the control group, nothing was done because very often nothing could be done for various reasons, except to follow up their academic, vocational and other development 10 years later. This was essentially due to the fact that there was no cooperation for special provision either by the school or the parents or other agencies. Consequently, such children did not receive an enriched programme, acceleration or segregation or any other specific help based on their personal needs. This was despite advice from one or more educational psychologists that something should have been provided. In all cases, however, the intellectual and educational as well as personal assessment was carried out by the psychologist. In the case of the experimental group, there was pressure from parents that something positive had to be done to help their able children, and the school was influenced by such pressure. In some cases, the help was provided by the school without such pressure. The nature of the help provided is summarized in Table 2 on the following page.

Follow up study

Follow up studies are fraught with difficulties, especially when a long period of time has passed since the assessment. Only 74 members of the experimental and 68 of the control group responded to telephone calls and/or letters. The letters were purposely kept short and contained specific questions as well as an opportunity to respond to structured questions. A letter based on another followup study assessed the development of children diagnosed as maladjusted who had attended Allington Manor School and Therapeutic Community (Lowenstein, 1989). In telephone conversations, the same questions were asked as in the letter. The questions touched upon the following issues: postsecondary education, examinations successfully completed, work history, respondent's opinion about educational measures which would have provided a better start in life.

Table 1. *Description of experimental and control groups on the basis of age and problems assessed*

Age when assessed	Experimental	Control
7–10	26	20
11–14	47	46
14+	27	34
Total	100	100
Problems assessed		
Lower than expected academic achievement	54	43
Behavioural / emotional problems	65	57
Withdrawal from educational system, emotionally or otherwise	35	43
Intelligence of experimental and control sample		
IQ = 125–135	61	57
IQ = 135+	39	43

Table 2. *Predominant types of therapeutic remedial interventions following the diagnosis and assessment*

Intervention technique	Number of children receiving this help (Experimental group only)
1. Enriched curriculum provided in own school	67
2. Acceleration (move up one or more terms)	7
3. Segregation:	
(a) Taught by tutor at home	2
(b) Attending special schools or classes compromised of able children	11
(c) Receiving outpatient treatment in child guidance centres or private centres in addition to remedial education intervention	6

Results

Answers to the various questions are summarized in Table 3.

Table 3. *Outcomes of experimental and control groups on certain criteria of positive development*

	Experimental	Control
A. 1. Continuing education after secondary school	69	43
2. Passing 1 0 level	63	41
3. Passing 2–3 0 levels	59	38
4. Passing 4+ 0 levels	57	27
5. Passing 1 or more A levels	48	19
6. Attending university	36	16
7. Obtaining a degree	34	9
8. Obtaining subsequent degrees	21	1
B. Vocational achievement		
1. Unskilled work	3	19
2. Semiskilled work	7	16
3. Skilled work	19	13
4. Own business	17	12
5. Professionals	28	8
C. Personal relationship with life		
1. Very contented with life	59	27
2. Moderately contented	7	13
3. Not contented	6	13
4. Very discontented with life	2	15
D. Close personal relationships	64	29
E. What actions retrospectively assessed would have helped able children		
1. Education based on personal needs	13	61
2. Smaller classes	54	59
3. Being with others of the same ability and interest	54	59
4. Better teachers	44	37
5. Being less bored with my education	12	52
6. Other reasons	9	36

Conclusions

There was value in providing these able boys with special educational provision such as enriched curriculum, acceleration and segregation in some instances. Manifestations of improvement occurred in the area of educational performance in the future, vocational success and personal contentment with life. This was not the case for the control group, which proved to be considerably less positive in its development.

REFERENCES

Benbow, C.P. (1986). Physiological correlates of extreme intellectual precocity. *Neuropsychologie, 24,* 719-725.

Brody, L.E. & Benbow, C.P. (1986). Social and emotional adjustment of adolescents extremely talented in verbal or mathematical reasoning. *Journal of Youth and Adolescence, 15,* 1-18.

Edwards, D. & Edwards, S. (1986). A parent's I-view. *Roeper Review, 8,* 172-173.

Farrell, D.M. (1989). Suicide among gifted students. *Roeper Review, 11,* 134-139.

Freeman, J. (1986). Up-Date on gifted children. *Developmental Medicine and Child Neurology, 28,* 77-80.

Greenlaw, M.J. & McIntosh, M.E. (1986). Literature for use with gifted children. *Childhood Education, 62,* 281-286.

Gross, M.U. (1989). The pursuit of excellence or the search for intimacy? The forced choice dilemma of gifted youth. *Roeper Review, 11,* 189-194.

Heller, K.A. (1986). Psychological problems in giftedness research. *Zeitschrift für Entwicklungspsychologie und Pädagogische Psychologie, 18,* 335-361.

Hillyer, K. (1989). Problems of gifted children. *Journal of the Association for the Study of Perception, 21,* 10-26.

Hollinger, C.L. (1985). The stability of self perceptions of instrumental and expressive traits and social self-esteem among gifted and talented female adolescents. *Journal for the Education of the Gifted, 8,* 107-125.

Horowitz, F.D. & O'Brien, M. (1986). Gifted and talented children: State of knowledge and directions for research. *American Psychologist, 41,* 1147-1152.

Janos, P.M., Sanfilippo, S.M. & Robinson, N.M. (1986). "Underachievement" among markedly accelerated college students. *Journal of Youth and Adolescence, 15,* 303-313.

Karnes, F.A. & Oehler-Stinnett, J.J. (1986). Life events as stressors with gifted adolescents. *Psychology in the Schools, 23,* 406-414.

Kaufman, A.S. & Harrison, P.L. (1986). Intelligence tests and gifted assessment: What are the positives? *Roeper Review, 8,* 154-159.

Kitano, M.K. (1986). Evaluating program options for young gifted children. *Journal of Children in Contemporary Society, 18,* 3-4.

Lajoie, S.P. & Shore, B.M. (1986). Intelligence: The speed and accuracy tradeoff in high aptitude individuals. *Journal for the Education of the Gifted, 9,* 85-104.

Lowenstein, L.F. (1972). The teacher and the gifted child. *Association of Educational Psychology Journal, 3,* 2.

Lowenstein, L.F. (1976). Helping children to achieve. *Journal of the Parents National Union, 2,* 1,2.

Lowenstein, L.F. (1979). Discovering gifted children in a Third World nation. *School Psychology International, 1,* 27-29.

Lowenstein, L.F. (1980). Is there a case for the segregation of the gifted? *The Journal of the Gifted Child, 1,* 23-24.

Lowenstein, L.F. (1982). Should there be special education for the intellectually and emotionally different? *School Psychology International, 3,* 65-84.

Lowenstein, L.F. (1989). Follow up of maladjusted academically children in a therapeutic community. *International Journal of Rehabilitation Research, 12,* 297-305.

Robinson, N.M. & Chamrad, D.L. (1986). Appropriate uses of intelligence tests with gifted children. *Roeper Review, 8,* 160-163.

Roedell, W.C. (1986). Socio-emotional vulnerabilities of young gifted children. *Journal of Children in Contemporary Society, 18,* 17-29.

Silverman, L.K. (1986). Parenting young gifted children. *Journal of Children in Contemporary Society, 18,* 73-87.

Thornburg, H.D., Adey, K.L. & Finnis, E. (1986). A comparison of gifted and non-gifted early adolescents movement towards abstract thinking. *Journal of Early Adolescence, 6,* 231-245.

Warkany, J. (1986). Unusual children. *Developmental Neuropsychology, 2,* 147-154.

Chapter 11
The inner life of children from ethnic minorities

ALI EL-HADI

The impact of cultural differences

Introduction

The aim of this chapter is to review some of the theoretical and clinical issues which often present to professionals who are working with children from certain ethnic minorities. The focus here is on children from non-western ethnic minorities, that is from African or Asian cultural backgrounds, mostly children who are either first or second generation immigrant to Britain.

I hope to demonstrate how different cultural and religious traditions and practices influence psychological development. There is an inherent danger in any discussion about culture or ethnicity of stereotyping or giving a false impression of cultures as monolithic entities. In this context culture is seen as a dynamic creation, a complex set of accommodations and identifications. This is particularly relevant here because the children we are concerned with are part of families who have embarked on a process of ethnic redefinition and creation of new arrangements which do not fit either those which exist in their traditional setting i.e. their home country, or those in the new context i.e. Britain.

I shall only be dealing with individual psychological development from a psychoanalytic perspective and not with epidemiological data regarding the incidence or prevalence of psychological problems in such groups of children. I shall be drawing on literature from various disciplines, psychoanalysis, psychology, anthropology, sociology and mythology. I will be relying on my own clinical experience, in the field of child and family mental health for clinical and case examples. Finally, I will also draw on my own childhood experiences, growing up in a non-western culture in the Middle East, and some clinical experiences in that environment.

Definition

The inner world or inner life is a psychoanalytic concept. It is usually used to describe feelings, impulses, or wishes which can not be directly observed, but are mostly inferred, in the case of children, from their conversation and preoccupations and by observing their play, games and behaviour.

Culture, personality and development

I think it is relevant at the outset to review how psychoanalytic and psychodynamic theories view the interaction between psychological development and cultural and environmental factors. Freud in 1897 suggested an antagonism between man's instinctual demands and the social restrictions of his culture. He returned to the subject in *Civilisations and its discontents* in more detail. His insights have endured but they have been taken up and modified by other writers. There has been a shift in psychoanalytic thought, so that the focus has moved from an inherent opposition between wishes, drives and impulses of individual personality on the one hand and the repressive constraints of culture on the other, to exploring how such forces complement each other.

The American psychoanalyst, Erikson, expresses this well: 'Instead of emphasising what the pressures of social organisation are apt to deny the child, we wish to clarify what the social order may first grant to the infant as it keeps him alive and as in administering to his needs in specific ways, it introduces him to a particular cultural style.' It is more interesting to consider how particular psychological themes fit cultural styles.

The Indian psychoanalyst, Kakar, has pointed out the importance of the adaptive point of view in clarifying the evolutionary aspects of individual and cultural development. He pointed out the way in which western social scientists writing about non-western cultures e.g. Weber, have ignored the adaptive view, and instead have interpreted the social institutions such as the extended family as oppressive, hindering growth and independence or initiative in the individual. Kakar believes that such interpretations are related to historically determined, culturally specific western European ideals of the 'healthy personality'. The question is, how universal are the basic intra-psychic processes, e.g. conflict, defence in human development? It is difficult at present to answer this question satisfactorily, due to the dearth of cross cultural studies. However there is a small body of literature which is primarily descriptive and anecdotal on child development in non-western cultures from a psychoanalytic perspective. Most of the research carried out in Britain on children from ethnic minorities is epidemiological.

Let us now focus on Freud's basic notion about cultural influences on individual development. He recognised that cultural traditions are internalised during childhood in the individual super-ego; 'The super-ego of the child is not really built on the model of the parents, but the parents' super-ego. It takes over the same contents, it becomes the vehicle of traditions and of all the age long values which have been handed in this way from generation to generation'. However for Kakar, 'The roots of culture in the psyche penetrate below the crusty layer of the super-ego'. Such a view is now more widely shared by psychoanalytic writers e.g. Klein, Winnicott: they view the development of the ego as intrinsically linked to and interdependent on the society in which the infant is born and which is represented by the mother or the culturally sanctioned caretaker. The ego is the organising principle of the personality that differentiates and mediates between the 'I' and 'you', between what is 'inside' and what is 'outside'. Naturally a mother's response to a child depends on her own history, her own cultural image of motherhood and of the nature of the child.

Individual development

The psycho-social quality of infancy in western societies chronologically from birth to two years is extended in non-western cultures through to the age of four or five. Generally this phase is characterised by an intense attachment to the one caretaker who is often the mother. This is an exclusive attachment despite competition from siblings. So even in the extended family situation the child will still direct his or her demands and affections towards the mother, despite the presence of other figures and potential caretakers. Father does not play a significant part in this phase. Ideas from attachment theory, Bowlby and Ainsworth, have had a radical influence on child rearing or childcare practices in western European societies, where the nuclear family is the dominant family structure. It is not clear if such patterns of attachment behaviours are universal. Certainly my clinical experience suggests that child rearing practices in non-western cultures do not accept the notion of one exclusive attachment which develops during a critical period (6-18 months according to attachment theory). Children are left with or looked after by members of the extended family for periods of days or weeks. Periods of long separation from the main caretaker/mother are common and are not seen as harmful to the child's future development.

Case example

Nabilah was 22 months when she was brought to see me by her mother. The mother reported that Nabilah had become clingy and fearful since her family returned to London from the Middle East where they had been visiting their extended family. Mother gave the following history:

When Nabilah was three months old her mother, due to financial pressures, decided to work full time, so she took Nabilah home and left her with her own mother in the Middle East. Nabilah was looked after by the grandmother until she was about one year old when her mother decided to bring her back to London. The mother said how surprised and puzzled she was when Nabilah clung on to her grandmother, and remained quite distressed when they returned to their own home. Nabilah's mother told me that she thought Nabilah was too young to notice or be upset by such changes. She felt that the fact that Nabilah had been so well looked after and quietly indulged by the grandmother and herself was all that mattered. Therefore she was puzzled by Nabilah's behaviour and was worried in case there was something seriously wrong with her psychologically.

Nabilah's behaviour of course could be seen as evidence of an insecure pattern of attachment, and this would suggest that this developmental process is universal to human development. However it is difficult to generalise from single cases. By the age of four or five the child begins to move away psychologically and confront the tasks of separation and individuation. The close attachment during this period is enhanced by the physical closeness of the infant to the mother e.g. it is customary for the child to sleep in the mother's bed or by the mother's side at night. There is a great deal of intense physical contact between the infant and the mother, and other caretaker figures in the extended family. The caretakers will move to pacify the child at the slightest whimper or sign of distress. During mother's absence it could be an older sister, an aunt or a grandmother who will perform the tasks of soothing, cleaning etc.

Case example

Gurpreet, who was three-and-a-half years old, was referred by the family's GP after mounting concerns about her behaviour by the staff at the nursery where she attended and by her young parents. She was described as disobedient, not following the parents' instructions, and had tantrums when she did not get her own way. At the interview with the whole family, I noticed that she had little speech, and behaved in a determined and controlling manner. She would not let her younger brother play with the toys in the room, and at times was physically aggressive towards him. The parents' reaction was mostly either to appease or distract her. The impression was of a child who expects her demands and needs to be met or gratified instantaneously without any delay. The history was quite relevant and, I think, highlights the above observations regarding beliefs about child development and child rearing practices. The family had lived with father's family in an extended family household until six months prior to the referral, when they moved to their own home. In that household the paternal grandmother was the authority on childcare, Gurpreet's mother and the other daughter-in-law referred to her. At a later interview with her and the family, she explained how she thought that Gurpreet was too young to tolerate any frustration or understand any boundaries. I noticed that whenever Gurpreet got into a conflict, e.g. when someone said no to her, and she started to get angry or have a tantrum, her mother would place her on her knee, cuddle her and try to distract her by offering her sweets or food. The work with the family focused on getting the parents to realise that Gurpreet was old enough to understand boundaries and limits,and would not be harmed if they were firm and consistent with her. This might sound as if one is imposing Eurocentric or western views about childcare on the family. However, in Gurpreet's case parental management seemed to be problematic or inappropriate; it did not help her to adjust to the nursery environment or prepare her for life outside the cosy and indulgent atmosphere of the family. In practice one has to tread a delicate course between respecting parents' beliefs and views which are different from the dominant culture and helping them to change their practice when they run into problems.

Such child rearing practices might, I think, help to reduce separation anxiety aroused by brief separations. Unlike western cultures there is total indulgence of the infant/child until he or she is four or five years old. For example, feeding is on demand, usually breast feeding. My experience working on paediatric wards in London showed that feeding is an area of potential difficulties. Parents will insist on physically feeding children as old as three or four years old, rather than leave the child to feed themselves. This will often create conflict with the nursing staff who regard this practice as inappropriate. Feeding difficulties or failure to thrive are often attributed, by professionals, to such practices. In talking with these parents, their main concern seems to be that the child is likely to make a mess with his food if they are left to feed themselves. They believe that they are too young to be able to use cutlery appropriately. I think this is also about non-western cultures, not emphasising independence or separateness for children, as is the case in western cultures.

Kakar observes that an Indian child tends to experience his mother almost totally as a 'good mother'. He refers to his clinical experiences in treating Indian men: how at the beginning of therapy they rarely express dislike, fear or contempt for their mothers. He believes this is also reflected in Indian literature, where mother is portrayed in her benign and nurturing aspects with nostalgia, uncomplicated by the slightest trace of hostility or guilt. It seems the idealisation of mother is more noticeable in male children and men, whilst girls or women describe mother as an earthy presence, not benign but always there. This theme is also reflected in Indian mythology where loneliness and separation are linked to a desire for and a yearning for the presence of the 'good mother' which is portrayed as a an enduring lifelong presence for the individual. One can see the link with the idealised mother/child relationship. Kakar contrasts this with the view held in western cultures, that yearning for the loved one could be seen as 'childish' or 'immature'. One possible negative consequence of such early experience is that children might grow up to be helpless, dependent adults unable to cope without their family.

Western psychoanalytic and sociological writers have described the behaviour of adults in non-western societies as 'regressive strivings', or 'oral fixation'. However Kakar sees it as more to do with a different model of human relationships which emphasises the need to avoid isolation or share the responsibility for one's life with others. However, separation anxiety is more likely to stem not from indulgence or spoiling but from the time in infancy when mother withdraws her attention. Anthropological observations based on retrospective accounts from adults suggest that this is a widely used method of disciplining young children. More significant in non-western cultures is the use of threats, so it is quite common for a mother or caretaker to tell a child that if he doesn't behave she will leave him or that he or she will be taken by a ghost. Such threats of ghosts, goblins, locking-up in a dark room, or threats of isolation and abandonment form the basis for separation anxiety and are used for disciplining children.

Psychosexual development

The intensity and duration of the mother-infant relationship in infancy has special implications for psychosexual development, particularly in a patriarchal society. I think the cultures we are concerned with here can be described as patriarchal. So male children are favoured and women are devalued. For a mother the birth of a male child will crystallise her motherly identity and enhance her status in the family. In turn she is likely to perceive the son as a kind of saviour and nurture him almost with reverence. It is common to find families with six or seven children where the five older children are girls and the youngest is a boy, so having more children in order to achieve the socially desirable aim of having a son. Sometimes if this doesn't happen after six children or more, a husband will leave his wife to remarry in order to achieve this aim. In certain Islamic societies, where bigamy is religiously sanctioned, the husband will have a second wife who can bear him a son.

It is likely that at an unconscious level the mother will demand that the child serve as an object for her own unfulfilled desires and wishes which might in turn conflict with his own. This could lead to feelings of confusion and helplessness in the child who feels overwhelmed by mother's closeness but unable to get away. Anthropological writers note that in all ancient cultures the fantasy image of the 'bad mother' lives at the opposite pole of the 'good mother'. It is likely that deep psychic ambivalence towards the mother is quite universal. But in the cultures we are concerned with here it is characterised by intense pervasiveness. It is possible to speculate that the apparent and conscious idealisation of the mother is evidence of repressed powerful hostile and negative feelings.

I would like to turn to another and still related aspect of the non-western cultures under discussion here. In such patriarchal cultures women are often discriminated against, and devalued. As a function of the power struggle in the relationship between the sexes, mothers will struggle with strong unconscious ambivalence towards their male children. In such cultures the expectations and the image of the 'good mother' implies a woman who is very close to and finds emotional fulfilment in the relationship with her children rather than the marital relationship. An implication of this is that mothers are likely to seek satisfaction in the relationship with their sons. This is combined with the social pressures to repudiate sexuality with the advent of motherhood, not the long periods of post-partum taboo on sexual intercourse and the confinement to women's quarters. This inevitably leads to intensification of erotic feelings towards the male child. So we arrive at an image of the 'bad mother' which combines both aggressive, destructive and erotic themes. The degree to which one theme will predominate over the other is more culturally specific.

Kakar observes that in Indian cultures it is the erotic or seductive theme which dominates. He cites the recurring theme in Indian mythology of the woman who turns men into eunuchs e.g. the castrating women in the Arundhati myth.

Kakar describes the following situation. The displacement of the mother's sexual longings from the husband to the male child poses the most difficult dilemma for the son. Mother's catering arouses intense feelings of anxiety. The child's dilemma is intense as he is still physically and emotionally dependent on his mother, but his contact with her arouses intense feelings which threaten to engulf him. As he gets older, he feels torn between his dependency on his mother and his need to get away, in order to protect himself. His feelings of wariness and the need to escape leave him in fear of mother's anger and disappointment in him, as he realises that he cannot satisfy her unconscious desires. Fears of being engulfed or devoured become focused on mother's body specially her genitals. This is exemplified by childhood fantasies about female genitals represented in concrete, frightening imagery e.g. a chamber full of poison causing death in the sexual act. This is also reflected in popular mythology, in which a woman character is portrayed with teeth in her vagina or womb who embraces people to devour them. To conclude, the sexual presence of the 'bad mother' looms large in the unconscious experience of male children.

Clinical experience with adult male patients suggests that an important consequence of this is heightened anxiety regarding actual or feared sexual impotence. The almost collective fear of female mature sexuality accounts for the age gap between husband and wife, something that is seen as desirable socially and culturally. It is also linked, in my opinion, to the practice of female circumcision, which is widely practised in some parts of the Middle East and Africa. The practice is aimed at lessening or destroying sexual pleasure and reducing the temptation as a way of safeguarding the daughter and the family honour. I think at an unconscious level this can be seen as an attack on, and a revenge against dangerous and threatening women's sexuality.

The Oedipal situation

Freud postulated that all children between the ages of three and five go through a phase of development which is dominated by unconscious feelings and wishes about possessing the parent of the opposite sex and eliminating the same sex parent. According to Freud, the Oedipal phase is a universal phenomenon built in phylogenetically. Melanie Klein believed that Oedipal manifestations may be present earlier, during the first year of life. Resolution of the Oedipus complex is by identification with the parent of the same sex and temporary renunciation of the parent of the opposite sex.

However, Deleuze and Guattari have attacked the primacy or universality of the Oedipal pattern in theory and argued that the Oedipal triangle (father, mother, child) already exists as part of the modern bourgeois self-conception. It is less an existing social structure than an ideology.

Kakar believes that the resolution of the Oedipal conflict in Indian culture for boys is different from that in western societies. 'Carrying the weight of a strong pre-Oedipal feminine identification with mother and lacking a vivid, partisan father with whom to identify, the boy is more likely to adopt a position of 'non-partisan' feminine submission towards all older men in the family'. This resolution by means of submission is different from the resolution in western societies where the boy's aggressive feelings towards his rival/father triggers anxiety which is reduced by his identification with his father. Kakar believes that this situation leads to the passive - receptive attitude adopted by boys, and later men, towards authority figures.

Ozturk, a Turkish psychotherapist writing about the special relationship between mothers and sons in Turkish society makes interesting and relevant observations. He acknowledges that the special or privileged position of the male child might be related to other socio-economic factors, still it has important consequences for the psychosexual development of boys. He links the close idealised relationship between mother and son with what he observes clinically, that boys or men present as self-centred, selfish and with a contemptuous attitude towards women. He describes the mother's preoccupation with hopes and fears regarding her son's future happiness in finding a suitable bride. He warns the psychotherapist, who is faced with this situation clinically, against formulation based entirely on psychoanalytic understanding i.e. in terms of unresolved Oedipal conflict or anxieties. He believes that there are socio-economic factors at play here, e.g. the economic and financial value of children, especially sons.

He gives an example of a 24-year-old man who presented asking for help and requested admission to hospital. The history was that he had fallen in love with a women and wanted to marry her but felt guilty about leaving his mother to marry. So he thought admission to hospital might provide him with a solution to his dilemma. The father died when he was seven,and there was an older brother who still lived at home. Ozturk describes how during a family session, the patient was able to express his anxieties regarding his future. His older brother supported his plans to have his own separate family, saying that he wished his brother would be successful in doing something which he himself had not achieved. At this point the mother said that she too supported his plans to get married, and wished that her older son would do likewise, so she could get a job working in the hospital as a nurse. Ozturk, comments on how such an action on the mother's part will serve to increase the son's feelings of self blame and guilt, given the social and cultural traditions and expectations in a traditional and conservative society. But when he put this to the mother, she vehemently denied the implications of such action; she soon became quite agitated and hysterical and fainted. Apparently the son eventually got married but compromised by having a house next door to his mother's so he could continue to meet the expectations of looking after her.

According to Ozturk, another example in which social and cultural factors are as significant as psychodynamic ones is the long term effect of male circumcision. In Islamic societies, boys are circumcised before the age of five. Ozturk believes the long term psychological effects of such experience, as observed in the clinical setting, are more to do with the socio-cultural meaning of the event or ritual rather than at an unconscious level, i.e. an initiation ceremony or ritual rather than intensifying Oedipal and castration anxieties.

Identity and ego development

In the non-western cultures we are concerned with here, ego development takes place according to a different model from the western model. This stems from the infant child's early experiences, where the mother/caretaker is more likely to accede to the child's wishes rather than attempt to control or help them to control them. Unlike western cultures, there is no gradual experience of frustration or disappointment, instead a state of mother-infant symbiosis persisting until the child is four or five. Luciani makes observations about Egyptian children that ' until they are six or seven they are greatly indulged and given free rein, for no one can tolerate making a child unhappy', and 'parents believe that they can remedy any unacceptable behaviour later in a child's life'. Thus separation or differentiation takes place chronologically later and results in a weaker ego, a less clear and weaker sense of self. This also leads to the persistence of modes of thinking which are, psychoanalytically speaking, described as primary i.e. concrete and magical, as opposed to secondary process thinking which is abstract and based on reality. Primary process thinking is characteristically dependent on visual and sensory images, unlike secondary process thinking which is conceptual and abstract. So one can observe primary process thinking in older children: unlike children in western cultures they are encouraged to continue to live in a mythical, magical world for a longer period. This is also reflected in the common or wider cultural beliefs in ghosts, spirits, and possession. This is well expressed and represented in innumerable folk tales in which trees speak and animals have human characteristics. There is also the belief in nuances of non-verbal communications, i.e. the 'inner eye', and the strong belief in the 'evil eye ' and the destructive influence of envy. To compensate for this I think the developing and undifferentiated ego is supported, in dealing with the demands of outer reality and to control inner reality, by social institutions and organisations. For the young child it is the family network, not just the nuclear family. This includes an array of uncles, aunts, grand-parents. Activities such as reasoning, weighing pros and cons are group activities rather than individual ones. The emphasis is on the individual as a member of a group rather than on his own. Linked to this is the myriad of rules and regulations which govern social interactions and relationships and which make the experience of social relating encounters predictable.

The social institutions or organisations which govern adult life tend to reflect childcare practices in a given society. Attitude towards authority is a good example. The hierarchical nature of the extended family and the cultures we are concerned with here are reflected in the way children are praised for compliance and submission and subtly or blatantly punished for independence. Hierarchical status is linked to gender and age. So in an extended family environment children's concerns are tolerated, but not necessarily acted on or used to influence decision making.

Children learn to avoid confrontation as they internalise the hierarchical tradition. Open expression of aggression or anger is frowned upon and discouraged, so is critical questioning. Instead, one observes in older children and young people a sense of helpless and impotent rage. The anxiety about losing the nurturance and approval of older parental figures in the extended family makes the compliance stance much safer.

Clinical and practical issues

There is a dearth of literature on dynamic psychotherapy with children and adolescents from Asian and African cultural backgrounds. This might be linked to the wider phenomenon that patients from non-western cultures are seldom referred for psychotherapy. The debate about psychotherapy and non-western cultures is beyond the scope of this chapter. So for our purpose here I shall summarise some of the issues identified by clinicians who are working with such children. I shall use my own clinical experience and refer to examples from my own practice to illustrate some of the points made.

Cultural and racial identity

For children from non-western cultures or certain ethnic groups living in Britain the question of cultural identity is quite complex. Cultural identity is both inherited and passed down the generations, or something created from history and experience: no one can construct an identity for themselves. As Andreou put it: 'Such children have to cope with being different and feelings of difference. This stems from their experience of society which could be markedly different from their experience at home or the experience of their upbringing'.

The following case illustrates this:

Dolly was a 15-year-old Bangladeshi girl who was admitted to a medical ward after taking an overdose of paracetamol. When I saw her on the ward it emerged that she had been removed from her family and placed with an English foster mother after she disclosed that her father had sexually abused her. She took the overdose following a weekend visit to her family. Over a series of sessions Dolly's difficulties unravelled. She spoke about how she had become more attached to her English foster mother, which caused conflict with her own mother, who made her feel that she was disloyal to her family and culture. Dolly spoke about her conflict and turmoil between her identification with her home and family culture and traditions and her attachment to and identification with the outside world, friends and school culture. She told me that was proud of being Asian and Muslim, but found this to be in conflict with getting on and being successful socially. Her experiences with the foster family intensified her dilemma especially as she became quite close to the foster mother. She had tried to keep up with her cultural background with the help of the foster mother, who was very sensitive to this issue, by attending language and Islamic evening classes. After Dolly had been seen on several occasions, she returned home to her family and started attending a group for Asian girls who had been abused.

For children from Asian and African cultures feeling different or being different sometimes focuses on physical appearance, particularly skin colour. In Dolly's case it was also dress, ways of behaving in public, music and interests.

For Maxime, interests and research in the area of identity have neglected racial and cultural identity, and have been mainly concerned with self-concepts or self-esteem. She believes that personal identity consists of universal components which must contain racial identity. Maxime emphasises the importance of race and skin colour and regards both as central to the formation of personal identity. She believes that professionals who are working with children from different ethnic groups, particularly African and Asian, need to recognise the importance of nurturing racial identity. She believes this to be central to the psychological wellbeing of such children. Maxime's central thesis is that 'For these children the 'ideal self' is seen as synonymous with white Caucasian identity'. So for many of such children to achieve positive identity involves rejecting their own inferior racial identity. She refers to a process of 'self-hatred' which can be observed in 'black children', which is a form of 'racial identity confusion/crisis'. She describes specific therapeutic work to deal with this which proceeds along five stages.

I believe there are inherent dangers in seeing racial or cultural identity as determined by skin colour. Such a view ignores the subtle differences and variations within such a category as 'black'. Of course the impact of racism and prejudice cannot and should not be ignored. But describing a whole range of cultures and ethnic groups as 'black' or 'white' is problematic.

Case example

Zahir was a 16-year-old Pakistani boy who presented with a range of concerns about his behaviour from his parents and teachers. The parents' main concerns were that he took no notice of them and showed no respect for their boundaries. At the initial interview with the family only the parents came; Zahir refused to attend for the appointment. Zahir, as the eldest son of three children, has been quite a disappointment to his parents. They were concerned not only by his rudeness and his attitude of disrespect but also about the way he dressed and his haircut, and the music he listened to. Father was concerned that Zahir did not observe Islamic restrictions about drinking alcohol and eating pork, nor did he escort him to the mosque on Fridays and important religious festivals. The parents felt that he had turned his back on the family's culture and religious tradition. They feared that he had become totally identified with the local western youth culture. At the next interview with Zahir and only his father, Zahir seemed despondent at what he saw as the gulf between himself and his parents. The father kept criticising the way Zahir was dressed, and the fact that he spent little time at home with the family. Father presented as quite a simple man who was quietly dismayed at the way his son was turning out. He spoke about a plan to send Zahir to their home town in Pakistan, to ensure that he continued his education away from distractions. Zahir reacted to the idea with scorn.

At the next interview the father came escorted by a teacher and youth leader from the local mosque, but without Zahir. This man explained that the father had approached him for help and had also asked him to help me understand the situation. He told me that Zahir's father, being uneducated and of humble origin in Pakistan, had difficulty keeping up with his son or offering him a positive role model as someone to emulate. He had met Zahir and invited him to join the youth group in the mosque and Zahir had responded positively. We agreed that he would keep in contact with Zahir and the father on an informal basis. At the next interview, Zahir was present. I learned from the father that Zahir's behaviour had changed at home and he was quite surprised when, on the occasion of an important religious festival, Zahir got up early to escort him to the mosque. Father sounded more reassured and less fearful about Zahir's future. It seems that through the contact with the youth leader and others at the mosque Zahir had found a way to reconcile himself with his family culture and tradition. In turn his family had become more tolerant of him.

Separation and leaving home

In some extended family settings the close psychological identification with the group or family can render the task of separation or leaving home quite difficult. This is because to move away from the family, as well as causing a feeling of insecurity, carries a sense of loss of 'significant others' who provide a sense of continuity and affirm inner continuity. The practice of adolescents or young people leaving home to live independently is almost entirely restricted to western cultures. Indeed, in my experience with non-western ethnic groups in this country, young people still do or are expected to live at home until they get married.

Of course in some eastern and middle eastern societies there are social and economic reasons for individuals remaining at home with their families. My own experiences in the Middle East are that attempts by the adolescent to move away or establish a sense of separateness from the family often result in a psychotic breakdown. Kakar, writing about Indian culture, has observed that it is not uncommon for family members to accompany the adult patient for the first and subsequent interviews and to complain about his autonomy as a symptom of the problem. This is consistent with my own experience. Of course the extended family provides protection and supports some kind of life insurance. So an individual's identity is bound up with his family's standing and reputation. In that context individual actions are not seen as reflecting aspiration or individual efforts. Instead they are interpreted in the context of the family's reputation in the wider society. To conform and remain part of the family is admired, to deviate and strike out on one's own is scorned.

Case example

Rajvinder was a 15-year-old Indian girl who was brought to see me by her mother because of a long history of non-compliance or what her mother saw as rebellious behaviour. On occasions when the mother felt provoked by Rajvinder's behaviour she resorted to physical chastisement, something she knew was illegal. Rajvinder used this to threaten her mother saying that she would report her to the local authority, which left the mother feeling more undermined. The main cause for the mother's deep concern was that Rajvinder, unlike her two sisters, did not seem to care about her own family or what she might be doing to their standing within the extended family and their local community, i.e. the threats to inform the authorities or the police. Mother cited the example of Rajvinder's dress and make-up. She could not understand how Rajvinder seemed only interested in furthering her own interest, refusing to take into account the family's concerns. Rajvinder saw her mother as completely out of touch with her needs, which she felt to be legitimate concerns of someone of her age. At the interview battle lines seemed to be clearly drawn, leaving little room for compromise. All attempts to get either party to negotiate failed and in the end Rajvinder was removed from home and accommodated by the local authority.

Unlike Rajvinder's extended family which seemed riven by infighting and factionalism, having a harmonious and a closely knit extended family could enhance individual merit and identity. Another important aspect here concerns cultural and religious rituals which are means for families to strengthen and extend family ties and bonds. This applies to big events, such as celebrating marriages or births, and also to small events as in certain Indian cultures e.g. a boy's first haircut. Such events reaffirm an individual's position in and belonging to the family, and confirm the belief that family ties are the most durable and reliable of all social relations.

Conclusion

I have tried to describe in fairly general terms common patterns or paradigms for certain cultures as they affect or influence the individual psychological development of children. I have been only concerned with what I have described as non-western cultures. I realise the inherent danger in stereotyping and presenting cultures in some caricature forms. It is imperative, therefore, that the reader bears this in mind.

References

Andreou, C. (1992). Inner and outer reality in children and adolescents. In R.Littlewood and J. Kareem (Eds.), *Intercultural Therapy*. Oxford: Blackwell.

Ainsworth, M.D.S.(1982). Attachment: retrospect and prospect. In C.M. Parkes and J.Stevenson-Hinde, (Eds.), *The place of attachment in human behaviour*. Tavistock.

Bowlby, J.(1966). *Attachment and Loss, Vol.1 Attachment*. London: Hogarth Press.

Deleuze, G. and Guttari, F. (1984). *Anti-Oedipus. Capitalism and Schizophrenia*. London: The Athlone Press.

Erikson, E.H. (1950). *Childhood and Society*.New York: W.W.Norton.

Freud,S. (1913). Totems and Taboo. *Standard Edition* vol.13. London: Hogarth Press.

Freud, S.(1916). Introductory Lectures on Psychoanalysis.In J. Strachey (Ed.) *The Standard Edition of the Complete Works of Sigmund Freud*. London: Hogarth Press.

Freud, S. (1930). Civilisations and its discontents. *Standard Edition* Vol. 21. London: Hogarth Press.

Kakar, S. (1981). *The Inner world: A psychoanalytic study of childhood and society in India*. Oxford: Oxford University Press.

Kakar, S. (1985). Psychoanalysis and Non-Western Cultures. *International Review of Psychoanalysis*, **12**, 441.

Kareem, J. (1993). The Nafsiyat Intercultural Centre:Ideas and Experiences in Intercultural Therapy. In: R. Littlewood and J. Kareem (Eds.). *Intercultural Therapy*. Oxford: Blackwell.

Klein, M. (1932). *The Psychoanalysis of Children*. London: Hogarth Press.

Littlewood, R. (1992). Towards an Intercultural Therapy. In: R. Littlewood and J. Kareem (Eds.) *Intercultural Therapy, Themes, Interpretations and Practices*. Oxford: Blackwell.

Luciani, D. (1982). Reflections on child development and primary health care in Egypt. Unpublished.

Ozturk, O. M. (1993). Psychotherapy and Culture Sensitivity. *Cultural Psychology*, **15**(4), 48.

Maxime, J. (1993). The Importance of Racial Identity for the Psychological Wellbeing of Black Children. *Association of Child Psychology and Psychiatry Review, Newsletter*, **15**(4), 173

Taylor,W. S. (1948). Basic Personality in Orthodox Hindu Culture Patterns. *Journal of Abnormal Psychology*, **43**(3).

Thomas, L. (1994). How can psychotherapy be relevant to black people? Paper presented at Working Across Cultures Conference at St. Georges Hospital, London, October.

Winnicott, D.W. (1971). *Playing and Reality*.London: Tavistock Publications.

Chapter 12
The art of communicating with secretive children

ALICE MORRIS

But then I promised ne'er to tell
How could I break my word?
So go your way and I'll go mine . . .

(Emily Dickinson)

. . . my parents would have about two haemorrhages apiece if I told anything pretty personal about them. They're quite touchy about anything like that, especially my father. They're nice and all - I'm not saying that - but they're also touchy as hell.

(Salinger)

The secret conflict in *Hamlet* is so effectively concealed, says Freud, that it was left to him to unearth it (1985). The play reveals the enormous capacity of a secret to cause chaos, madness and death; its tendrils entwine themselves around the psyche, paralysing action and contaminating creative impulses. Hamlet's great talent and promise are spoiled by holding the terrible secret inside him.

A child may become secretive because she or he possesses information which it is considered necessary to withhold from others, which often focuses around a stigmatizing condition. The need for secrecy may arise in the child's mind because a surface level secret in the family is seen as being rather shameful and must not be told, for fear that the family may suffer from negative consequences and adverse evaluation. A child may be encouraged to disclose information with a trusted practitioner which will enable a particular type of practical help or advice to be given, particularly when the issue seems to fall within the range of 'normal', or acceptable difference; some secrets are, indeed, pleasant to communicate even if there is an edge or 'frisson' of discomfort around them. However, when the secret is loaded with complex unconscious material which has accrued within family systems over a long period, or has its origins in painful and incomplete personal development arising from the primal relationship with the initial caregivers, it has a much more complex aetiology which will require more indirect methods to unravel. Pincus and Dare (1978) see secrets as being:

> . . . private to one family member; or tacitly shared with others or unconsciously subscribed to by all family members, often from generation to generation, until they become a myth.

Whether originating in the individual or in families, secrets have a facility to function in an invasive way, like deposits, the intruding psychic 'chemical' entering the network drip by drip, until a cumulative mass is formed, layer upon layer, developing the power to inhabit the mind in a parasitic way. The more threatening and dangerous it becomes, as if calcified, the more the recipient gets caught up in a circle of denial of its existence, causing the secret to receive yet more deposits, energy, and potential for greater disruption and pain.

Another characteristic of secrets is that they belong in the deep recesses of the mind which are associated with primitive development, because their existence is connected with life and death issues, destruction and annihilation. Freud (1986) links the origin of secrets with the uncanny and the grotesque in our natures, with something which ought to have remained hidden but which has come to light, often giving the impression that the bearer may have 'secret injurious powers', a capacity that disturbed children sometimes feel they possess, regarding themselves as being dangerous unless their secret remains hidden. The type of communication required to address this labyrinth of secrets, particularly as it operates in the lives of young people showing disturbed and delinquent behaviour and experiencing emotional difficulties, is the particular focus of this chapter.

The quality of the techniques used to challenge and break up secrets housed in the confused internal world of these youngsters is as important as the actual methods used. Many practitioners have a natural way of communicating with youngsters who find the very act of communication difficult and a threat to the secret part of the self: some use humour in a startling and zany way; others use a kind of 'ordinary' informative and amiable conversation, a kind of infill, as a parent uses to a toddler, eager to expand her or his knowledge about the world; many disturbed children will not have experienced this particular form of holding. For some this filling up space with dialogue which expects nothing in return is a gift they never had and offers a temporary respite from the void within themselves.

Several writers emphasize approaches which are lateral, indirect and unexpected (Skynner, 1987; Laing, 1959; Pitt-Aikens and Thomas Ellis, 1990). These have the potential to break through ordinary consciousness to jolt the unconscious processes and states, a task which is central to this kind of work. Skynner (1987) speaks of the need to address the fantasy at the core of the magical thinking by which many families are seduced, to startle people into:

> . . . a new awareness of reality by . . . dissipating the fantasy that constantly
> engulfs and controls . . . by showing how shadowy and unreal it is.

He refers to the use of methods which have an effect on entrenched behaviour and unconscious blocks, such as paradox, double binds, koan-like questions, crazy statements, zany interventions and antithesis - tasks and instructions which break up established structures and shock the family out of their dreams and self-fulfilling negative prophecies into a 'level of higher awareness'. The character of the fool in *King Lear* is a personification of this process. Using nonsense rhymes, riddles, songs and paradoxical questions, he forces reality on the king until he begins to make contact with his unconscious. Lyward, at Finchdean Manor, based a whole provision on this non-linear approach, using myths, stories, music and idiosyncratic interactions to break into the inner lives of the boys there.

In a therapeutic community setting, Dockar-Drysdale (1993) discusses the particular form of communication she used with primary-age disturbed and secretive children. She emphasizes a form of 'being' with the children, as their therapist, in which she makes adaptation to them, rather than providing interpretations - they may have built up such elaborate defence systems around the secretive part of their nature that direct action and interpretation will be experienced as exploitations, which may be felt as a 'terrifying maternal object' (Winnicott, 1971). Winnicott also observes the dangers when the therapist makes 'clever' interpretations based on her or his own agenda without following cues from the child, thereby losing sight of the child's position and need. This tactic has been taken to its extreme in some recent abuse cases concerning 'false memory', where there has been some question as to the motives of the therapists. Mistimed interventions 'outside the ripeness of the material are indoctrination' and will produce compliance (Winnicott, 1971). The technique developed at the Mulberry Bush involves the therapist being aware of the interpretation but responding to it at a deeper level of meaning, by picking up the emotional content, the 'affect' of the communication and responding to this without the exchange at any moment losing its emotional impact.

It is helpful to be aware of the need to address problems according to when the environment failed the child, for the point at which traumatic interruption has taken place will determine the nature of defence mechanisms used by the child (Dockar-Drysdale, 1993). Nevertheless, there are characteristics common to disturbed children which produce a comprehensive picture for which a generalised treatment plan can be formulated. This can be based on characteristics arising from Klein's paranoid-schizoid phase of development (see appendix); if these character-features are left unresolved and unworked through at the primary stage they may take on a new life and energy at the time of adolescence. A portrait of the delinquent character may be drawn from this early formation of characteristics as so many of the symptoms can be seen to have their sources here. Problems and secrets arising from the depressive position, such as loss and depression, give rise to types of secrets which are by their nature more accessible to a less specialised form of treatment, being based on a certain amount of earlier integration, and may be more readily worked through in the more usual psychotherapeutic and analytical methods. This is never clear-cut, for as Klein (1988) states, there is no clear division between the two stages of development, which interact and intermingle in the gradual process of modification and synthesis of inner and outer phenomena. Symptoms and syndromes predominantly based on these earlier omissions in the paranoid-schizoid phase need more specialist approaches, often involving a team and/or adapted environment in addition to personal therapy.

One feature common to secretive syndromes is that of fantasy, or 'phantasy' to use the Kleinian spelling, distinguishing the unconscious type of fantasy from the conscious. The work of Melanie Klein is particularly helpful for work with EBD children because of her emphasis on the presence of pathology even in normal development, the necessity for the analyst to draw out and accept negative feelings, and the awareness of the aggressive characteristics she attributes to young babies, an idea which at first was considered exaggerated by her contemporaries. Practitioners working with delinquent and disturbed youngsters may often find no other terms in which to understand the powerful material in the form of panic, aggression, and destructive annihilatory rages which are hurled at them. She discovered in her work that children relate to the whole world through their unconscious phantasies, creating a kind of magical thinking unmodified by reality. Nothing is seen simply as it is: instead some sort of unconscious phantasy is added to every perception of the world, structuring, colouring and giving meaning and significance to it (Segal, 1992). Phantasies give 'body' and expression to emotional states, bringing them alive. Klein used the concept of phantasy to describe the active and 'concrete' nature of manifestations of inner life - the child imagines them as literally existing. Pincus and Dare (1978) consider that many secrets arise at adolescence, from feelings and attached phantasies which surround a child's relationship with the parent and the opposite sex - this stage echoing the earlier one when the baby looked to the father to take on the primary responsibility for the mother and save her 'from the baby's own attacks'(Segal, 1992). Bly (1990) speaks of the necessity for a boy to 'resonate to the masculine frequency', but laments that this does not happen as much as it should; we have not yet seen the real impact of the loss of fathers on their sons through divorce but the phantasies surrounding this wound must give rise to secrets which threaten the very essence of their developing manhood.

A child who has not managed to separate out the reality and phantasy of these early stages may at adolescence present a mysterious, ineffable air as described by Fairburn (1994). He depicts a secretive youngster who has a 'sense of inner superiority' and feels different from others. Such a child shows pathological behaviour arising from schizoid tendencies, but Fairburn claims that it still remains a significant factor in the unconscious situation in less schizoid states. His table of the sources of secret qualities is useful in showing how internalized secretive material manifests itself: (my emphasis)

1. The development of the conviction that *their mother did not value and love them as persons in their own right,* either through apparent indifference or possessiveness and emotional dependency.
2. They suffered a sense of *deprivation and inferiority* which caused extreme *fixation* on the mother.
3. The libidinal attitude caused by this fixation gave rise to dependency, self-preservation and narcissism as a defence against *the severe threat to the ego* presented by the anxiety of this situation of loss.
4. *The internalization of objects and part-objects became excessive* so the child failed to move towards a state of integration.
5. There has resulted a *general over-valuation of the internal at the expense of the external world.*

The inner necessity responsible for the secretive exterior is partly determined by the loss of, or fear of losing, internalized objects which appear infinitely precious - as precious as life itself. Much energy is expended in trying to keep the inner life intact, but this is not always a success - it will spill over into ordinary life by some means or other. It is made all the more potent and inscrutable by the fact that, on the conscious level, it seems unknown and unknowable to the carrier of this secret.

Bion's (1967) theory of alpha and beta elements helps to explain the essential dynamic of a secret and the havoc it can wreak on the psyche. Alpha elements are based on a function of the psyche to transform sense impressions (images, emotions, senses, sounds) of all raw elements into alpha ones, which are used for dreaming and thinking, and storable in the normal way. The beta elements are 'accretions of stimuli' which can be ejected, relived or got rid of into other people or re-experienced, sometimes with repetition compulsion. Under normal circumstances, the mother will convert these beta element projections into a form assimilable by the child, rather like a mother bird predigests the food for her fledglings, but should this fail to happen they will be driven into secret pockets in the psyche and felt as dangerous objects liable to destroy all around them. Bion (1967) explains the energy and potential for destruction inherent in these pockets, giving the example of a man who may murder his parents and so feel free to love because the anti-sexual parents are supposed by this act to be evacuated. Dockar-Drysdale (1993) calls this tendency an 'integrating round a hole' and relates a fascinating account of how her conversations with a young boy allowed him to make links between his early life and his delinquency. In his baby state he was excitedly waiting for food but giving up when none was forthcoming. However, the excited part of him remained alive in a separate compartment later demanding a repetition of the excitement and gratification through his delinquency.

In general terms the creation of a secret causes splitting mechanisms to operate which, if the original need remains unmet, will recur at later stages of development and will not change until they are actually met (Dockar-Drysdale, 1993). The split-off parts are inclined to turn into a serious dissociation which in turn causes the development of false-self syndromes and false-self relating (Winnicott, 1971; Laing, 1959). Breger (1989) describes this process vividly when writing about Dostoyevsky and in particular his literary creation, Godyalkin, in the story, *The Double* (1846). As is the case with many disturbed children, the split in Dostoyevsky's own nature manifested itself strongly in adolescence, where the outward young man was secretive and isolated, going through the motions of the role allotted to him but remaining aloof and uncommitted to it. In *The Double* the split-off, shameful parts of the hero's nature are imagined as residing in another person, so he encounters another version of himself in a way that seems real to him. Another life is going on in terms of the dissociated, cut-off and rejected part because it contains unacceptable shadow qualities. The substantial, tangible nature of this abstraction is highlighted by Breger's description of this process as a 'concretization of projection'; a theme which is explored in detail by Otto Rank (1971) who traces its use in literature, showing how it is used by those who are unsure of their identity. The artist may present her or his creation in an acceptable form, 'justifying the irrational in the midst of our over-rationalised civilization', while the 'neurotic individual' is left to deal with the material by other less socially acceptable or prestigious means.

This state of affairs can be compared with what happens to many disturbed children when a part of their character gets away from them, appearing to take on an autonomous identity and existence, which may be hated by another part of them. This may express itself through all sorts of derring do, criminal and antisocial and daredevil deeds, attacks on others and things, essentially based on adrenalin rushes, which seem to promise excitement and 'buzz' and may divert attention from the more demanding and difficult task of ego development. This is a diversion from having to painfully face those sides of themselves whose energy is in fact partially dissipated through the acts themselves. Whilst this is happening the youngster may for a time escape and be freed from the intense anxiety states which characterise her or his inner life; temporary oblivion may take away the confrontation with the gap inside. Because this fantasy or inner-self state has existed in isolation it has not been tempered by reality testing. It can therefore remain grandiose, heroic, egocentric and omnipotent and appear to be possessed of great powers; in the youngster's being the embryonic identity hovers, looking for something to attach to which might offer a seductive promise of doing justice to its exceptional qualities and provide a fulfilling way of being. Failing this, she or he is left to face the frightening inner emptiness and the feeling that there is nothing to give anyone - 'the austerity and fear of loss in relating' (Wood, 1984). Artists such as Magritte, Bosch, Chagall, Salvador Dali and Escher create hallucinatory, fantastical and enigmatic landscapes and drawings which often fascinate disturbed children. These

> . . . evoke disturbing echoes from a world of unpredictable objects and people, having no permanent nature, size or substance, location nor relationship with other objects; and where space is a mystery. (Wood, 1984)

Conforming to social norms and doing things within the infrastructure of society is not seen as 'doing' anything; instead it is perceived as offering no choice at all, so they look for a reality beyond the social, through doing startling acts designed to disturb the non-beingness they see around them, and so escape the nihilistic, surreal one inside them.

This type of personality Breger (1989) describes as consisting of a number of 'poorly integrated self fragments', while Winnicott (1987) considers how the tenuous link with creativity which usually belongs to the approach of the individual to external reality, is suppressed. People with splits in their character would, he says, like to be helped to achieve:

> . . . unit status or a state of time-space integration in which there is one self containing everything instead of dissociated elements that exist in compartments or are scattered around and left lying about.

Lacking this unit status, the child will often present a compliant self to the world, afraid to let the inner self make its debut for fear of its badness, madness, its inadequacy and the suspicion that it does not posses the ability to cope with everyday reality. Failure is too strong to risk, as is success, for it may lead to expectations from others, impossible to live up to. The false-self is based on the early formation where the mother has not made a good enough adaptation to the child who has then had to defend or even parent her; now the adolescent continues this early pattern by torturing her or his personal shape to fit a space left by the rest of the world, instead of the space it needs to choose in order to express its unique individuality. So many secrets are surrounded by deep shame, a central characteristic of secrecy, because the mother did not love her child as she or he deserved. The thought of this is too terrible to conceive and name.

The kind of therapy needed to address such secrets needs to be deep and ongoing. This may be set up on a one-to-one basis, in groups such as family therapy, personal growth groups, or in art therapy or drama therapy. Challenging entrenched secrets in disturbed children requires a tenacity and patience in the practitioner often pressurized to produce quick changes, when the process is essentially a slow one and needs to be based on the child's own rhythm. Winnicott's gentle, tactful and respectful approach can provide a compensatory environment where the origins of a sense of self may be formed and built on. However, Kleinians are less afraid of disturbing people's defences than they are of leaving people alone with hidden fears and anxieties if 'the therapist' could face the anxiety involved (Segal, 1992). The central aim of an approach based on Kleinian principles is to use therapy to enable the child to move from the 'pre-concern', paranoid-schizoid stage to reach the depressive position, or the 'stage of concern' (Winnicott, 1958), making it possible for the child to be neurotic, with the hope of moving towards ultimate recovery through the ability to make permanent relationships and to communicate in a way which shows awareness of the needs of others - a taking on of self-responsibility, what Pitt-Aikens (1990) calls an 'objective view of the self', in which we become accountable for our own process. For many children, regression is part of this treatment which calls for an environment making suitable adaptation, such as therapeutic communities (Lyward, Rose, Dockar-Drysdale, Wills, Balbernie) which can be seen as the ultimate form of communication, the totality of the place becoming a kind of symbolic representation of the mother, where:

> '. . . therapy should actually arise from the transactions with every aspect of life, and of these the physical and material aspects can be at least as important as any.' (Rose, 1990)

Having reached the depressive position a child may then move on to treatment involving interpretation and transference, as real communication takes the place of the broken-down type used in acting out syndromes. This will not happen until there has been some restoration of a primary bond in which the therapist/community takes on a vital adaptive function.

But how do we take the initial step to enable the child to even want to communicate in the first place and find a space in which to undertake the task of releasing the blocked energy around the secret? There is at first a need to negotiate boundaries. Some will be inclined to disclose all at once with a hope, even a desperation, that something will finally be done with it; others may give the impression that work has begun to loosen the boundaries, only to confront the practitioner with a brick wall. Checking boundaries with questions such as, 'Now let's check what it is you want to be known here'; 'What makes you think you want to tell me this?'; 'What might change if you tell me?' and 'How will you know when you want to tell me?' may open up a new way of thinking and learning about the problem, empowering the child to begin to consider the idea that she or he has some control over boundaries and what is disclosed. If this fails to happen, the therapist may evoke a sense of invasiveness, of a controlling parent who colonizes the child. It is important for something to happen so that the bonds of secrecy begin to break up, although it is not always necessary for the 'whole story' be told for a therapeutic outcome to occur. Dindia (1994), talking about the process of self-disclosure, sees it as occurring in three ways; firstly it is an act - the act of making yourself manifest, of showing yourself so that others may perceive you; secondly as an intrapersonal and, thirdly, an interpersonal process. In the intrapersonal process self-disclosure functions as a form of self-expression, for self-clarification and social validation. Interpersonal self-disclosure may take place in family groups and will be discussed below. Self-disclosure is essentially an anxious and contradictory process; the child might make a tentative foray to test the environment and to test how much the therapist or the environment will take. Limandri (1994) talks of the dialectical nature of disclosure - an offering followed by retraction and denial, an opening-closing pattern.

Communication with the child in personal therapy will involve similar tentative and sensitive movement into psychic areas which are protected by, among others, defences of shame. The therapist becomes a kind of 'transitional object' (Winnicott, op. cit.) to be utilized by the child according to emotional needs, as the first part of the movement towards integrating reality into the mind by balancing the polarities of inner and outer reality. Bion's idea of containment (1967), based on Klein's work, includes both a warm accepting presence and the use of words to convey and hold significant emotional meaning and truth (Segal, 1992). The intent of analysis, according to Jung, (quoted in Samuels, 1986) is to 'facilitate the assimilation into consciousness of unconscious fragments and hence overcome the dissociation'. Casement (1990) stresses the 'non-doing' role of the analyst, the emphasis instead on being - the child is active in the situation in a held way, in which she or he can be allowed to take responsibility and exercise choice; paradoxically, the meeting of needs is not provided by the analyst but yet 'can be found by the child'. It then becomes possible for development and growth which had been retarded through early environmental failure to be resumed. It is the 'intensified tie to the analyst' (Winnicott, 1958) which becomes a compensation for the faulty attitude to reality. Within this, many of the needs are met as a matter of course in the analyst's usual responses to the child and do not necessarily require any particular alteration of technique, so much as a sensitivity to the changing needs of the patient and adequate responsiveness to them on her or his part. It is also necessary that the analyst communicates her or his capacity to withstand attacks, to survive the 'danger' of disclosed secrets.

The particular medium and atmosphere to be created in the thera-peutic situation arising from this approach is based on the conditions of early play, in a concept central to the approaches of Winnicott and Klein, which for the former is almost mystical. It is as if in 'ordinary' conditions and life there is an inherent connection with the unconscious, a reach-ing out into that realm, a promise of its breaking through to provide a rich creativity - an area mysteriously offered to the child through the rela-tionship with the mother. Winnicott's concept of play and its particular quality and function is central to work with disturbed children. It becomes a central motivating force in therapeutic communities such as Finchdean Manor and Peper Harow - the former enveloped in a kind of 'flow', an ever-available poetic and transcendental environment, the latter an 'atmosphere' which was more like a kind of permanent play which had a restorative function. The 'potential space' (Winnicott, 1958) originally used in connection with mother and baby can be re-created in the therapeutic situation. It is essentially experiential (Axline, 1947), creating the conditions wherein the child may 'surprise' himself or herself with insights and it offers a peaceful, reflective space. The play must be 'spontaneous and not acquiescent' and interventions can only be made effectively 'when the immediate interest is momentarily centred' (Winnicott, op. cit.).

An account of an analysis of an adult documented by Winnicott has relevance to the process for damaged children. A woman for whom fantasy had become a powerful defence mechanism began to change, as Winnicott adapted to her need, so that material which had been formerly locked in the 'fixity of fantasising' was now being released for the more reality-based occupations of living and dreaming, described as the core of the personality. He states that creative playing is allied to dreaming and living but not to fantasising, while fantasy, for this woman, has interfered with both. As the analysis progressed, she found the means of achieving an identity. However, this discovery is not partic-ularly comfortable and it is helpful to keep in mind the shock and disorientation which can arise as the defence system is challenged by the impingement of reality; this woman retained nostalgia for the 'certainty of the illness pattern, the power of the defences to protect, and great anxiety that goes with the freedom to choose'. In our enthusi-asm to create conditions of change it is useful to keep in mind the degree of investment, energy and fear which have gone into these formations so that we tread carefully. Many children have been desper-ate to pretend to choose when they do not perceive themselves as having any choice. Extreme behaviour of all kinds at least looks like obvious choice, while the reality of choice is so much more mundane and restricted and indeed often inaccessible to them.

The main clues we are offered in the process of following the child's lead lie in studying how the material offered in acting-out syndromes reveals the nature of the unconscious processes, particularly through the transference and also by the 'unconscious search for new solutions', often expressed in the form of projective identification; the antisocial tendency; repetition compulsion; the communication of hate and sadism and identification with the aggressor (Casement, 1990).

The following parts of case studies illustrate experiences in which some of these phenomena, particularly through the transference, act as a means of receiving and understanding secrets. Another clue to inner reality can be found in children's repetition of everyday, even clichéd words as the expression of their recurrent themes: Karen's response of 'shameful' to various deeds (even if they were not, particularly), revealed her deep feelings of shame, and Jamie's attack on teachers because they didn't care for him (whereas he felt he had a better chance of gaining the care he had lacked from care staff) was an oblique comment on his terrifying absence of parental care.

Case study 1

Projective identification

Projective identification belongs to the paranoid-schizoid position and is based on an aggressive object-relating. It involves a more intense process than projection as such; a more active getting rid of, a discharging of unwanted feeling into someone else and evoking in them aspects - nasty, 'mad', shameful parts of the self - which are unbearably painful. It can involve a destructive attack, a 'making you feel' something which is calculated to destroy the perceived peace of mind, or superiority youngsters see as residing in you or in others (often causing intense envy) and sadly absent, they imagine, from themselves. In the transference with Karen, an intelligent and witty girl, I found that she had developed survival mechanisms based on the shame of her rejection by her mother whom she could never please. Her secret was this failure of the primal and childhood relationship and she was having to think of cutting off all communication with her mother, who had pressed enormous responsibility on her from an early age, including, in effect, bringing up siblings. Her coping mechanism was to force this on others; she took on great power in the community home by manipulating events and people and demanding that they fetch and carry for her. In the transference I felt small, insignificant and rather ashamed and found myself running around providing her with what she needed; also that my words (and actions) were never good enough and would be received with sarcasm. When I realised this was like her role with her mother I played out an obsequious role as if she were a queen. On an unconscious level she seemed to sense I had uncovered and spotted her secret: on the one hand this felt comforting; on the other it threatened her rigid defences which she was not ready at the time to address.

Case study 2

The communication of hate and sadism

From visits to his home it was clear that Jamie's mother belittled and humiliated him. At first I had a close relationship with him in which he attached to me as a baby to its mother. Suddenly, this behaviour changed radically (had he concluded I could never provide him with the symbiosis he wanted?) and he began behaving sadistically and outrageously towards me, with real annihilatory attacks. In the transference I felt such strong feelings of uncontainment, a boundariless state like floating in space together with *shock and incomprehension that I could be treated like this*. I also had feelings of humiliation, shame and powerlessness that were unbearable. I had an image of a baby left alone in the cot unattended for long periods; transferred feelings from that stage had split me off into the bad mother so as he could annihilate me as the bad mother whilst keeping the good one intact.

When the secret evolves not from personal experience but is imposed from outside, such as sexual abuse (in which secrecy takes on an enormous convoluted power and significance on all levels) or other defects transmitted in a covert way, the delinquent may become a kind of container for family themes. This concept, evolved by Pitt-Aikens (1990); treats the presenting delinquent as a victim, almost a kind of 'symptom', rather than the cause, as she or he often seems to be regarded, of the family's malaise. She or he becomes identity-less, a kind of 'non-person' by unwittingly taking on this role. A common causative factor in this scenario is loss, which has occurred either in their own or in the parents' or grandparents' generation, and is unacknowledged, unmourned and unworked through; or else some other repetitious character defect or omission has become taboo and locked up and is demanding energy and attention obliquely through the vessel of the young person:

> Often we are faced with a silent frustrating youth who will not satisfy our need to know about the problem. On a conscious level it might be to do with the fact of delinquent 'knowing' – 'being in the know' in other words having all the family thematic unconscious material packed tightly within (her or) him. (Pitt-Aikens, 1990)

Pincus and Dare (1978) widen the concept of secrets transmitted in this way to include 'secret convictions' which, unchallenged, may turn into personality flaws, and can motivate a person to behave in a maladaptive way if not dealt with at the time they arise. They may exact a terrible revenge in terms of the wellbeing of succeeding generations, particularly the next, until such time as the underlying issue is addressed. Pitt-Aiken's central tenet of a three-generational approach to delinquency is based on a 'loss of good authority' which he sees as a failure to take some necessary and realistic actions or exercise meaningful authority at a point in a family's history resulting in the creation of dominant 'themes', which will then cast round and look for a psychic space in which to reside in whoever seems to be receptive. It is a kind of psychological explanation of the Mosaic formula of the sins of the fathers being visited on the children.

A particular feature of this bizarre form of 'passing the buck', a psychodynamic transmission of psychic contents, is that certain events when unperceived and unacknowledged, may be repeated in the psyches of following generations in ways which have an uncanny similarity, in some element, to the original event, i.e. they may be re-enacted at a similar time or place or in a parallel way if not in some symbolically representational way. Rose (1990) describes a Peper Harow community meeting in which the antisocial behaviour of a boy who broke into a family tomb at nights to 'have a smoke' was discussed. He became conscious of the significance of what had previously looked like random behaviour when another boy pointed out that the death of his smoker father had occurred at the same time in the night as he visited the tomb. The boy's unconscious acting-out had released in him understanding from which he could move towards mourning his father's loss. The loss of fathers in the two wars is shown through Pitt-Aikens' work to have created a space in the mind of sons and daughters who, in a sense, pass on this gap - hard as it may be to conceptualise passing on 'a gap'! The 'containing' delinquent is then faced with the task of trying to draw attention to something of which she or he has no conscious understanding.

When the good authority, having moved out of parental control, resides in the hands of the professionals, the practitioner has to keep a very clear and uncluttered mind in the face of the 'themes' pressing down upon her or him so as not to be drawn into the family's pathological communication system, often kept in place by the use of secretive subcodes and powerful non-verbal interactions. In all types of settings, including courtrooms, the seductive pathology of a family can press down, fill up the room, and seem to smash the power of clear thinking: it is essential that practitioners develop the necessary staying power, strength and insight to confront delinquent and other behaviours to re-link them to their original source in the family network, thus giving those concerned a fresh chance to become aware of their nature and power.

Such a process is charted in Skynner's (1987) description of the principles operating in an open systems family therapy group, showing how secret themes can surface. Working on the level of the presenting family, he uses the transference as a major tool of communication in an exercise which moves towards unification of the group; on the conscious level the therapist has to refuse to accept any secrets from individuals, for this would 'disconnect elements of a structure which must remain connected if it is to be capable of intelligent response and change'.

Yet the transferential process he describes places the therapist in a position where she or he actually receives experiences and absorbs the secret material as though acting as a container. At the same time she or he operates like a detective, unravelling clues and promptings and following up hunches. He describes the various stages of the process, at first remaining open and responsive to what is given and resisting any tendency to 'do' anything. This is a painful stage for the therapist as there is a sense of confusion and chaos and fear of being overwhelmed by unrelated fragments and by feelings of likely failure. Pitt-Aikens (1990) speaks of a method in the sixties where therapists were encouraged to do without notes and conduct sessions from the material which surfaced, trusting that this would be pertinent.

Gradually the therapist becomes aware of puzzling emotional responses inside, which gain in clarity and insistence until they begin to feel increasingly as if they are somehow information about the family. Finally a conviction arises that this aroused response is exactly what is needed to be put into the family system; it has been missing throughout and can be defined as a feeling or emotional attitude conspicuous by its absence.

Like Pitt-Aikens, for whom loss and 'missingness' (the latter defined as a syndrome containing unconscious fantasy or other accumulations around a painful event e.g. a father leaving) often constitute the missing link in the family's dynamic towards health, Skynner tries to define a concept which evades elucidation, partly because it has, in the family's mind, for so long remained unnamable but also because of its elusive nature. It can only be 'seen' experientially, but when it is realised it happens with a sudden flash of insight which he compares to a photographic flash in a darkened room. This places the person or family in a position where old paradigms are no longer tenable, and a Gestalt switch occurs. Skynner conceptualizes it as a 'figure': the therapist having accumulated enough 'public' information to make up a background, the figure, which is defined as an 'empty space in the pattern of facts', may then become visible. This is explained as a 'figure/ground phenomenon' and is based on the idea that the real family problem is always contained in what is not communicated, what is missing from the content of a session.

The therapist may then communicate the material back to the family broken down into an easily assimilated form, using behavioural and educational task setting, advice, restructuring and communication of skills by example and modelling. By becoming a sort of personification of the very qualities the family disowns, the therapist takes on the scape-goat role, often in the place of the designated delinquent or other 'malfunctioning' family member. This 'exposure' can be very frightening for a family who have spent so much time keeping the lid on their secret monstrous material to find that it is now present in the room, having gone 'inside' the therapist, who has now become an even more terrify-ing and threatening monster than the original secret. The final interven-tion, Skynner claims, will take into account and be sensitive to the defences and resistance of each family member as well as revelations and uncovering of secrets. Using the transference in this way the therapist will absorb the projective system of the family in its entirety and will find that the final solution, if reached, will be 'exactly tailored to their partic-ular defence system'.

Whether individually or in families or other group settings, chal-lenging entrenched secrets in disturbed children requires a tenacity and single-mindedness which may at times be threatening to the privacy of that child. This may occur not so much from individuals but from our systems, which are not always respectful of the child's own boundaries and right to privacy. Children in care systems suffer from a lack of 'information control' (Goffman, 1968) over their lives: the possession of a Social Services file in itself constitutes a type of stigma and the right to confidentiality is often negated, as information disclosed is not clearly defined by boundaries. Also, it has the power to create change in the youngster's life over which she or he has little control but instead may be passed on to agencies and used to deter-mine placements, treatments and create other momentous changes in the child's life. Dockar-Drysdale (1993) stresses the need for communi-ties to provide their own therapy as part of their provision to offer a more comprehensive and unified treatment plan rather than relying on outside agencies.

For some children, particularly those who have had numerous place-ments, discontinuity of depth counselling has eroded their respect for therapists in general and the process in particular. Behavioural approaches which govern the 24-hour curriculum in some settings, while effective in providing containment and setting goals for some, may be inadequate for the child whose secret is so deep-seated that she or he cannot help but discharge the expression of 'themes' of loss into the environment, however injurious these are to the other members of the community. Young people such as these, the group in most need in our society, often fail to receive the kind of therapy which is ongoing and consistent, committed to their personal needs and which assures them of confidentiality, not least because of the large number of placements they have had.

On the educational level, Rose (1990) speaks of the difficulty for teachers who may have had only a basic psychological training, in coping with a class of disturbed youngsters they are trying to educate. The group situation in itself may be threatening, the child may be acting out feelings of sibling rivalry and envy, both of the other students and what appears to be the ease of skill with which the teacher operates, and there may be unconscious attempts to destroy what is being offered. Subjects like English often threaten the child anxious to keep the lid on feelings, but when enough trust has been established can provide opportunity for discharge of feelings. Some youngsters will use a GCSE psychology course as a means of understanding their own turbulent feelings; often insights gained in this way will reduce acting-out behaviours and loosen the bonds of a secret: for example a girl terrified of madness ceased her compulsive window-breaking after increasing her understanding of herself through this kind of study.

The secret self of the child arises naturally and healthily in normal development from the good enough care given, for example, when a space for quiet self-reflection and self-development is created within the primal relationship and the baby lies contentedly in the cot, thinking her or his own thoughts. Such a state can only be achieved when the baby feels secure enough to move out of the original circle of play and safety created in the mother's presence as she holds the baby in her mind, enabling the baby eventually to hold *her* in her or his mind. The pathology which surrounds secrets should not let us lose sight of the positive nature and function of secrets which contain not only the potential for pain and conflict but also are the source of our imagination and creativity. Winnicott (1964) makes a passionate commitment to the privacy of the self: 'Each individual is an isolate, permanently non-communicating, permanently unknown, in fact unfound.'

He suggests that the traumatic experience, which so easily evolves into a secret and belongs to the organisation of primitive defences, is based on the

'. . . threat of the isolated core, the threat of being found, altered, even communicated with. The defence consists in further hiding of the self.'

However much we categorize and tabulate the features of early experience which are common to humanity we cannot pin down or take apart that mysterious variable, the uniqueness and surprisingness of the individual whose forms of communication are often fresh, idiosyncratic and stimulating, the creativity that is the path leading to the culture, for which Winnicott had so much respect.

How the cathecting, internalizing of sense impressions and moments of experience are drawn in by the baby, seemingly in a random fashion, is expressed by Shaffer's character of the psychiatrist Dysart in *Equus* (1980):

A child is born into a world of phenomena all equal in their power to enslave.

Appendix
Klein's paranoid-schizoid position - negative outcomes and their connections to adolescent behaviours

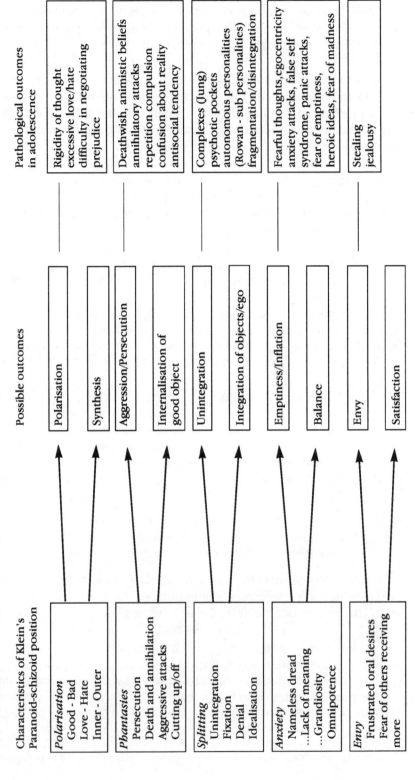

Characteristics of Klein's Paranoid-schizoid position

Polarisation
Good - Bad
Love - Hate
Inner - Outer

Phantasies
Persecution
Death and annihilation
Aggressive attacks
Cutting up/off

Splitting
Unintegration
Fixation
Denial
Idealisation

Anxiety
Nameless dread
...Lack of meaning
...Grandiosity
Omnipotence

Envy
Frustrated oral desires
Fear of others receiving more

Possible outcomes

Polarisation

Synthesis

Aggression/Persecution

Internalisation of good object

Unintegration

Integration of objects/ego

Emptiness/Inflation

Balance

Envy

Satisfaction

Pathological outcomes in adolescence

Rigidity of thought
excessive love/hate
difficulty in negotiating
prejudice

Deathwish, animistic beliefs
annihilatory attacks
repetition compulsion
confusion about reality
antisocial tendency

Complexes (Jung)
psychotic pockets
autonomous personalities
(Rowan - sub personalities)
fragmentation/disintegration

Fearful thoughts, egocentricity
anxiety attacks, false self
syndrome, panic attacks,
fear of emptiness,
heroic ideas, fear of madness

Stealing
jealousy

It sniffs, it sucks - it strokes its eyes over the whole uncomfortable range. Suddenly one strikes. Why? Moments snap together like magnets, forging a chain of shackles. But why at the start they were ever magnetized at all - just those particular moments of experience and no others, I don't know . . .

Part of this spectrum is operating also to produce the 'creativity which belongs to being alive' (Winnicott, op cit.), which widens out from play to creative cultural experience of all kinds, and which is the ultimate goal of the delicate process which constitutes the art of communicating with secretive children.

References

Axline, V.M. (1947). *Play Therapy: The Inner Dynamics of Childhood.* Boston: Houghton Mifflin

Bion, W.R. (1967). *Second Thoughts.* New York: Aronson.

Bly, R. (1990). *Iron John.* Shaftesbury: Element.

Bowlby, J. (1983). *Loss: Attachment and Loss, Vol. 3.* Harmondsworth: Penguin.

Breger, L. (1989). *Dostoyevsky: The Author as Psychoanalyst.* New York: University Press.

Burn, A. (1964). *Mr. Lyward's Answer.* London: Hamish Hamilton

Casement, P. (1990). *Further Learning from the Patient.* London: Routledge

Dindia, K. (1994). In: Duck, S. *Dynamics of Relationships.* London: Sage.

Dockar-Drysdale, B. (1993). *Therapy and Consultation in Child Care.* London: Free Association

Dockar-Drysdale, B. (1993). *Consultation in Child Care.* London: Free Association

Fairburn, W.R.D. (1994). *Psychoanalytic Studies of the Personality.* London: Routledge.

Freud, S. (1985). *Art and Literature.* Harmondsworth: Penguin.

Freud, S. (1986). *The Essentials of Psychoanalysis.* Harmondsworth: Penguin.

Goffman, E. (1968). *Stigma: Notes on the Management of Spoiled Identity.* Harmondsworth: Penguin.

Gogol, F. (1930). *The Double.* London: Everyman.

Klein, M. (1988). *Love, Guilt and Reparation.* London: Virago.

Laing, R.D. (1959). *The Divided Self.* Harmondsworth: Penguin.

Limandri, B. (1994). Disclosure of Stigmatizing Conditions: The Discloser's Perspective. In Duck, S. *Dynamics of Relationships.* London: Sage.

Pincus, L. and Dare, C. (1978). *Secrets in the Family.* London: Faber and Faber.

Pitt-Aikens, T. and Thomas Ellis, A. (1990). *Loss of the Good Authority: The Cause of Delinquency.* Harmondsworth: Penguin.

Rank, O. (1971). *The Double: A Psychoanalytic Study.* New York: Meridian.

Rose, M. (1990). *Healing Hurt Minds: the Peper Harow Experience.* London: Routledge.

Salinger, J. D. (1951). *Catcher in the Rye.* Harmondsworth Penguin.

Samuels, A. et al. (1986). *A Critical Dictionary of Jungian Analysis.* London: Routledge.

Segal, J. (1992). *Key Figures in Counselling and Psychotherapy: Melanie Klein.* London: Sage.

Shaffer, P. (1980). *Equus.* Harmondsworth: Penguin.

Skynner, R. (1987). *Explorations with Families.* London: Tavistock/Routledge.

Winnicott, D. (1958). *Collected Papers, through Paediatrics to Psychoanalysis.* London: Tavistock.

Winnicott, D. (1964). *The Child, the Family and the Outside World,* Harmondsworth: Penguin.

Winnicott, D. (1971). *Playing and Reality.* London: Tavistock.

Winnicott, D. (1987). *Home is Where We Start From: Essays by a Psychoanalyst.* London: Pelican.

Winnicott, D. (1988). *Human Nature.* London: Free Association.

Wood, M. (1984). In Dalley, T. (ed.) *Art as Therapy.* London: Routledge.

Index

able children 147–8
MLD 45, 56
SDLD 125, 132, 134, 136
see also speech
visual impairment 1–14
autism 81
PMLD 64, 65, 67, 69
SDLD 125, 126

vocabulary
autistic children 81
MLD 57
SDLD 132, 135, 139, 141

wheelchairs 28–9, 32, 33, 37
word finding 131, 132–3, 135, 139